Turning
Team Performance
Inside OUT

Turning
Team Performance
Inside OUT

Team Types and Temperament
for High-Impact Results

SUSAN NASH

Davies-Black Publishing
PALO ALTO, CALIFORNIA

Published by Davies-Black Publishing, an imprint of Consulting Psychologists Press, Inc., 3803 East Bayshore Road, Palo Alto, CA 94303; 800-624-1765.

Special discounts on bulk quantities of Davies-Black books are available to corporations, professional associations, and other organizations. For details, contact the Director of Book Sales at Davies-Black Publishing, an imprint of Consulting Psychologists Press, Inc., 3803 East Bayshore Road, Palo Alto, CA 94303; 650-691-9123; Fax 650-623-9271.

03 02 01 00   10 9 8 7 6 5 4 3 2
Printed in the United States of America

Library of Congress Cataloging-in-Publication Data
Nash, Susan Marie
Turning team performance inside out : team types and temperament for high-impact results / Susan Nash.
p.   cm.
Includes bibliographical references and index.
ISBN 0-89106-136-3
1. Teams in the workplace. 2. Performance. 3. Leadership. I. Title.
HD66.N37   1999
658.4'02—dc21

99-33220
CIP

FIRST EDITION
First printing 1999

Dedicated to

MY FATHER, WHO ENVISIONED MY
POTENTIAL, AND MY HUSBAND AND CHILDREN, WHO
HAVE SUPPORTED ME AS I REALIZE IT

Contents

Foreword

This book is all about making teams work more effectively. There is no doubt in our minds as to the importance of this subject.

In her career management practice, Judy frequently encounters teams that falter or even fail. Either the human aspects of these groups are overlooked or in conflict, or the systems to make them work are not in place—or both. *Turning Team Performance Inside Out* shows us how to combine a personal behavior analysis with a performance strategy to improve team effectiveness. Using the well-researched personality theories of temperament and the *Myers-Briggs Type Indicator®* (MBTI®) to examine the behavior of teams and their members and her own unique method for examining team performance, Susan Nash explores and illustrates the differences between teams that operate well and those that do not. She finds that high-performing teams combine a healthy balance of differing personality characteristics with a set of team systems common to most good group efforts. She applies these two complementary techniques in teaching us how to diagnose a team's potential strengths, challenges, and remedies for the problems uncovered.

In Bob's book *Adhocracy: the Power to Change,* he argues that ad hoc forms of organization—that is, teams of various shapes and sizes —are the wave of the future. The reason is that in today's world, issues seldom come packaged in ways that fit normal bureaucracy. Issues almost never wait until conventional bureaucracy can reorganize itself to meet the needs. On a grand scale, the early 1980s turnaround at the Ford Motor Company can be directly attributed to Team Taurus, a huge team effort that cut through every layer of Ford's conventional organization. On a much smaller scale, teams are the not-so-secret key to innovation at some of the most successful organizations. At 3M, when two people with very different backgrounds, from very different parts of the organization, got together to form the nucleus of a team, they launched a product that would change the company: the Post-it® note. At Rubbermaid, the company that was introducing one new product for every day of the year, the last time we looked, teams were doing the innovating. Assigned to each team are representatives from all the key functions required to get a product from idea to consumer—marketing, research and development, manufacturing, sales, and finance.

The importance of Nash's book is threefold. First is its focus on teams: the ad hoc part of life in today's organizations, which we view as so critically important. Second is the very important message that well-functioning teams not only must represent a variety of disciplines, as Bob argues in *Adhocracy,* they must also comprise a healthy balance of personality types. Too many artists on the team, and the ideas may be beautiful but the work never gets done. Too many doers on the team means things may get done but the result may be pretty pedestrian, falling far short of the inventiveness the times require. Third, Nash shows us how to figure out team composition and determine where the weaknesses, predictable conflicts, and potentially deadly swamps are likely to be. She goes further and tells us what to do about these problems long before they turn into real team-busting issues. In many cases, she shows us how to first analyze and then compensate for both our own weaknesses and those of other members of the team. In other cases, she shows us that although understanding these weaknesses can help greatly, the team composition may have to be changed to make the team truly effective. Further, she helps us figure out just what characteristics a new team member needs to have.

Just as Nash suggests that team members are very different and teams can thrive on these differences, we suggest that the same probably is true of her readers. For those of us who like systematic approaches to understanding the dynamics of organizations, the plethora of exercises and examples will be greatly satisfying. These individuals should read the book carefully, complete the exercises, develop their own analysis of the teams they work on, and help other members of the team understand their own views of the team's dynamics. People on the other end of the spectrum, those with a more "let's get on with it" personality, will also find the book helpful, but may wish to use it differently. These individuals could easily get bogged down in the analysis and thoroughness required to complete all the work and in the order Nash suggests. But even if they read the book in a different way, these people will want to be just as familiar with the book's content, its way of looking at personality differences, and its ideas for making teamwork more systematic. All of us can profit from knowing better how to combine what's known about skilled team functioning with the personal dynamics and work styles of teams and their individual members.

One central message in the book can barely be repeated enough. That theme is this: Each of us routinely gets frustrated at work and in life because others, in Nash's phrase, are NLM: not like me. They think differently, approach work differently, act differently, solve problems differently. Unless well understood, and respected, these differences repeatedly cause failures in organizations (even civilizations). On an everyday basis, however, to understand and appreciate the NLM phenomenon, and to go on to the next step—to learn to deal with it effectively—that is the key to the most powerful problem-solving mechanism we have in today's arsenal of organizational tools: the team.

Bob Waterman, author, *What America Does Right*
Judy Waterman, CEO, Career Management Group

Preface

You have the best and brightest people in your industry, a looming deadline, and the full resources of the organization behind you. . . . So why doesn't your team deliver the results you need when you need them?

Chances are you're on some kind of work team, probably more than one. It may be called a task force, committee, coalition, or work group—formed to help your organization do more with less. It doesn't matter if you sit in a cubicle or the executive suite, if your team is traditional or "virtual," if you're the team leader or an individual contributor—you're part of a team and responsible for its results.

For almost twenty years I wondered why the work teams I was a part of often didn't work. It seemed that we had everything we needed—smart people, an achievable goal, and the resources to accomplish our task. So, what was missing?

I had this epiphany in the early '90s when I was first introduced to the *Myers-Briggs Type Indicator* (MBTI®) and temperament theory. It was instantly clear to me that this scientifically based work is the missing element in work team performance. Normally, if a team isn't performing, we assume that we need to fix some system, policy, procedure, or process: the "Outside In" approach. The result is that individuals continue to respond the way they always have because the focus is on systems, policies, procedures, and processes, not on the impact of what they say and do on team performance.

I realized that we needed to consider the most important part of any task involving human beings—individual patterns of behavior and their impact on team productivity. When individuals understand the impact the differences in the way they gather information and make decisions has on others, then the team can capitalize more effectively on each individual's strengths to immediately improve team performance—from the "inside out."

This book will outline the approach to teamwork from the inside out and is designed for anyone, whether a team leader or team member, who is trying to make team performance a fact, not a fantasy.

WHAT IS TEAMWORK FROM THE INSIDE OUT?

Teamwork from the inside out is a step-by-step methodology to diagnose and immediately impact team performance comprising the following steps:

1. Assess your team SCORE.

2. Profile individual team members' personalities.

3. Create a team profile.

4. Create a plan of attack to raise your team SCORE based on your team profile.

ASSESS YOUR TEAM SCORE

In order for a team to be able to perform successfully, certain key factors need to be present. These important characteristics are captured using the SCORE acronym. The SCORE concept is illustrated in Figure P.1. A successful team will SCORE if it has the following:

S: Strategy

- Shared purpose
- Clearly articulated values and ground rules
- Understanding of risks and opportunities facing the team
- Clear categorization of the overall responsibilities of the team

C: Clear Roles and Responsibilities

- Clear definition of roles and responsibilities
- Responsibility shared by all members
- Specific objectives to measure individual results

O: Open Communication

- Respect for individual differences

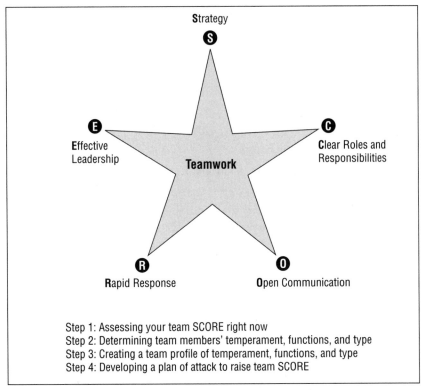

Figure P.1   How to Raise Your Team's SCORE

- Open and nonjudgmental communication environment among team members

R: Rapid Response

- Rapid response to the team's problems, as well as to customers' needs
- Effective management of and response to change in the internal and external environment

E: Effective Leadership

- Team leader who is able to help members achieve the objective and build the team
- Team leader who can draw out and free up the skills of all team members, develop individuals

Teams begin the process of improving teamwork from the inside out by assessing their current performance level within each of these categories.

PROFILE TEAM MEMBERS' PERSONALITIES

The next step involves assessing each team member's personality profile. In this book we will provide you with three ways of profiling human differences within a team:

- First, team members may have different temperaments—there are four temperaments with different core needs and values.

- Second, team members will use different functions to gather information and make decisions.

- Third, team members have different approaches to the world of work, or operating styles—often assessed by the *Myers-Briggs Type Indicator,* providing sixteen psychological types.

The methodology we will use combines the systems theory of temperament (which has been around for over twenty centuries) with the personality theory most commonly associated with Carl Jung and the *Myers-Briggs Type Indicator* (MBTI).

CREATE A TEAM PROFILE

The data on team members' temperament, functions, and type is then combined to create a team profile showing team temperament, functions, and type, combined with an analysis of the team's potential strengths and challenges. The team profile provides an indication of how the team will SCORE against the backdrop of the characteristics of high-performing teams, thereby affecting team performance from the inside out.

CREATE A PLAN OF ATTACK TO RAISE TEAM SCORE

Once you have a picture of your team's profile, you can implement performance strategies, customized to your team, to affect team performance right now. In my work with more than forty organizations and over five thousand individuals, I have found again and again that by helping team members understand their team's habitual patterns of behavior they can "self-diagnose" potential problems, capitalize more effectively on their individual and team strengths, and achieve better results.

Using these data, the team will be able to

- Achieve more effective group process and one-on-one interactions

- Provide effective assignments to maximize individual skills, abilities, and motivations

- Shift habitual responses and decision-making patterns to embrace other, previously unseen opportunities
- Minimize potential for failure
- Capitalize on performance possibilities
- Respect and reveal team historical values

READING THIS BOOK

Purpose

The purpose of this book is to provide individuals in organizations with skills and techniques to optimize their team effectiveness based on understanding, valuing, and utilizing individual differences.

Approach

In this book we use the Inside Out methodology for improving team performance. In Part 1 we assess team members' personality using three steps: understanding temperament, functions, and type.

Chapter 1 allows readers to assess their own temperament by providing information and definitions, and then using exercises and examples of temperaments in real-world teams. Chapter 2 allows team members to understand and then "try on" the functions they might use to either gather information or make decisions, and then provides examples of these functions in a real-world case study. Chapter 3 ties temperament and functions together to allow team members to identify their type and understand the strengths of each type and possible challenges each might face on a team.

In Part 2 we examine team behavior and show how team performance is influenced from the inside out by the team members' personality profiles. Each chapter includes examples, exercises, case studies, and a plan of attack for you to apply the principles introduced to improving team performance immediately.

Chapter 4 provides a basic introduction to the team profile and the critical elements of high-performing teams. Readers are introduced to skills and techniques to enable them to profile the "personality" of their teams, diagnose strengths and potential challenges, and then create a general action plan to raise their team's SCORE. Chapters 5 through 9 describe in detail each of the elements of high-performing teams, and then enable teams to analyze their profile against these key performance requirements, with customized implications and actions for improving team performance in each one.

Chapter 10 gives you ideas and tools to use for maintaining your team at peak performance level.

Using This Book

The following approach is recommended to optimize your use of this book.

Step One: Understanding Team Member Behavior

- Read Chapters 1, 2 and 3 first. This will enable you to assess your own personality profile and get an indication of the profiles of your fellow team members. (Remember not to jump to conclusions about team members' "type"—what you see is not necessarily what you get!)

- Ask your team members to also read these chapters so that all can build an understanding of each team member's personality profile.

- Remember that this book is no substitute for an in-depth counseling session with an MBTI expert but that it can provide valuable data to help you improve team performance.

- Remember not to use this information as a labeling tool—no one is completely one temperament or type or uses just one function. As human beings, our personalities represent a complex adaptive system. The purpose of this information is to help you recognize in yourself and others behavior that might be hindering or helping team performance and understand why.

Step Two: Profile Your Team

- Read Chapter 4. This will introduce you to the five elements of high-performing teams and enable you to assess your current team's performance.

Step Three: Turning Team Performance Inside Out

- Based on your team's assessment, completed in Chapter 4, you can pick and choose the chapters and the sequence you wish to follow, based on your team's needs (Chapter 5, "Strategy," through Chapter 9, "Effective Leadership"). For instance, if there were a conflict in your team, you might elect to start with Chapter 7, "Open Communication" (the O in SCORE).

This book is based on centuries worth of knowledge about different personalities and years of work with teams as they struggle to survive in today's business world. I hope the tips, techniques, concepts, and strategies are useful to you in working with your teams, producing better results, having more fun, and learning more.

Acknowledgments

Writing a book on a theoretical subject such as type and temperament involves an intense collaboration with an expert support network and comprehensive, often unquestioning support from family and friends.

I want to acknowledge the contributions of David Keirsey in *Please Understand Me* and *Please Understand Me II* and for his role in bringing temperament theory to the current century. I also want to acknowledge the contributions of Linda Berens of Temperament Research Institute in two ways—first for introducing me to the personal enlightenment that the knowledge of temperament has given me, and second for the time she invested in providing guidance and feedback on the temperament and functions chapters, the building blocks of the book. Her analytical perspective and knowledge were pivotal.

Second, I would like to acknowledge my partnership with Courtney Bolin in the development stages of the book. Her research, development of content, critical questioning skills, and insights on introversion represent essential contributions to the book.

Next, I would like to thank Julie Khademi for the expert support she provided in brainstorming ideas and developing concepts as she lived and breathed with me the methodology as it developed. Many other consultants, including Meg Ellis, Kelly Herrick, Jerene DeLaney, and John Kinsella, willingly provided their time, viewpoints, analyses, and ideas.

I also want to thank my clients, whose openness and willingness to change provided the business content for this book.

Finally and most important, I have to offer thanks to my family and friends. To my husband of twenty-five years, Derek: no words could express my appreciation for the consistency of his unrelenting support and tolerance for temperament and functions talk at breakfast, lunch, dinner, and holidays, and for proving such a wonderful Guardian role model for the content in the book. To my young adults, Antony and Laura, who shared and cared for me during the gestation of the book. And finally to my good friend Tessa in England, who has always helped me with her calm yet caring voice of reason.

About the Author

Susan Nash is owner of EM-Power, Inc., a consulting firm that provides organizational development and training services to help businesses achieve results by optimizing their people resources. EM-Power has been in business for more than five years, and currently revenues exceed half a million dollars working with a wide range of Fortune 500 organizations. Nash is also the author of *Becoming a Consultant* (1999) and the forthcoming title *Exceeding Customer Expectations* (due February 2000) and is currently writing a book on type, temperament, and relationships.

Born in the United Kingdom, Nash graduated from the University of Birmingham in England with a first class honors degree in business studies. She began her career in management with Marks and Spencer, completing the company's management development program. She then worked for Time Manager International, a Europe-based training company specializing in time management and customer service training. In her time with the organization (over seven years) the company grew from 5 people to 150, and from $250,000 to $20 million, and became Europe's largest training company. Her responsibilities there included establishing and managing the sales support group, being part of the Executive Management team, spearheading the organization's strategic marketing efforts, and finally acting as general manager for the business unit on the West Coast of the United States after moving to California in January 1987.

After leaving TMI, Nash spent three years subcontracting for a training organization in the U.S., during which time she was responsible for designing and delivering a wide range of programs under a

$3 million ETP (Employment Training Panel) contract for Certified Grocers.

As director of training for Williams-Sonoma, Inc., she completed several successful training projects including the following:

- Rolling out a basic selling-skills program to over 4,500 retail employees during a six-week period for two successive years, resulting in a comparative store sales increase of 17 percent and 16 percent, respectively

- Designing and implementing a comprehensive leadership training curriculum to all 300 managers based on the *Myers-Briggs Type Indicator*

- Negotiating, managing, and implementing an ETP program for over 400 employees resulting in collection of over $200,000 from ETP funds

In October 1994, Nash established her own training business, EM-Power, to continue to supply a wide range of training services, including extensive work with the *Myers-Briggs Type Indicator,* to more than fifty organizations and over 10,000 individuals throughout the U.S. and Europe. Nash combines practical business management experience with strong facilitation skills to help clients develop training needs assessments, in-house training curriculum plans, and train-the-trainer programs. She has designed and delivered training in a number of subject areas including leadership skills, interpersonal communication, sales and marketing, telephone sales, and career development.

Nash's current role involves extensive travel in the U.S. and Europe, consulting with clients on customer service initiatives, increasing team effectiveness, and developing customized learning interventions for other business needs. She is a member of the Association for Psychological Type and won the Employee of the Year award while at TMI.

When not working directly with clients, Nash enjoys traveling and exercising.

PART ONE

Profiling Your Team

The Inside Out approach begins with diagnosing the different personalities within a team and defining the team profile, so that you can then implement strategies for improving team performance. In the first three chapters of this book we will focus on understanding individual team members' behavior. In Chapter 1 we will examine different patterns of core needs and values by building an understanding of the four temperaments. In Chapter 2 we will examine the functions you and other team members use to gather information and make decisions. Finally, in Chapter 3 we will integrate temperament and functions to determine type. After we have built a firm comprehension of team member behavior, we will be prepared for Part 2 where we can apply this knowledge to improving team performance from the inside out.

1

Understanding Temperament

WHAT MAKES ME TICK?

"We do not see things as they are, we see them as we are. We do not hear things as they are, we hear them as we are."
—The Talmud

The first step in creating a team profile is to understand the four temperaments, which can give us valuable insight into our own and other team members' core needs and values. We use examples, exercises, self-assessment, and case studies to enable you to build a comprehensive picture of how each temperament approaches life, and the types of skills and roles each temperament demonstrates in a team. Understanding temperament can also provide insight into the core values and motivations of your team as a whole.

"BLM" SPECTACLES

As we see the world through our own paradigm, we tend to assume that everyone sees or at least should see things the same way we do. Each of us has his or her own pair of "BLM" (be like me) spectacles (Berens, 1998). We have all been frustrated when a mate, a friend, or a co-worker is fundamentally different from us in some particular way: disorganized, too organized, too talkative, or too quiet. The differences were fine at first, maybe even attractive and exciting, but then they became irritating. We wonder, Why can't he or she be like me? I like me. We might start to view the person as incompetent, disagreeable, or uptight. At this point we begin to forcibly cram him or her into an ill-suited mold of our own seemingly perfect self. Yet even if it were possible to do so, a world without differences would be as mundane as the Mona Lisa without her enigmatic smile. Resisting the "Pygmalion Project," the temptation to sculpt another into our own "perfect" image, is truly a difficult endeavor (Keirsey, 1998). Only when we work to understand our differences will we be able to celebrate our diversity rather than bemoan the supposed faults of others.

DEFINING TEMPERAMENT

We all view the world through a unique set of lenses, distorting reality to match our own mental picture. We are all unique individuals with our own complexities and idiosyncrasies, but four basic patterns have been consistently and cross-culturally recognized in the human personality. Temperament theory is based on these four basic patterns. The human personality is complex and varying, but temperament reveals the underlying, inborn foundation on which it is built. In temperament theory we start with an understanding of the core themes and then examine our basic psychological needs, core values, favorite talents, common approaches, and habitual worldview. People with the same temperament share the same core needs and values. However, this similarity does not mean that these people are all the same. There is wide variation, but with strong shared needs. For example, stringed instruments are a family of musical instruments, but a guitar is quite different from a double bass.

As the basic pattern of our personality influences our daily actions and interactions, awareness of our temperament can be invaluable. Once we understand our own basic patterns, it becomes much easier to make more effective choices and communicate with others. The four temperaments can be described as follows.

- *Artisans* live one day at a time, seizing all the freedom they can get. Alert to opportunities, they respond to the needs of the situation and want to make an impact on their environment. In teams, Artisans are often tacticians, troubleshooters, firefighters, and negotiators.

- *Guardians* are driven by responsibility and duty, wishing to serve and protect those they care about. They are pillars of society, stable and supportive, yet they also need membership and a sense of belonging. Guardians' roles in teams have included logistic and process managers, stabilizers, builders, and traditionalists.

- *Rationals* seek knowledge and competence in all they take on. They try to understand the operating principles of all around them and create their own destiny. Rationals' roles in teams have included strategists, inventors, engineers, and innovators.

- *Idealists* are soul-searchers who constantly quest for meaning and significance in their lives. They want to make a difference and are on a lifelong journey to find themselves and help others do the same. Idealists' roles in teams have included coaches, collaborators, advocates, and mentors.

ORIGINS OF TEMPERAMENT

Scholars have observed and written about these four distinct patterns of personality since nearly the beginning of recorded time. As far back as 450 B.C. the Greek physician and father of medicine, Hippocrates, described four types of people based on body "humors" (fluids): the Sanguine as excited and impulsive, the Melancholic as morose and serious, the Phlegmatic as calm or impassive, and the Choleric as sensitive and emotional. Similarly, in the Middle Ages another physician responsible for the application of chemistry to medicine, Paracelsus, recognized "four natures" found in humans. Four different spirits of nature guided his four dispositions: the Salamander of fire, the Gnome of earth, the Sylph of air, and the Nymph of water. In America the Medicine Wheel of the American Plains Indians also recognized four similar personality themes: the bear way of connecting to the environment, the mouse way of staying grounded and close to the roots of life, the buffalo way of logic and analysis, and the eagle way of seeing patterns and floating above the details. The task of each individual in the Plains society was not only to master his or her own innate way of seeing the world but also to move around the wheel and understand the perspectives of others.

Despite the historical consistency of the descriptions and the centuries of validation, the idea of four temperaments was virtually abandoned until David Keirsey, a behavioral scientist, developed the modern theory of temperament in 1956. Keirsey was impressed by the consistencies in temperament portraits throughout history and spent over forty years researching and integrating the descriptions into a comprehensive systems theory of temperament. In *Please Understand Me,* the million-copy best-seller Keirsey (1978) coauthored with fellow psychologist Marilyn Bates, he originally called the temperaments the Dionysians, the Epimetheans, the Prometheans, and the Apollonians after the Greek mythological characters that were most like each personality theme. He later referred to them as the Artisans, the Guardians, the Rationals, and the Idealists. With twenty years of observational data on individuals in their daily lives, he put together portraits of these different temperaments based on their behaviors, needs, values, and pathologies. These descriptions are consistent with behaviors observed in twentieth-century corporate cultures.

SELF-ASSESSMENT

Before we consider detailed descriptions of each of the four temperaments, use Exercises 1.1 through 1.4 on pages 7 through 11 to stop and think about you.

DESCRIPTIONS OF THE TEMPERAMENTS

We are now ready to describe some broad characteristics associated with each of the four temperaments.

The Artisan Temperament—Carpe Diem

> *"Things turn out for the best for the people who*
> *make the best of the way things turn out."*
> —John Wooden

Artisans live and act in the moment. They live by the carpe diem philosophy and need freedom to act and let their creative energy flow. They hate being forced to do something. With flexibility as their priority, they go with their impulses and move at the speed of life. Although they do not see themselves as whimsical, they feel their impulses are usually right and go with them. Easily bored, they highly value excitement, variety, and stimulation and are action oriented. They like to keep things moving, mentally or physically, their minds racing. They feel they can multitask their thoughts. Fun-loving, they move and change to avoid boredom.

Artisans love to make an impact, realizing that people may see them as unpredictable. Making an impression on people and affecting outcomes energizes them. They crave immediate results, and sometimes if they don't get a response they will push on until they do. In a sense, they are performers who love to wow the fans, to entertain for a group or one on one, although they may need to feel comfortable in the situation first. They can take something boring and make it fun, but whatever they do, they want to do it gracefully and skillfully. Class clowns as children, they are now the group comedians. With little rehearsal or planning, they can usually pull off anything, and they are great at thinking on their feet. Impressed by fellow performers, they will do anything to encourage them.

Exercise 1.1

BEST TEAM/WORST TEAM EXPERIENCE—STEP ONE

Most of us have had a positive team experience. Think of that team. What characteristics made it successful? What skills were you able to utilize that made it enjoyable? What were some of the assignments or activities? What made it fun?

Think of your worst team experience. What characteristics made it so unpleasant? What skills were you unable to utilize? What were some of your gripes? What were some of the projects or activities that made it so unbearable?

Write your thoughts in the space provided. We will return to this list after a brief discussion of the four temperaments.

Best Team Experience

_____

_____

_____

_____

_____

_____

_____

_____

Worst Team Experience

_____

_____

_____

_____

_____

_____

_____

_____

Exercise 1.2

QUICK TEMPERAMENT SORTER

Currently no accurate assessment for temperament exists. The following "quick and dirty" sorter is designed to help indicate which temperament(s) you should consider. It is not a formally validated, reliable assessment, but it does serve as another tool for self-discovery.

1. Read the word or words in the left column.

2. Choose the response that is most like you, not the one that you want to be like.

3. Rank the choices in each row from 1 to 4, with 1 being the most like you and 4 being the least like you.

4. After answering all the questions, total each column.

	1	2	3	4
Value...	Authenticity	Expertise and competence	Honor and duty	Excitement and adventure
Need...	To make a difference	To be logical	To be responsible	Freedom to make things happen
Want more...	Romance	Precision	Ownership	Stimulation
Enjoy...	Growth and development	Theory and debate	Nurturing and being needed	Making an impression
Descriptive verb...	Becoming	Knowing	Protecting	Doing
In setting a direction, need...	Meaningful purpose	A strategy	A step-by-step approach	An action plan/goal
Give feedback on...	Individual strengths	Accuracy and competence	Areas for improvement	What was done with skill and style
Like feedback that is...	Genuine and specific	Expert and specific	Constructive and specific	Frequent and direct

Exercise 1.2 (cont'd)

	1	2	3	4
Words are...	Dramatic and flowing	Precise and sophisticated	Specific and clear	Colloquial and to the point
Admire...	Realized potential	Knowledge and design	Achievement	Skill and beauty
Seek in life...	Meaning	Knowledge	Membership	Opportunity
Would hate to be...	Average	Incompetent	Excluded	Confined
Ideal work environment...	Expressive and personal	Innovative and intellectual	Organized and secure	Stimulating and varied
Learning is easier when...	Relationship centered, growth oriented	Knowledge centered, competence oriented	Authority centered, practical in application	Experiential based, practical/ tool oriented
Core abilities...	Diplomacy/ building relationships	Developing strategies/ analyzing frameworks	Logistics/ operations	Tactics/ performance with skill
Motto...	"Be all that you can be"	"Knowledge is power"	"To protect and serve"	"Carpe diem"
Total				

Total each column in the boxes provided. If your lowest total is in column one, this could be an indicator for the Idealist temperament. If your lowest total is in column two, this could be an indicator for the Rational temperament. If your lowest total is in column three, this might be an indicator for the Guardian temperament. A lowest total in column four might indicate that you should consider the Artisan temperament.

Exercise 1.3

BEST TEAM/WORST TEAM EXPERIENCE—STEP TWO

Now let's take a moment and review the "typical" answers to Exercise 1.1 for each of the temperaments.

The Best Team/Worst Team Experience exercises are a clear reminder that different people have different needs and values in any situation. While we may adapt our style in the business environment, our core needs, values, and favorite behaviors will most likely emerge in our evaluation of the experience.

Temperament	Best Team Experience	Worst Team Experience
Artisan	• Fun and exciting • Tons of variety • Immediate, concrete result • Challenging • Room for breaking the rules • Instant feedback/gratification • Sense of urgency • Lots of concrete, tangible actions • In control	• Boring • Dead-end • Pointless details or theories • Repetitious • Lots of useless rules/policies • No challenge • No ability to make an impact/difference • No one cared about the result • Drawn-out, unproductive meetings
Guardian	• Part of a group • Saw a tangible end result • Clear step-by-step approach • Defined roles/responsibilities • Recognition for completed tasks • Minimal changes in direction • Same people consistent over time • Every team member fulfilled his or her responsibilities	• No ownership • Constant changes in direction and people—change for change's sake • People not living up to their responsibilities or not meeting deadlines • No social interaction • Poor or no communication • Isolated or left out of group • No clear team spirit
Rational	• Able to learn new concepts • Intellectually challenging • Working with experts • Opportunity to analyze abstract data • Being the "expert" • Ability to solve problems • Strong future focus • Clear strategic direction • Ability to control own destiny	• Dealing with minutiae and details • Working in an area of little competence • No ability to influence direction • Repetitive, mindless, and mundane work • Bureaucratic overload • No vision or strategy • Surrounded by incompetence

Exercise 1.3 (cont'd)

Temperament	Best Team Experience	Worst Team Experience
Idealist	• Meaningful work with a sense of purpose • Personal connection with others in the team • Working in an area where learning and growth were possible • Helped others learn and grow • Served as diplomat and catalyst to group unity • Opportunity for creativity • Lots of positive feedback	• No positive feedback • Pointless work • Drawn-out, unproductive meetings • Isolated • Stressful interpersonal interactions and conflicts • Poor communication • Repetitive, detailed, practical work • Individual contributions unrecognized • Ethics compromised

Exercise 1.4

TEMPERAMENT SELF-ASSESSMENT

Based on the previous information, please do the following:

1. Review your ideas in Exercise 1.1 (see page 7) for best team experience and worst team experience. Compare them to the typical answers in Exercise 1.3 and list next to "Step One" in the following grid which temperament you believe is the closest fit.

2. Review the Quick Temperament Sorter (Exercise 1.2) on pages 8 and 9 and list the temperament it indicated next to "Step Two" below.

3. Now on pages 11 through 23 read the description for the temperament with which you identified most closely throughout these exercises. Feel free to try on multiple descriptions until you are comfortable with the one that feels like the "best fit." Read the other temperament descriptions to increase your awareness of how those with other temperaments view the world. As you read the descriptions, think of the other members of your team and consider which descriptions sound most like them.

Exercise	"Best Fit" Temperament
Step One: Best Team/Worst Team Experience	
Step Two: Quick Temperament Sorter	
Step Three: Read the temperament descriptions. Which temperament feels like the best fit?	

Because Artisans live in the here and now, they can adapt easily and are chameleonlike, able to fit into any group. Walking into a scenario, they immediately take in the lay of the land, sense what motivates others, and can meet them there. Artisans find themselves surrounded by camaraderie when working on a project and always form a good group of "buddies," although they don't necessarily keep in touch when things are over ("We had a good time, the situation ended, so it's time to move on"). They are up on the latest of everything: jokes, lingo, events, trends, you name it.

Artisans are contextual thinkers. Just as they can think on their feet, they think best within the context of a given situation. Yet when asked what they would do theoretically, it's hard for them to say; it is within a context that they can best see how everything fits and works. They like troubleshooting: "Send me into a mess and set me free to fix it." They recognize, define, go straight for the bull's-eye, and then move on, using their ability to read a situation and negotiate or fix the problem. Extremely persuasive, they know just how far people are willing to go and can get two sides to agree. (For Artisans, nonverbal cues are a dead giveaway.) They also see opportunity coming before anyone else does and quickly take advantage of it, before it can even knock. In fact, they respond quickly to everything, being tacticians. They know what needs to happen and get it done in the most expedient way possible, often hurdling red tape and sprinting around protocol. Their motto is "just do it and move on to the next project."

Intensely observant of sensory detail, Artisans need frequent sensory stimulation. They live for the thrill of the moment, for intense, over-the-edge excitement, and push themselves to the outer limits for the experience. So in tune are they with the here and now that what appears to be a risk to others seems grounded to them. They have a handle on the concrete, tangible, and real, and therefore trust their impulses. A risk, they say, is merely another skillful performance easily done when you're in tune with your senses. Their love of taking chances plays itself out not only in situations involving physical danger but also in working around the rules and in financial wheeling and dealing. For Artisans, adventure keeps life fun.

Their sensory awareness also provides them with a keen eye for aesthetics; they notice details and variety. They consider themselves connoisseurs of taste, touch, smell, sight, and sound—all that is sensual. They are also adept with tools and gadgets, which satisfy their "function hunger." Everything has a function (or at least should), they say, so why not put it to use? With hands-on projects they are in their sensory element. Others may see them as fidgety tinkerers. When bored and unable to make an impact, they crave stimulation and their body language shows this. Tools help them speed up the process and aid in getting the desired results.

As learners...

Artisans like to learn in an experiential manner, to jump right in and try things out for themselves. Hands-on simulation, role-plays, and vivid examples can also help. They are active learners and want lots of tools and processes to aid in figuring everything out. It is imperative that the material be useful to them in some way. They learn best when the material is relevant to their goals; they want practical application. "How can I use the theory if I don't know where it fits?" they ask. Their whole motivation is based on the results they will get, and they are encouraged by immediate feedback. They want just enough theory to explore the details fully and move on to something new. They learn best in a stimulating environment where special attention is paid to variety and making things fun.

In the process of change...

Artisans thrive on change and variety. In fact, they sometimes change things just for the sake of fun. They feel that if you keep doing things differently you're bound to find a better or more enjoyable way, and they usually go along with any transformation for the novelty of something different. But they don't want the change to be confining.

Under stress...

Artisans experience stress when they feel fettered. Easily bored, redundancy drives them crazy. When they feel that life is completely lacking variety and excitement, they are at their wit's end. They react to stress by retaliating. Although this is the negative side of their need to make an impact, it doesn't necessarily mean they will "go postal." They have the ability to chew people out, manipulate, and work their art to make an impact without retribution. They may also overindulge in sensory pleasures, whether it's a night on the town or at home. The danger is in taking such pleasures to self-destructive extremes.

Overall...

As fun-loving individuals who value variety and stimulation, Artisans have strong sensory abilities that allow them to push the envelope of life. They need freedom to follow their impulses, prefer immediate results, think on their feet, and can adapt to any situation. Artisans live in the here and now, enjoying what the present has to offer.

The Guardian Temperament—To Protect and Serve

> *"Every right implies a responsibility; every opportunity,*
> *an obligation; every possession, a duty."*
> —J. D. Rockefeller, Jr.

Being needed and living up to their responsibilities is of primary importance to Guardians. Completely dependable, they work hard to fulfill all their duties and meet others' expectations. With family, team, club, or group, they need to feel valued. One of their biggest fears is being excluded from an organization they care about. Usually they are assigned the role of "the responsible one," whether they want it or not. They tend to take care of those important to them, as looking after others is second nature. They see themselves as preservers of traditions and history, of the comfortable and familiar ways that everyone can turn to for stability. Loyalty, reliability, and trustworthiness are some of the characteristics they most value in themselves. They approach the world with structure, sequence, preparation, and a desire to nurture.

Guardians like a structured environment. "Tell me what and how and I will diligently get the project done," they say. They want to put effective processes and procedures into place so that things are accomplished correctly and consistently over time. Experience has shown them that step-by-step processes provide a reliable course of action and result in the established expectations. For this reason, they feel, it is imperative that methods are standard and repeatable. They also want to know all the guidelines and regulations, so that they can abide by them without upsetting anyone. The rules are there for a reason, they believe, and we must all respect them so that everything runs smoothly. Guardians often find that they are the ones who end up setting guidelines and defining procedures, bringing the gift of stability to their world. However, they also feel compelled to be the enforcer at times when unreliable people don't follow the clearly stated directions. For Guardians there must be a determined hierarchy, a chain of command that dictates who is responsible for what and establishes accountability. They respect authority and do not confront it head-on. For them, roles and responsibilities need to be clearly defined so that each person knows his or her duties.

Guardians are also sequential thinkers. They naturally view things in a sequence and want each component to be in its proper place. Follow-through is never lacking in a Guardian's performance, as they always continue step by step through the entire sequence. They can't stand it when they have to sit though an unorganized program or meeting. While they organize their thoughts and ideas in this manner as well, they prefer to deal with what is material and tangible. They can manipulate large amounts of concrete data or material and find a suitable place for everything. Excellent at data monitoring and administrating over details, Guardians know that organization is one of their strongest abilities. When they look at any task or prepare to meet a goal, they can clearly see the appropriate place to start. Extremely talented with logistics, they get the right things to the right place at the right time, taking on jobs with a meticulous eye and noticing all the particulars others might not see. "Sometimes people think I am critical because I always notice when something is missing or done incorrectly," says the Guardian, "but I only want things to be done properly down to the smallest detail." They also remember clearly what worked or did not work in the past and adjust the process accordingly, not wanting to take chances on the future and preferring to learn from history.

But while Guardians like life to proceed according to plan, they also take into account the unpredictable things that cannot be structured and organized. Because they are very economical and hate to waste time, resources, or money, they plan and prepare diligently. Practice, practice, and prepare, prepare is the Guardian's motto. "I like to have everything tied up," a Guardian might say. "Loose ends only get tangled into a mess." Thus they are extremely provident and proactive in building up contingencies in case plans go awry—which is just what their fatalistic side knows will happen because that's life. Others say Guardians worry a bit too much about things they can't control. Sometimes their lack of faith in the way things go does cause them to overplan, which in the end, they realize, is really a waste of time. However, they are cautious and careful, always alert to the possibility of danger and wary of risk.

Furthermore Guardians consider it very important to protect and provide for their loved ones. Constant nurturers, they always place the needs of the group above their own. "I proudly provide for those who rely on me materially and supportively," says the Guardian. Possessions are important to them and they want those close to them to have all the comforts they can provide. Similarly, they take excellent care of their belongings. They also value practical application and want things to be useful. "Don't tell me your philosophies on life and the meaning of it all; I'd rather see solid common sense," says the Guardian. They believe in working hard to succeed and thus may not always give enough praise: "I expect everyone to meet his or her responsibilities, and that isn't anything special." Those who don't fulfill their duties or meet deadlines are especially frustrating for Guardians. On the other hand, they value those who do their best because they have exceeded what was expected of them. In addition, Guardians may take their desire to care for others to a larger arena and work to better their community in an effort to meet social responsibilities. Holidays and traditional celebrations are some of their favorite times; they love it when family and friends gather together and observe an important remembrance of their common heritage. Such things, they believe, must be done properly as we must respect our history and remember where we came from. For them, even at work it is hard to see old ways change, unless the new ways make a practical improvement.

As learners...

Guardians want material to be useful and pragmatic; learning information that is unnecessary to their goals bothers them. They want to see the applications of any theory taught and prefer to learn in an applied setting. For them, material should be clearly structured in a sequential order; it troubles them when an instructor jumps around without explaining why and indicating the specific changes, so that they can follow along. Guardians want to know all the specific details and like to be able to relate the information they are learning to their past experiences. The promise of practical results attracts them to a learning situation, but they need corrective feedback in order to stay motivated. They want to be able to do things correctly; they are diligent students under the right conditions and always respectful of the instructor.

In the process of change...

Change can be a big challenge for Guardians. They must be convinced that it is necessary and not just frivolous change for the sake of change. A detailed explanation of the benefits accompanied by supportive concrete data in writing allows them to assess the efficiency and effectiveness of the change. They prefer this information in writing so that they have time to review and prepare for the changes to take place. They also like to be able to provide verbal input and discuss their concerns.

Under stress...

Guardians are most stressed when they feel that the group has excluded them or someone "attacks" their group/family. A sense of insecurity can take over and leave them hurting. Irresponsibility and blatant disregard for the agreed-upon guidelines of the group also upset them. "I really need to feel that everyone respects everyone else and in doing so follows the predetermined standards," a Guardian might say. Along the same lines, insubordination stresses them, as it is one's responsibility to perform assigned tasks and duties. Guardians usually end up blaming and complaining when one of these issues sends them into stress. They recover best from stress when others appreciate and recognize their contributions. New membership provides that feeling of belonging that Guardians need.

Overall...

Reliable and caring, Guardians enjoy having a well-defined role and being part of a group. They prefer to structure their environment and plan ahead, and they value clear guidelines, respected by all, in order to live happily. "My trust is in my past positive/successful experience: what is tried and true," they say. "I am the keeper of tradition."

The Rational Temperament—Knowledge Is Power

> *"I don't think much of a man who is not wiser today*
> *than he was yesterday."*
> —Abraham Lincoln

Rationals' life is a search for knowledge. Intrigued by the workings of everything around them, be it animal, mineral, or vegetable, they want to understand why things work the way they do and constantly strive for a clear, certain mental perception. Before Rationals attempt anything, they want to know everything about it. One of their greatest fears is to be perceived as incompetent and ignorant, so they strive for expertise and mastery in their areas of interest, including hobbies. In this sense, some think they turn play into work.

Just as they like to attain mastery in their forte, Rationals want to master themselves. They believe they have the power to create their own destiny, that it is under their control. Self-control is also very important to them; they would not want to be perceived as overemotional or irrational.

Always looking for the underlying principles of the universe, Rationals often create their own conceptual models to organize and process information. They propose theories and hypotheses as their ideas formulate and their mental picture becomes clear. While they value knowledge gained by study, it is the insight this knowledge allows, the opportunity to develop their ideas and make something their own, that Rationals find most valuable. "I am an architect of ideas," a Rational might say. "I excel in design. In my eyes, there is always a new and better way of doing something." Thus, evaluating, critiquing, and redesigning are imperative in their thought processes.

Rationals have a keen ability to take in the whole picture, to see things in their broader context, but they also can hone in on the details to note exactly what is missing. They know that it is this capacity to assess everything from a critical thinking perspective that leads people to view them as harsh or critical at times. While they have a handle on the big picture and can see things as part of a system, they also have sharp differential thinking skills and naturally categorize information. Analysis, forecasting, and strategic planning are among their strongest talents. They can map out possibilities, project ideas, and devise complex stratagems, and they are excellent conceptual problem solvers.

Rationals demand logic and expect things to be consistent with the principles that govern them. Like scientists, they seek to understand, predict, and explain. With the ability to objectively analyze data and create appropriate categories, they feel confident to make logical and consistent decisions. "I try to be uniform in my system of beliefs," they say. "To be just and truly differentiate things, how can there be shades of gray?"

With their intense need to excel in their chosen field, their tendency toward perfectionism, they are in constant competition internally and with others. They love to meet challenges, especially those of a mental nature, and when they prevail, they feel it proves their competence. Performing a particular skill is, for them, a means to sharpen their abilities, which for them is important. Their standards are very high. They probe others for their competency areas and are disappointed when they don't find any of interest. They gravitate toward those with expertise, valuing their insight and intelligence, appreciating their feedback over the opinions of those they perceive to be nonexperts.

Rationals look to the future in order to develop strategies and long-range plans, but their conception of time is somewhat infinite. This is because their interests are in the universal principles that underlie everything and transcend time. Consequently they can sometimes be unaware of realistic time constraints and feasibilities.

Others say Rationals are oblivious to those around them, but Rationals prefer to see themselves as absorbed in their thoughts. "Besides," they protest, "emotional responses often have little bearing to me, so it is not such a mystery how I can be unaware of them." They would rather talk about ideas, concepts, and abstractions, about what might be the reason or rationale behind something. Favorite topics are those in which they have an in-depth knowledge, which, they realize, can lead some to conclude that they are arrogant. Always questioning, asking what and why, Rationals long to understand all that is around them and to make things better. They talk about systems and how things work; they philosophize and explain their theories and strategies to people. They also love to debate and pride themselves on their intellectual rigor. "I use reason and logic to argue and I expect others to do the same," they say. They carefully analyze people's rationales for their beliefs or statements, using their ability to pick out inaccuracy and inconsistency. "I am skeptical," they say, "and the burden of proof is on you."

As learners...

Perpetual learners, Rationals feel that erudition is in line with their core needs and moves them toward their goals. They approach learning from a "what and why" perspective, always looking for the underlying principles and preferring to deal with concepts and theories rather than be buried in facts. A conceptual picture overview is a necessary starting place for them. They learn best in an environment that is innovative and intellectual, and they want the material to be logical and objective. Competent instructors and expert feedback are essential.

In the process of change...

Open to change, Rationals enjoy designing better ways of doing things. Opinionated and generally enthusiastic about new ideas, they like to approach change with their intellect and fully design the best plan and strategy. Creating the processes and procedures to bring about the change also interests them. In fact, they tend to focus on the design, as it is more interesting to them, and thus they may delegate the actual implementation to others.

Under stress...

When feeling powerless or incompetent, Rationals tend to obsess and lose themselves in some detail of a project. They find it especially troublesome when they can't communicate concepts and strategies precisely enough or when others simply don't implement them as designed. Failure or feeling that they have appeared stupid tends to catapult them into a state of stress. Having a new project to focus on helps to reconfirm their perception of competence.

Overall...

In general, life is a process of learning for Rationals. They want to know all that they can in order to be competent individuals. "I search for truths, though I don't believe the truth exists," a Rational might say. They want mastery over themselves and all that they take on. Knowledge is power, they believe.

The Idealist Temperament—Be All That You Can Be

> *"When you cease to dream, you cease to live."*
> — Malcolm S. Forbes

The Idealist's life is a journey of self-discovery. "I want to be the best me that I can become," they say. Always searching for their purpose in life, Idealists want everything they do to be meaningful. They are passionate about what they believe in and have extreme difficulty doing something they feel has no value. They want to make a difference in this world, even if it's only a small one. One of their biggest fears is to be "average," living day to day without doing everything possible to make life mean something. They believe we can all contribute to the world in our own special way if we try. They want to be valued for their own unique contributions, and they view every other person as a singular individual with something special to offer.

Idealists believe in human potential. They say that we all have special gifts we bring to the world that are to be treasured and nurtured to their fullest. Idealists constantly ask themselves, Who do I want to be and what is my purpose? At the same time, they see the goodness in everyone and want to help others unleash their abilities. Striving to nurture and teach as much as they grow and learn, Idealists naturally give praise as they intuitively focus on people's strengths. They know just the right thing to say to make someone feel special, and when they lead people, they have a strong and charismatic commitment to helping them achieve their best. But although they are catalysts of self-actualization and mentors of hope for others, they can sometimes be very hard on themselves. Their desire to be all that they can be continually pushes them to go above and beyond in whatever they do and they can easily take on too much and end up overwhelmed.

Idealists view the world in light of their ideals, seeing the potential in everything. Others may say they need to be more realistic, but to the Idealist reality can be confining sometimes. "If we don't aim for our ideals, how can they ever become realities?" they ask. They feel they can believe in something so strongly that they can actually make it happen. "I am a strong advocate and enthusiastic spokesperson for any cause I believe in," they say.

Their ideals stem from the importance they place on ethics and integrity; Idealists have a strong sense of what is "right" and moral. Authenticity is also very important to them; they can't be someone they are not, and they work hard to put their beliefs into practice. In the same sense, they know when someone else is "fake" and they say it makes their skin crawl. They don't enjoy interactions with people who are not genuine.

On the other hand, they have an ability to draw people out, to bring out someone's true self despite surrounding superficiality. Compassionate and empathetic, they can easily and intensely identify with others' emotions. Sometimes this empathy is painful, and Idealists wish they were not so affected, but at other times they are glad for their rich emotional life. They value how close they can feel to others, even strangers. In this same sense, they are concerned about the personal lives and problems of those around them. When Idealists ask "How are you?" they really mean it. They can spend hours relating to friends or co-workers; when they are empathizing, nothing is more important. Good listeners, they are often sought out to discuss troublesome issues. Relationships are extremely important to them—not superficial acquaintances, but deep and meaningful connections with kindred spirits who understand them and whom they understand.

Idealists seek to create a harmonious environment. Conflict is gut wrenching for them. Diplomacy, however, is one of their special skills; they can build a bridge across what appeared to be an endless chasm, or foster communication between two parties in conflict. This interpreting ability often gives them the role of the peacekeeper, to facilitate understanding and strive toward cooperative, consonant interaction. Likewise, they can explain the same thing in different ways to different people without altering the content, allowing them to teach and communicate effectively. However, their desire for harmony and commitment to support those they care about can sometimes cause them to put the needs of others before their own. They know they must be careful about the sacrifices they choose to make.

Always focused on the future, Idealists can see all the possibilities. Their refusal to be confined by past and present allows them to freely explore ideas. They spend a lot of time philosophizing about how to make things better. Imagination and creativity are their tools in any task they take on. They love abstract ideas and are much more in touch with general impressions than with particular details. They see patterns and connections between seemingly disparate categories, and can link concepts and ideas that may not have an obvious association to others—a special ability called integrative thinking. Often they find that everything is like a living system; it's all connected and every part relies on the other in a giant collaborative effort. They also feel they can see the underlying meaning in everything. "I spend a lot of time predicting how others feel or what they think," the Idealist might say. "However, sometimes I can get hurt or into trouble by seeing meaning that was not intended."

As learners...

Idealists are very curious and love to learn as it provides them with a larger knowledge base and skills to work toward their goals. When learning, they need to know the purpose of the material, and they learn best when learning what is relevant to their aspirations and thus valuable to them. A supportive, flexible environment that focuses on individual needs and recognizes individual contributions is, to the Idealist, very valuable. Positive, constructive feedback is also necessary. Idealists like to be creative, to deal with concepts, and to discuss material openly, so that everyone can share and learn from different ideas. They appreciate innovation in teaching, as well as instructors who can show how various pieces of information relate so that they can synthesize the data into a comprehensive body of knowledge.

In the process of change...

Idealists approach change with the people in mind. It is imperative to them that important consideration be given to the human element before any changes occur. Just as they lead from an open and democratic point of view, they feel that in times of change we should all be able to contribute. Each person should have the opportunity to honestly discuss his or her feelings on the matter.

Under stress...

Idealists can become very stressed when they feel what they are doing is meaningless and without a higher purpose. "I can't stand to get bogged down in the picky details of day-to-day living," they say. When they feel that they have lost their identity and are nobody special, they can become depressed and disconnect from those around them. Their characteristic optimism also rapidly disappears if they perceive that people are being inauthentic or have betrayed them, especially those they care about. To get out of the doldrums, they have to make an effort to appreciate themselves, which is aided when they receive nurturing and support from others. Once they have found a new quest to believe in, they are back on their feet again.

Overall...

Complex and unique individuals, Idealists have characteristic patterns. They are always searching for who they are. They want to lead a meaningful life that will make a difference in the greater scheme of things. The Idealist's motto is, I believe in the potential of all of us, and my own goal is to be all that I can be.

TEMPERAMENT AND TEAM PERFORMANCE

In the first part of this chapter we examined the general theory behind temperament. Each temperament brings unique benefits to a team, while at the same time exhibiting certain behaviors that may inhibit team performance. Following are some general statements about each temperament's strengths and possible challenges in a team environment. You will be able to use this information in Part 2 of this book to diagnose your team dynamics and implement strategies to improve team performance. As we will learn later, when different individuals come together on a team, you can learn a lot about the overall team strengths and challenges based on an understanding of the different temperaments. Just as temperament reveals the motivations and core values of the individual, it also characterizes the culture of a team.

Table 1.1 provides some general statements about each temperament's possible strengths and possible challenges in a team environment.

Table 1.1 Strengths and Possible Challenges of Each Temperament on a Team

Temperament	Strengths	Possible Challenges
Artisan	• Dynamic, lighthearted demeanor, great storytelling • Quick thinking and great at seizing opportunities • Great tactical problem solvers • Strong drive to take action • Constantly looking for new ways of doing things • Create the most expedient solution • Short, concise communicators • Focus on the here and now • Flexible and adaptable in times of change • Understand the motives behind the behavior, able to persuade others to their way of thinking • Make good "buddies" on the team yet move on to new relationships easily	• May get bored easily and then disrupt the group • Impatient with those who are not as quick as they are • May react "play-by-play" rather than look for a proactive solution • May move to act without considering implications • May sidestep the rules in the process • May become impatient with what they perceive to be long-winded communication • May lose sight of long-term vision • May make unnecessary changes for variety and stimulation • May appear manipulative • May be viewed as superficial and uncaring
Guardian	• Strong team loyalty • Respect for authority • Provide historical perspective: what worked/didn't work in the past • Implement consistent systems and procedures to optimize resource allocation • Responsible, good follow-through • Contingency planning for all perceived eventualities • Bring continuity • Constantly monitor systems and procedures • Provide clear, step-by-step directions • Economical with resources and possessions • Can manage large amounts of information	• May want to maintain the group when no longer suitable • May not question authority when appropriate • May be viewed as inflexible and reluctant to change • May be too caught up in details and rigidly insist on existing processes • May follow through when they should move on • May be viewed as pessimistic and waste time overplanning • May be viewed as "anal" • May micromanage the details and find it hard to multitask simultaneously • May seem pennywise and pound foolish • May lose sight of the big picture in all the details

Table 1.1 Strengths and Possible Challenges of Each Temperament on a Team (cont'd)

Temperament	Strengths	Possible Challenges
Rational	• Strong strategic vision • Constantly looking for operating principles • Analyze a situation from multiple perspectives • Use precise language • Like to debate possible approaches • Will use critical reasoning to identify any possible weakness in a plan or idea • Constantly use theories and models to devise new ways of approaching work • Focus on ideas, new concepts, and results • Future focused in directing effort • Conceptual problem solvers, get to root causes	• May underestimate the detailed steps necessary to complete the tasks • May overcomplicate situations or lose themselves in theory • May overrationalize possibilities and postpone taking action • May appear "picky" with team members' word choice and use esoteric language • May appear to argue for the sake of arguing • May be perceived as overly skeptical, critical, and fault finding • May appear to change for the sake of change • May be oblivious to people and their concerns • May not be realistic about actual time requirements
Idealist	• Need a sense of "higher" purpose • Contantly see and wish to develop the potential of people in the team • Build bridges between disparate viewpoints • Innately assess the authenticity of those around them • Build strong team relationships to increase team cohesiveness and unity • Constantly see creative approaches • Bring passion and enthusiasm to the team when they feel the work is meaningful • Focused on possibilities in the future • Empathize and build consensus with the team • Give genuine feedback to team members • Emphasize communication	• May not draw the line quickly enough with performance problems • May appear wishy-washy because they see both sides of an issue • May fantasize negative meaning • May become overdependent on relationships or avoid conflict • Dislike detail and repetitive tasks • Will not enjoy work that is perceived as mundane or meaningless unless attached to a cause • May not be realistic, including about time requirements • May not make "tough" decisions • Need lots of recognition to maintain self-esteem • May "overcommunicate" or want to spend too much time getting to the bottom of issues

CASE STUDY OF TEMPERAMENTS IN TEAMS

Now let's look at a real-life team to show how the team members' temperaments influenced the team's performance. For the purpose of this case study, we will use an actual team responsible for the delivery of training in a large computer company. You will not only recognize each temperament's contributions but also notice how the interactions between the temperaments contribute to this team's performance.

Kelly: Team Leader

Kelly has an Artisan temperament. Before he started his team, he was in marketing, where he enjoyed the fast-paced, challenging environment. He was offered the opportunity to start up a new organization that would deliver national training to the internal population of the company. He seized the opportunity because he recognized the immediate impact he could make by forging the way in a new company department that would educate all those bright, new, enthusiastic employees. In addition, Kelly had the chance to learn lots of new, different, and "cool stuff."

Within the company the environment was constantly changing. The company was growing frenetically, so Kelly was able to grow his team to support the increased activity. With his team he continually adapted the direction to meet the needs of the organization. He also had eleven different bosses in a four-year tenure, but he didn't mind. Kelly changed his approach where necessary and knew instinctively how to get the support of each boss in order to take the team in the direction he wished it to go. He loved the freedom to chart his own course. His new bosses really weren't around long enough to keep up with him.

As director, Kelly helped put together persuasive promotional material supplemented by fun "trash and trinkets" that attracted people to programs and served as giveaways in training sessions. He also aided in designing a simulation-based training that allowed participants to run their own company. He loved experiential, hands-on learning opportunities and ensured that learning was fun yet practical for everyone. Kelly loved to travel, and in the new position he went to training programs all over the world, experiencing the immediate results of his team's actions.

Kelly attended a personality profiling session while he was in global operations and loved the information. At first he self-assessed as an Idealist, probably to be more like his boss, who was an Idealist (the chameleon in action!). Previously, he had felt he did not fit in anywhere. He believed he didn't behave as others behaved. He was always being chastised for having a short attention span, getting bored too easily, and not staying focused. Finally Kelly was able to understand the needs and values that were driving him as an Artisan, and as a result he felt relieved that it was okay to be himself.

The knowledge of temperament was also invaluable to Kelly in building his team; he realized that he could not be effective with a whole bunch of people exactly like him. The team might have a lot of fun and see things eye to eye, but they wouldn't be able to respond to the disparate needs of the job function. Recognizing that BLM (be like me) can influence the daily decisions we make, Kelly was committed to focusing on the qualities needed for each job and the person who would be the right fit. As he grew his team from eight people to over eighty, many people with diverse perspectives filled different positions within the team. As part of the new-hire orientation process, each team member attended a personality profiling session to enable him or her to understand the differences within the team and work productively together.

Gwen: Operations Director

Gwen has a Guardian temperament. She had been a purchasing manager for several years and enjoyed the methodical processes required to succeed in finance. She had progressed in a step-by-step manner up through the ranks, and she was now in a position where she wanted to move up to another level and into a management position with more functions. Gwen looked for a position in which she could use her sequential thinking skills and create and implement processes and procedures. She also felt that her role in purchasing was a little too individually focused; she wished to belong to a larger group with work that was more team based.

Kelly created the operations role for Gwen, in which she was responsible for the logistical organization of the training delivery process. Her group administered over classrooms, booking trainers, communicating with the field, and distributing course materials, rosters, checklists, and so on. Kelly knew that this was not something he himself would want to do but that the requirements of the position would be rewarding for a Guardian. It was critical that consistency and structure be established around this delivery process, to ensure customer satisfaction, and he thought Gwen was the right person for the job.

Gwen enjoyed her new position, and Kelly thoroughly appreciated the organizational strengths Gwen brought to the table. She had often perceived herself as boring and unimaginative, and now she was able to see the concrete results that her logistical ideas produced for the team. Creativity does not just involve thinking of crazy new possibilities (although that seemed to be Kelly's strength); it also involves looking at the way things have been done in the past and adapting those methods to new arenas.

Gwen also enjoyed being part of Kelly's management team. She initiated regular meetings that were well managed, with specific agendas, and therefore very productive. She was able to see where she was contributing, plus at the same time see what else the group was doing. Gwen was also responsible for hiring and training a new team to expand the capabilities of the group. She clearly defined the roles and responsibilities for her team members and then used behavioral interviewing to ascertain whether the candidates had the required skills and abilities.

In addition, Gwen clearly defined her own responsibilities. Beyond managing the group, she also managed the entire financial budget for Kelly's group. Gwen was horrified at the astronomical prices hotels charged for training room rental and food delivery. To be more economical, she gathered data on outside classroom costs and compared these with the costs associated with the company owning its own dedicated classrooms. Gwen discovered that the company could save approximately four million dollars, even including construction costs, if it bought and managed its own classrooms. So it did! With Gwen in the operations role, the team was consistently able to reduce the cost of training delivery, even though the costs of products and services increased. With Gwen's clever management of purchasing and negotiating agreements with vendors, the training cost per day went down by 5 percent a year.

Eileen: Field Education Manager

Eileen has a Rational temperament. She had been in the training and education business for many years and had always been on the leading edge of new educational learning systems. With two master's degrees, she placed import on expertise in her field. Eileen was looking for a position where she had more control over her own destiny. With her previous employers Eileen had been responsible for instituting new training delivery models at other major corporations. Kelly was looking for someone who had extensive knowledge and expertise in the training world to bring credibility to the team and help them have a more positive impact. Although the rest of the team had complementary skills and abilities, he needed someone who could help him envision a new framework for delivering training in the field. When Eileen joined the team, there were no delivery organizations in the field—all training delivery was managed from corporate head-quarters. With Kelly she envisioned a training delivery model that was more proactive. The group's work could be categorized differently to create a field delivery organization. The training functions would be associated with regional sales offices. The individuals in these functions would therefore be able to participate in assessing training needs, designing and delivering appropriate localized training, and coordinating with the corporate headquarters. Together they created the role of performance consultant for these field members. Performance consulting was based on a competency model of delivering training. For each position critical competencies were identified, and then training was identified for each one. The training did not have to be delivered in a traditional classroom setting but could use innovative, alternative delivery methodologies.

With Eileen's input the team also began a more formalized strategic planning process. Previously the group had engaged in tactical strategic planning emanating from Kelly's inherent strengths. The team would see future possibilities from the current data and plan projects accordingly. There was no clear overview of the group's responsibilities or any critical questioning as to why the team was performing in a specific way. Eileen brought that ability to the group. At its regular meetings the team reevaluated its strategic position, categorized the workload into Key Result Areas, and established strategies for each critical business function.

Suzanne: Technical Training Manager

Suzanne has an Idealist temperament and has been in the group since its origination. She had worked for the company for nearly six years when she was given the opportunity to establish a technical training group within a planning and scheduling function. She welcomed the new opportunity because it gave her the chance to begin a completely new department. Suzanne envisioned the new group as a valuable asset to the company. She knew there was an enormous need for effective training of internal technical experts, and she felt that the training designed for external customers would not meet the group's needs. Setting up the group gave her a sense of purpose, as she felt that this group could really help make a difference to the developers.

Suzanne felt that she was uniquely qualified to perform this function, based on her previous experience with another training company and her personal relationships with some of the key players, who would be her prime internal customers. Within the company she had consistently built meaningful relationships and excellent connections.

When Kelly joined, Suzanne welcomed him as a new director because there had been a great deal of upsetting conflict under the previous director. She was happy with Kelly's leadership style, which was very laissez-faire, and respected the way he was able to sell the benefits of the internal training group to the customer base. Once he was sure that his team knew the general direction, Kelly was happy to leave Suzanne alone to do her work but was there as a support if she needed help. The culture that Kelly established and reinforced was also aligned with Suzanne's ethics. Kelly was considerate and open to the input of all team members and great at providing positive feedback, which Suzanne really valued. She also appreciated the cohesiveness that Kelly was able to instill in the group, through a clear goal, a unified sense of direction, and regular meetings to build interpersonal cooperation.

In her work Suzanne enjoyed creating an approach for the delivery of training to the technical community, recruiting the key players, and then putting a plan in place to make it a reality. Many of the people she worked with were genuine individuals whom she trusted. She was able to see a variety of different components, functions, and skills located in several different functional areas, which could be integrated to more effectively provide internal technical training. While working for Kelly, Suzanne grew her group from three people to twenty, with no turnover, and established many innovative and valuable training programs, which were well received by the internal customers.

SUMMARY CHECKLIST

Understanding your and other temperaments is the first step in profiling your team. Remember, however, that your current "working hypothesis" on temperament may change as you experience more profiling tools in Chapters 2 and 3. The four temperaments are illustrated in Figure 1.1. Before moving on to Chapter 2, answer the following questions:

1. Have you identified your temperament?

2. Have you reviewed the in-depth description of your temperament?

3. Have you reviewed the other temperament descriptions so that you are familiar with the differences and complexities of each Temperament?

4. Did you see any of your team members in the temperament descriptions? Start thinking about your colleagues and keep track of your hypothesis for each team member, as you will use this information to create and analyze your team profile in Part 2. The grid below may help you take notes. However, keep in mind that individuals often adapt their style when at work, so you may be seeing their adapted style rather than their true temperament. While you can try to work with your hypotheses, they should be validated by the team members to whom they pertain. The personality profiling information in Part 1 should be shared with everyone on your team.

Team Member Assessment

Team Member Name	Artisan	Guardian	Rational	Idealist

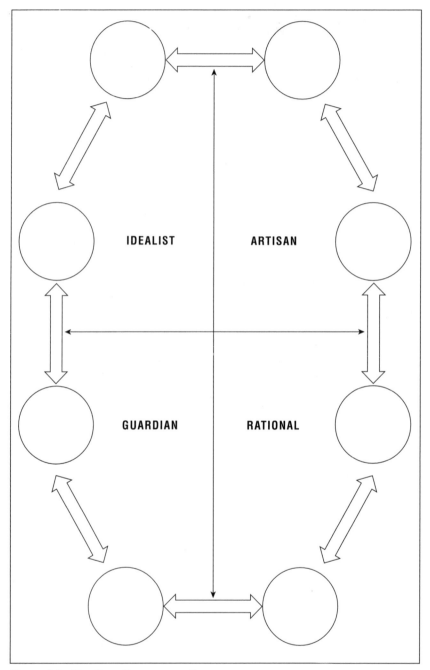

Figure 1.1   The Four Temperaments

2

Understanding Functions

HOW DO I APPROACH WORK?

"Knowing others is wisdom, knowing oneself is Enlightenment."
—Lao-tzu

In the first chapter we looked at the first step in creating your team profile, understanding temperament, and the impact of this on team performance. While temperament theory is very rich, it cannot explain the full depth of personality. In order to gain more insight into differences among team members, we need to examine team member behavior through other dimensions.

Therefore the second step in creating your team profile is to understand how team members prefer to gather information and make decisions. Then we will revisit the case study from Chapter 1 to demonstrate how team members use these preferences to meet their internal needs and contribute to team goals. Understanding how team members vary in the way they perceive information and weigh decision-making criteria will be a key input to the team profile, providing further perspective on how the team as a whole functions in these areas.

ORIGINS OF TYPE THEORY

Largely overshadowed by the work of Freud, Carl G. Jung's contributions to the study of personality were unappreciated during his lifetime. His work is best known in popular psychology for distinguishing the difference between extraversion and introversion. However, Jung's work delved much deeper into the elements of being.

As described below, Jung recognized two different ways of gathering information and two different ways of making decisions. Jung saw that different individuals preferred one function to the other when gathering information or making decisions—that is, the function was more natural or more consistently used. Rather like writing with your preferred hand (the hand you normally write with), a preferred function is smooth, requires less conscious thought, and takes less time. However, Jung also recognized that every individual uses all of these functions to a greater or lesser extent. This differing use of functions can explain many of the behavioral differences among team members. When we try to use functions that are not as natural for us, rather like writing with our nonpreferred hand, the function appears as awkward, requires conscious thought, takes more time, and produces less satisfactory results.

COGNITIVE PROCESSES

Jung's theory states that all individuals *meet their core needs* by either gathering information or making decisions. He identified two cognitive processes that account for this phenomenon: the *perceiving* (information-gathering) process and the *judging* (decision-making) process. He further described two functions associated with perceiving data (gathering information), which he called *Sensing* and *Intuition,* and two functions that are used for judging (making decisions), *Thinking* and *Feeling.* Furthermore, for each function there is an outward *(Extraverted)* and inward *(Introverted)* orientation, creating eight functions as listed in Table 2.1.

In our work with organizations we have found that the technical terms for these functions tend to be confusing and hard to remember—for example, Extraverted Sensing. For this reason, we have assigned a verb form that we believe, in one word, captures the essence of each function. This verb form does not necessarily represent the full depth and definition of the function, but it does aid memory and practical application of the theory. As you can see, in Table 2.1 we have added a word that helps to identify each function in "business language."

Each team member's personality includes all four information-gathering functions and all four decision-making functions. In fact,

Table 2.1 **Information-Gathering and Decision-Making Functions**

INFORMATION-GATHERING (PERCEIVING) PROCESS			
Sensing (S)		Intuition (N)	
Extraverted Sensing (S_E)	Introverted Sensing (S_I)	Extraverted Intuition (N_E)	Introverted Intuition (N_I)
Experiencing	Recalling	Brainstorming	Visioning

DECISION-MAKING (JUDGING) PROCESS			
Thinking (T)		Feeling (F)	
Extraverted Thinking (T_E)	Introverted Thinking (T_I)	Extraverted Feeling (F_E)	Introverted Feeling (F_I)
Systematizing	Analyzing	Harmonizing	Valuing

everyone uses all of these mental tools to some degree in daily life. While some situations may compel us to use all eight functions, the differences between individuals lie in the ease with which we can naturally access and use specific functions. A preference for a function, just like handedness, is an unconscious mental orientation or habit of the mind manifesting in individual differences. It is not the same as a conscious choice or liking one thing more than another. Therefore each team member will use some functions naturally and others with difficulty or not at all.

Before we define and explore each function in depth, imagine that you are in charge of organizing a team retreat. The process might push you to use all eight functions in the ways shown in Figure 2.1 on page 36.

The next sections of this chapter introduce you to each of these information-gathering and decision-making functions to enable you to assess which functions are most comfortable for you. Understanding the functions you use easily will provide you with greater insight into your own strengths and challenges and a greater comprehension of team member differences. Also keep in mind which functions your team members appear to use most easily.

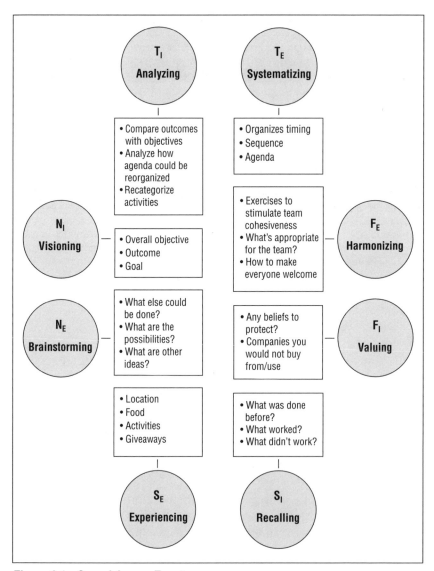

Figure 2.1   Organizing an Event

INFORMATION-GATHERING (PERCEIVING) FUNCTIONS

Learning About Sensing and Intuition

Jung described how each person gathers or perceives information; he referred to this as a cognitive function. If we prefer the Sensing (S) function, we tend to gather information primarily through our senses, using sight, sound, smell, touch, taste, and balance. We tend to trust whatever can be measured or documented, what is real and concrete. As a result, we doubt intuitive insights. If we prefer Intuition (N), we gather information through ideas, patterns, possibilities, hypotheses, and inferred meanings. We tend to trust abstract concepts, ideas, and hunches and minimize the importance of practical experience.

Learning About the Information-Gathering Functions

There are two versions of Sensing and Intuition, one being more externally focused (S_E and N_E) and one more internally focused (S_I and N_I).

- *Extraverted Sensing (S_E): Experiencing* is defined as moving outward for the acute uptake of sensory data (sight, sound, touch, taste, smell, and balance) in the immediate external world. Those who use Experiencing with ease approach life with a zealous hunger for experiences and adventure.

- *Introverted Sensing (S_I): Recalling* is defined as moving inward to recall past experiences and compare the present information to a historical data bank of sensory data and internal thoughts, feelings, and sensations. Those who use Recalling with ease approach life with care, valuing the lessons they have learned in the past.

- *Extraverted Intuition (N_E): Brainstorming* is defined as moving to the outer world for the unlimited creation and exploration of new ideas, new possibilities, and the perceptions of patterns and meanings in the moment. Those who use Brainstorming with ease approach life with a constant enthusiasm for possibilities and a desire to create new options.

- *Introverted Intuition (N_I): Visioning* is defined as moving inward for the unconscious correlation of conceptual ideas, possibilities, and symbols that enter consciousness as a whole system or idea. Those who use Visioning with ease approach life with intensity, seeking to understand the meaning of things and, through the perception of future implications, actualize their own intuitive insights.

Exercise 2.1 allows you to "try on" the four information-gathering functions.

Exercise 2.1

TRYING ON THE INFORMATION-GATHERING FUNCTIONS

Below is a short exercise to enable you to experience each of the information-gathering (perceiving) functions. As you conduct the exercise, think about which function seems easiest for you. Try rating them on a scale from 1 to 10, 1 being easiest to use and 10 being most difficult. When we find a function easy, it normally means it is a well-developed function. When we lose patience with the exercise or it is particularly difficult, it likely means that we are using a less-developed function. Think about the extent to which you use each function in day-to-day life. If you use it frequently, mark it with 1. If you rarely use it, mark it with 10.

Extraverted Sensing (S_E): Experiencing

Take a moment and focus on the here and now. Do not allow your mind to wander into conjectures or possibilities, or to recall past data. Observe intensely the sights around you. Listen carefully for all sounds, smell the air, and tune into every detail of the physical environment.

Notes:

_____

_____

How did this exercise feel? How easy was it? How often do you use this function without being prompted? Rate on the scale below your ability to naturally use this function.

A 1 means relatively effortless; you tend to use this a lot in your day-to-day world. A 10 means that this was difficult for you to do; you wanted to move on. You don't normally use this function in your world.

Rating   1   2   3   4   5   6   7   8   9   10

Introverted Sensing (S_I): Recalling

Think of a project you are working on. As you think of the project, review a similar project you tackled in the past. What did you do? How did it work out? Go back to that project and experience it as though you were there again. See that past environment in all its detail, feel your movement, listen to the sounds, replay the sequence of events, and recall the outcome. Try to replay the experience in its entirety, rather like operating a video camera. Compare and contrast this project with the last one.

Notes:

_____

_____

Exercise 2.1 (cont'd)

How did this exercise feel? How easy was it? How often do you use this function without being prompted? Rate on the scale below your ability to naturally use this function.

Remember, 1 means relatively effortless; you tend to use this a lot in your day-to-day world. A 10 means that this was difficult for you to do; you wanted to move on. You don't normally use this function in your world.

Rating   1   2   3   4   5   6   7   8   9   10
_____

Extraverted Intuition (N$_E$): Brainstorming

Think of the subject matter of this book, individual behavior and personality as they relate to team performance. List possible alternate applications for these concepts, as many as you can imagine. Think outside the box. What are some completely new applications for this body of knowledge? Anything goes!

Notes:

_____

_____

How did this exercise feel? How easy was it? How often do you use this function without being prompted? Rate on the scale below your ability to naturally use this function.

Rating   1   2   3   4   5   6   7   8   9   10
_____

Introverted Intuition (N$_I$): Visioning

Think about a time when you had a complex problem. You stepped back from the problem. Later you got an "aha!" and the solution came to you in its entirety. To what extent do you get such "shower solutions" and epiphanies? To what extent do you rely on them when gathering data?

Notes:

_____

_____

How did this exercise feel? How easy was it? How often do you use this function without being prompted? Rate on the scale below your ability to naturally use this function.

Rating   1   2   3   4   5   6   7   8   9   10

(If you were asked to generate lots of options for uses of a concrete object such as a plate, and you found that easier than the Brainstorming exercise, this is normally an indicator of Experiencing, not Brainstorming.)

Models of Information-Gathering (Perceiving) Functions

On the following pages, in Tables 2.2 through 2.5, models are used to help you understand Extraverted Sensing (S_E): Experiencing, Introverted Sensing (S_I): Recalling, Extraverted Intuition (N_E): Brainstorming, and Introverted Intuition (N_I): Visioning in more detail. Please review each of the diagrams and read the examples shown to begin to build a more in-depth understanding of the information-gathering functions. In order to help you with self-assessment and team profiling, think about whether each of these functions is something you or your team members appear to do with ease. *Note that the functions in these models are defined and characterized according to how they would appear as a first, or easy-to-use, preference. Each function would look different if it were one of your less-used functions.*

The center of each diagram provides the definition of the function. The other boxes explain the four different facets of each function. Under each facet are details on the types of behavior clues and signals you might observe from individuals using these functions in day-to-day life. Keep in mind that the process of information gathering is, to a certain extent, unconscious. Thus, in self-selection, the bulleted behaviors and approaches may give the best indication of our function and the functions others are using as they interact with us.

Information-Gathering Functions in Action

After you have tried on each of the information-gathering functions (S_E, S_I, N_E, N_I) and read the detailed charts (Tables 2.2 through 2.5), Table 2.6 on page 45 gives you two different "in action" examples of these functions as you might see them in a team work situation. The first column provides examples of what each function looks like in a meeting. The second column shows how a team member might approach a new job and some of the thoughts that might be evoked by using each function.

Self-Assessment: Information-Gathering Functions

Now complete Exercise 2.2 on page 46 and assess which information-gathering function appears to be easiest to use.

Table 2.2   Extraverted Sensing (S$_E$): Experiencing

ATTUNE TO NEW SENSORY EXPERIENCES	AWARE OF PHYSICAL FACTS IN THE ENVIRONMENT
• Constantly search for the new and various sensory stimuli including variety, excitement, and the newest/best tools rather than depth and meaning of experience • Value all experiences: If it is meant to be experienced, experience it! • Seek to explore and adventure • Seek constant stimulation or activity • May increase movement (touching, fidgeting, playing with tools) when not getting adequate sensory stimulation	• Accurately at a glance notice all the details and changes in the physical environment • Keen to clues in human reactions and body language • May appear disorganized but know where things are • Know lots of facts and details • Have a strong sense of spatial awareness—maneuver through the physical world with natural skill • Aesthetic awareness—pick up on what looks good and what doesn't • Individual sense of style appreciated in self and others

Moving outward for the acute intake of sensory data in the immediate external world

DRAW ON WHAT IS THERE NOW, NOT ON WHAT WAS OR MIGHT BE	PRACTICALITY ORIENTED— WANT ACTION
• Are present, in the moment • "What can we do now?" • Constantly improvise, using existing tools and techniques (tools, time, and physical skills) • Cut to the chase and implement an effective solution to get more stimulation • Aware of and use current resources, even if not a usual use • Take things at face value	• Action oriented, fast-paced • Act on a trial-and-error approach • Get to the point quickly in words • Economize effort in actions • Respond quickly to current circumstances

Table 2.3   Introverted Sensing (S$_I$): Recalling

ATTUNE TO OWN VIVID DATA BANK OF PAST SENSORY EXPERIENCES	**AWARE OF PAST EXPERIENCES AND TRADITIONS**
• Recall memories more vividly than present experience • Remember the physical world and subjective impressions in detail • Observe current information and file it internally for retrieval when needed • Internally file details that coincide with personal interests and experiences; discard other information	• Highly trust their own vivid data bank of knowledge and experiences • Communicate "shoulds" and "oughts" related to respect or traditions • Uphold traditions and ceremony, talk about heritage and history • Know and describe how things have always been • Value experience in others • Ask, "What is your experience?" Say, "In the past...," "In my experience..."

> **Coming forward into awareness of a historical data bank of sensory experiences**

DRAW ON PAST EXPERIENCES AND APPLY WHAT IS RELEVANT TO THE PRESENT SITUATION	**PRACTICALITY ORIENTED— CAUTIOUS**
• Perceive connections between current information and past experience • May show no immediate response while accessing data bank of past and processing information • Recall previous relevant experiences to generate new ideas • Compare and contrast present and past • Project the past into the future: "I did this last time and this happened, therefore the same thing will happen again"; can become pessimistic—"Things always go wrong"	• Research thoroughly and collect data before acting • Strong sense of reality—like to deal with what is concrete and tangible • May resist new ideas, especially if there is no experience to reference or it did not work well before • Appear steady and reliable • Conserving or economical • Reluctant to change unless change is practical

Table 2.4 Extraverted Intuition (N$_E$): Brainstorming

ATTUNE TO NEW IDEAS AND POSSIBILITIES	AWARE OF CONNECTIONS AND MEANINGS
• Live in a world of ideas, a stream of consciousness • Think out loud/hypothesizing, speculating • Constantly explore new options • Perceive potential • Energize others to act on possibilities • Constantly transforming—optimistic about change	• Read between the lines—may infer meaning or intention that is most often accurate • Talk about trends • Recognize patterns and connections in a given situation • Quickly understand complexities • Able to reframe and look at things differently

> Moving to the outer world for the unlimited exploration of new ideas and possibilities with a perception of pattern and meaning

DRAW ON WHAT IS THERE TO BRAINSTORM WHAT MIGHT BE	ABSTRACTLY ORIENTED— WANT NO LIMITS
• Constantly brainstorm and envision, as everything sparks an idea, "what if," "all we have to do is...," and so on • Take the information and go straight to possibilities inherent in the situation • Seek interaction to develop ideas—need a sounding board to help stimulate the flow of possibilities • Always see how things could be better	• Suffocated by routine • Explore future possibilities • Focus on generating insights, not implementing • Focus on the conceptual picture rather than details • Imagination runs free, often without consideration of the constraints imposed by the environment or the time and energy limitations of individuals

Table 2.5   Introverted Intuition (N$_I$): Visioning

ATTUNE TO INTERNAL REFRAMING AND ENVISIONING	AWARE OF PATTERNS AND MEANINGS
• See situations from a fresh perspective • Reflectively imagine possibilities • Experience random acts of illumination—"aha!" experiences/ "shower solutions"/epiphanies • Project intellectually independent ideas • Aware of future implications	• Perceive the whole pattern or system • Notice patterns in seemingly unrelated things • Understand archetypes and symbols • Able to simplify the complex • Cut through distractions and get to the meaning • Exhibit intense depth of understanding

Coming into consciousness of conceptual ideas, future possibilities, and symbols as a whole system or idea

DRAW ON OWN INSIGHTS AND VISIONS OF FUTURE	ABSTRACTLY ORIENTED— WANT REFLECTION
• Sharp, uncanny insights into what will be • Trust "flashes of insight" without concrete supporting data • Seek to develop innovative ideas • Long-range view • May suddenly change their model or approach for no obvious reason, as a new vision is realized • Complex ideas; may seem ahead of their time • May have difficulty articulating their vision; others may see them as rigid about their ideas	• Like to attack complex problems but prefer to work on them alone • Prefer innovative solutions over practical ones • Absorbed in thought—refuse to act until their internal picture is formed • May ignore or dismiss details that don't fit into their inner perspective • Seek solitude to perceive connections and integrate new ideas • Ideas come after a time delay

Table 2.6 Information-Gathering Functions in Action

Function	Looks Like in a Meeting	Approach to New Job
Extraverted Sensing (S_E) **Experiencing**	Notices every detail: what's not said, what people are wearing, and so on. Sees body language cues. Practical suggestions about what to do now. Interactive and alert. Restless with abstract theory; easily bored.	Picks up information in the environment: What's the building like, what's on the walls? What equipment/tools will they have? Aware of key players. "Reads" people based on their body language and other subtle cues.
Introverted Sensing (S_I) **Recalling**	Quietly observes what's going on. Tells what has been done in the past in like situations. Warns of what can go wrong. Asks for information about others' experience. Will question untried approaches. May appear overly cautious or negative.	Can remember vividly the sounds, sights, and emotions of first days on jobs. Will think back to the steps necessary to get established and the process for learning the new job. Compares this company with previous companies in all ways.
Extraverted Intuition (N_E) **Brainstorming**	Verbalizes ideas and possibilities; enthusiastic. May jump between seemingly unrelated topics. Constant verbal brainstorming. Uses one idea to jump to the next. May not consider practical application; shows frustration if mentioned. Notices meanings of nonverbal behavior.	Thinks about the possibilities in the new position in terms of potential and projects. Will ask questions and think about future, where the company is heading, what are the possibilities. Will consciously look for hidden patterns and meanings.
Introverted Intuition (N_I) **Visioning**	Integrates ideas presented into one cohesive possibility. Sees future implications. Will participate in discussion about possibilities, but then will appear to withdraw. Will then suggest a complete solution seemingly unrelated to previous discussions. Avoids questions and has difficulty describing a model in detail or explaining where the idea came from.	Thinks about the position and subconsciously creates a picture for how the job should look, desired role. Will think of personal model and approach for the job and may be unwilling to discuss or have difficulty discussing ideas with others.

Exercise 2.2

INFORMATION-GATHERING FUNCTIONS
SELF-ASSESSMENT

1. Write your score for each of the functions in Exercise 2.1 in the top row in the chart below.

2. Read the tables describing each function (Tables 2.2 through 2.5) and mark in the box below which function sounds most and least like you. Mark 1 for most like you, 2 for next most like you, 3 for next most like you, and 4 for least like you.

3. Finally, read Table 2.6, "Information-Gathering Functions in Action," showing how the functions are used in a meeting and in starting a new job. Rate each function 1 (for the one that is most like you) to 4 (for the one that is least like you).

4. Total each column. The lowest total number indicates the function that is probably easiest for you to use. We will revisit this page in Chapter 3.

5. Circle the function with the lowest number.

Gathering Information	Extraverted Sensing (S$_E$): Experiencing	Introverted Sensing (S$_I$): Recalling	Extraverted Intuition (N$_E$): Brainstorming	Introverted Intuition (N$_I$): Visioning
Exercise 2.1 Rating on a scale of 1–10 1: Easy/ Use frequently 10: Difficult/ Use infrequently				
Tables 2.2–2.5 1: Most like me 4: Least like me				
Table 2.6 1: Most like me 4: Least like me				
Total				

DECISION-MAKING (JUDGING) FUNCTIONS

Learning About Thinking and Feeling

The second of Jung's cognitive processes relates to how we make decisions and come to conclusions. If we make decisions based on Thinking (T), these decisions tend to be made impersonally, logically, and analytically. We see criteria as black and white: the facts, ma'am, just the facts! If we make decisions based on Feeling (F), we are more interested in subjective criteria such as personal values, the people involved, and special circumstances. We see criteria as shades of gray. Both are rational decision-making processes; they simply use different criteria.

Learning About the Decision-Making Functions

Team members use two versions of Thinking and Feeling, one version being more focused on data in the external world (T_E and F_E), and one version more focused on internal decision-making criteria (T_I and F_I).

- *Extraverted Thinking (T_E): Systematizing* is defined as quickly making decisions using logical, objective criteria to organize, structure, and achieve goals in the external world. Those who use Systematizing with ease approach life with drive and assertiveness, looking to organize the environment in a logical way.

- *Introverted Thinking (T_I): Analyzing* is defined as making decisions where external information gathered is synergized into a model using internal logical criteria. Those who use Analyzing with ease approach life as objective observers, desiring to develop the rational principles by which they gain insight into the workings of the world.

- *Extraverted Feeling (F_E): Harmonizing* is defined as making decisions using subjective criteria to optimize interpersonal harmony. Those who use Harmonizing with ease approach life as facilitators of group consensus, seeking connection with all those around them.

- *Introverted Feeling (F_I): Valuing* is defined as making decisions based on subjective values and an internal belief system. Those who use Valuing with ease approach life wanting all humankind to live in congruence with what is right.

Exercise 2.3 allows you to "try on" the four decision-making functions and see how well they fit.

Exercise 2.3

TRYING ON THE DECISION-MAKING (JUDGING) FUNCTIONS

Below are some short exercises to enable you to experience each of the decision-making functions. As you do the exercises, think about which function seems easiest for you. Try rating them on a scale from 1 to 10, 1 being the easiest to use and 10 being the most difficult. When we find a function easy, it normally means that it is a well-developed function. When we lose patience with the exercise or it is particularly difficult, it normally means that we are using a less-developed function.

Extraverted Thinking (T_E): Systematizing

Think about a trip you would like to take. List the places you would visit. Decide how you would research these places to identify what specifically you would like to do at each site. (How many days would you spend in each place? What would you see at each location?) Put a detailed plan in place for your trip, in order to ensure that you achieve what you want from the journey.

Notes:

_____

_____

How did this exercise feel? How easy was it? How often do you use this function without being prompted? Rate on the scale below your ability to naturally use this function.

Remember, a 1 means relatively effortless; you tend to use this a lot in your day-to-day world. A 10 means that this was difficult for you to do; you wanted to move on. You don't normally use this function in your world.

Rating   1   2   3   4   5   6   7   8   9   10

Introverted Thinking (T_I): Analyzing

List all the information that you associate with England (for example, castles, monarchy). Try to list at least twenty factors. Now try to group this information so that it falls under approximately six headings, for instance, geography. Make sure you have no more than six major categories. What different headings could you have used? How could you have grouped items differently? (The headings are likely to be different depending on who categorizes the list.)

Notes:

_____

_____

How did this exercise feel? How easy was it? How often do you use this function without being prompted? Rate on the scale below your ability to naturally use this function.

Rating   1   2   3   4   5   6   7   8   9   10

Extraverted Feeling (F~E~): Harmonizing

Think of a decision you need to make. Think of the people who might be affected by this decision. Write down what you believe would be their point of view. Decide which would be the most appropriate decision for the group, and the one that would make the most people feel comfortable. Think of possible conflict that this decision could create and identify how to reduce that disagreement.

Notes:

How did this exercise feel? How easy was it? How often do you use this function without being prompted? Rate on the scale below your ability to naturally use this function.

Rating   1   2   3   4   5   6   7   8   9   10

Introverted Feeling (F~I~): Valuing

Think about your ideal company. List your work values and then pick a company and compare how what you know about its values meshes with your own. Where are its values different from yours? What could you live with? What would you not be able to tolerate?

Notes:

How did this exercise feel? How easy was it? How often do you use this function without being prompted? Rate on the scale below your ability to naturally use this function.

Rating   1   2   3   4   5   6   7   8   9   10

Models of Decision-Making (Judging) Functions

The charts on pages 51 through 54 (Tables 2.7 through 2.10) will help you understand in greater detail Extraverted Thinking (T_E): Systematizing; Introverted Thinking (T_I): Analyzing; Extraverted Feeling (F_E): Harmonizing; and Introverted Feeling (F_I): Valuing. Please review each of the diagrams and read the examples shown to begin to build a more in-depth understanding of the decision-making functions. Understanding how you approach decisions compared to other team members can be useful in optimizing team cohesiveness. In order to help you with self-assessment and team profiling, think about whether each of these functions is something you or your team members appear to do with ease. *Note that the functions in these models are defined and characterized according to how they would appear as a first, or easy-to-use, preference. Each fuction would look different if it were one of your less-used functions.*

The center of each diagram provides the definition of the function. The other boxes explain the four different facets of each function. Under each facet are details on behavioral clues and signals you might observe from individuals using these functions in day-to-day life. Keep in mind that the process of decision making is, to a certain extent, unconscious. Thus, in self-selection, the bulleted behaviors and approaches may give the best indicator of our function and the functions others are using as they interact with us.

Decision-Making Functions in Action

Table 2.11 on page 55 gives you two different examples of how team members would use the decision-making functions. The first column gives you examples of some of the behaviors you might see from team members as they use these functions in a meeting. The second column shows how a team member might make a decision on selecting a vendor for a project and some of the thoughts that would be sparked by using each function.

Self-Assessment: Decision-Making Functions

Now complete Exercise 2.4 on page 56 and assess which decision-making function appears easiest for you to use. Then complete Exercise 2.5 on page 57. In Chapter 3 we will revisit these data as we link temperament, functions, and type.

Table 2.7 Extraverted Thinking (T$_E$): Systematizing

SEEK TO LOGICALLY ORDER THE EXTERNAL WORLD	PUT FACTS AND LOGIC FIRST
• Look for the organizing principles	• Work with established facts and proven data
• Create a library of principles, knowledge, and rules	• Convince with fact-based logic
• May use models and frameworks to organize and explain information	• Demand proof
• Tend to see right or wrong/black or white	• Critically question the logic of others—may appear cold
• Take a definite stand	• Want logic—can get along without harmony
• Want things and information in a logical sequence	
• Want order for order's sake	
• Order thoughts and rationale out loud—can be verbose with verbal pros and cons list	

Decision making using logical criteria to organize, structure, and achieve goals in the external world

EXPECT A RATIONAL WORLD	FOCUS ON IMPLEMENTING—ACT
• Expect consistency between principles and outcomes—even with factors such as behavior	• Organize resources (people, things, objectives) to accomplish strategies
• Mechanistic approach—if this happens, then this will happen	• Quick, decisive action—impersonal decisions
• Point out possible flaws in systems, procedures, and ideas	• Deal with problems quickly, move to contingencies, anticipate consequences
• Need to be treated fairly and equally	• Skill in logistics—break things down into achievable components
• Control "irrational" emotions—relatively unaware of own and others' emotions	• Implement—plan, direct, delegate
• Normally have a logical reason/rationale that can be expressed clearly in detail	• Need closure and put boundaries in the external world
• Impatient with inefficiency and ineffectiveness	

Table 2.8   Introverted Thinking (T_I): Analyzing

SEEK TO DEVELOP INTERNAL MODELS	PUT THEORIES, DATA, AND LOGIC FIRST
• Develop internal system for understanding external data	• New views more important than new facts
• Create precise data banks	• Work with theories or underlying principles
• Look for the inherent principles of data	• Rarely express opinions and logic unless challenged
• Check ideas and data for consistency with internal mental models	• Believe their theories are objective and totally logical
• Easily dismiss information that doesn't fit into the model	• Can be stubborn about their own ideas—difficult to persuade
• Clarify distinctions between theories: will provide an independent rationale and philosophy	• Focus on truth and accuracy—people and relationships of secondary importance

> **Decision making where information gathered externally is evaluated and sorted based on an internal standard/model of logical criteria**

EXPECT THEIR MODEL TO WORK	FOCUS ON ANALYSIS—REFLECT
• Can confuse mental model with external reality	• Approach people and events as objective observers
• May not easily and clearly articulate the model they perceive	• Prefer to work out problems and make decisions internally and alone
• Rigorous standards take precedence over their own and others' needs	• Analyze for precision, accuracy, and clarity
• Defend ideas/internal realities voraciously	• Constantly evaluate and improve their ideas and models
	• Critiquing comes naturally—hone in on inconsistencies
	• Disengage to analyze and observe
	• Internally evaluate pros and cons
	• Trust their own carefully considered decisions

Table 2.9 Extraverted Feeling (F$_E$): Harmonizing

SEEK TO CREATE A HARMONIOUS ENVIRONMENT	PUT THE NEEDS OF THE GROUP FIRST
• Constantly change style and approach to optimize group harmony	• Tune in and adjust to the values of others
• See what is positive, harmonious, and uplifting; may disregard negative, limiting messages, situations, and conclusions	• Put the needs of others first in making decisions; suppress their own position and may appear codependent at times
• Desire to alleviate concerns and suffering of others	• Strive to treat others with unconditional positive regard
• Exude warmth and enthusiasm; can appear "gushy"	• Take care not to hurt others' feelings
• May appear moody; affected dramatically by the mood of the situation	• May sacrifice an individual for the sake of the group
• May recognize logical criteria but fly in the face of logic, making decisions to bring about harmony	• Able to build group dynamics and make connections
	• Welcome everyone and try to include them

Decision making using subjective criteria to optimize interpersonal harmony

EXPECT APPROPRIATE BEHAVIOR FROM SELF AND OTHERS	FOCUS ON CONNECTING—ACT
• Protocol—people should comply with the implied standard of behavior	• Empathize; feel others' emotions
• Know the appropriate behavior for a given situation	• Seek to establish rapport and feel a disconnect when rapport is broken
• Able to tell appropriate stories—self-disclosure	• Ask questions that cut to the core of the issue
• Constantly evaluate objects, ideas, and events under the strong influence of societal norms	• Epitome of the people person—outgoing, friendly, and focused on relationships
• Readily make judgments that are "fitting" to the situation	• Know the right thing to say to make someone feel good and important
	• Reveal their feelings on their face and in their body language; easy to tell how they feel

Table 2.10 Introverted Feeling (F$_I$): Valuing

SEEK TO DEVELOP BELIEFS AND CREATE INTERNAL HARMONY	PUT VALUES AND BELIEFS FIRST
• Live by internal convictions	• Reject data inconsistent with their values; can be stubborn about a belief
• Sensitive to contradictions between internal values and external requirements	• Value individuality and uniqueness—find diversity immensely appealing
• Constantly strive to clarify beliefs and values	• Are deeply disappointed when those they care about do not share their values
• Decide who and what to support	• Firm and uncompromising in their beliefs when related to their values system
• Talk about what is meaningful and important to them	
• Have intense emotions regarding beliefs and values	• Tend to be the ethical backbone of a group—attempt to influence by example
	• Hold their values deeply—choose when and if to divulge them
	• Disclose with trusted confidants and like-minded individuals

> **Decision making based on subjective values and an internal belief system**

EXPECT A "GOOD" AND MORAL WORLD	FOCUS ON EVALUATING—REFLECT
• Have a vision of utopia	• Evaluate right and wrong regardless of objective evidence and decide what is worth standing up for
• Believe in a better world	
• Focus on what is good in others, downplaying their faults, often to be disappointed later	• Sense who is genuine; avoid superficial conversation
	• Try to understand others by putting themselves in others' shoes
• Habitual worldview is forgiving—cherish hope	• Reveal so little of themselves that they can appear indifferent
• Feel misunderstood—hard to articulate their values	• May appear mild, modest, and self-effacing, but all is evaluated internally

Table 2.11   Decision-Making Functions in Action

Function	Looks Like in a Meeting	Selecting a Vendor
Extraverted Thinking (T_E) Systematizing	Talks about ways to organize and mobilize people, structures, and equipment. Decisive, eager to push to conclusion and action. Aware of the agenda and timeframes. Will comment on what won't work. Has lengthy logical reasons for all decisions	What is their proven track record? What published data are available about their products and services? How quickly did they respond to the request for proposal? How well structured was their proposal? What specific actions did they recommend and when? Will make a quick, firm decision.
Introverted Thinking (T_I) Analyzing	Analyzes proposals logically. Will check ideas and data for consistency, then comment on what is missing or inconsistent. Able to bring clarity to discussion by sorting and defining categories. Firmly defends own ideas. Talks about own philosophies. Will present alternative rationale for actions.	Concerned with how well the vendor's proposal links with own mental model of how the project should be tackled. Takes vendor's data and integrates them with own internal system or framework. Will disengage to analyze what will work before making a decision.
Extraverted Feeling (F_E) Harmonizing	Ensures everyone gets to participate. Mediates conflict. Addresses the impact of possible ideas on morale and people involved. Friendly and warm; self-discloses. Meets, greets, and welcomes. Shows feelings on face and in body language.	What is the existing relationship with the vendor? Is everyone comfortable with the vendor? Do you trust them? Will they be easy to work with? Will they fit in with the team?
Introverted Feeling (F_I) Valuing	Silently weighs ideas and proposals against personal value system. Likely to be amenable to ideas yet will push back if idea crosses personal values. Will verbalize ethical issues.	What are the company's ethics and beliefs and how do they mesh with my internal values system? Is their behavior in line with what I believe is right? Will they deliver on their commitments?

FUNCTIONS AND TEAM PERFORMANCE

While every team member has the ability to use every function, some are easier to use than others. When we are young, we tend to rely primarily on one information-gathering and one decision-making function. If we use other functions, they are not as easy and take more

Exercise 2.4

DECISION-MAKING FUNCTIONS
SELF-ASSESSMENT

1. Write your score for each of the functions in Exercise 2.3 in the top row in the chart below.

2. Read the table describing each function and mark in the box below which function sounded most and least like you. Mark 1 for most like you, 2 for next most like you, 3 for next most like you, and 4 for least like you.

3. Finally, read Table 2.11, "Decision-Making Functions in Action," showing the functions in a meeting and selecting a vendor. Rate each function 1 (for the one that is most like you) to 4 (for the one that is least like you).

4. Total each column. The lowest number indicates the function that is probably easiest for you to use. We will revisit this page in Chapter 3.

5. Circle the function with the lowest number.

Making Decisions	Extraverted Thinking (T_E): Systematizing	Introverted Thinking (T_I): Analyzing	Extraverted Feeling (F_E): Harmonizing	Introverted Feeling (F_I): Valuing
Exercise 2.3 Rating on a scale of 1–10 1: Easy/ Use frequently 10: Difficult/ Use infrequently				
Tables 2.7–2.10 1: Most like me 4: Least like me				
Table 2.11 1: Most like me 4: Least like me				
Total				

Exercise 2.5

COMPLETING YOUR SELF-ASSESSMENT

1. Go back to Exercise 2.2.

2. Which information-gathering function had the lowest score (closest to 1)? Write that function in the space below.

_____

3. Go back to Exercise 2.4.

4. Which decision-making function had the lowest score (closest to 1)? Write that function in the space below.

_____

time and conscious effort. As we grow up, we hope to develop fluency in other functions. By understanding which team members are using which functions, you will be able to recognize the conflicts that occur over perception of data and decision making, which can appear to pull the team in different directions. In addition, when a group of people come together as a team, they develop a set of functions that provides clues as to how the team as a whole naturally gathers information and makes decisions. It is important to understand the group momentum in these areas, as they are strongly linked to team performance. Let's look at the different strengths and possible challenges each function brings to the team, shown in Table 2.12 on pages 58 and 59.

In a team, often team members use different information-gathering and decision-making functions and, as a result, can appear to be acting at cross-purposes. Once we understand this process, we can use this diversity as a strength (to ensure all viewpoints are considered) rather than as a weakness (as a source of conflict). As we get older (and, we hope, mature!), we tend to expand our approach and use other information-gathering and decision-making functions. Understanding which team member is proficient in which functions is a vital element in maximizing team productivity. In the next chapter we will tie together temperament and functions into a more complete personality profile for you and your team members. But first let's revisit the team we met in Chapter 1 to show how their functions manifest themselves in team performance.

Table 2.12 Strengths and Challenges of Functions on a Team

First Function	Strengths on Team	Challenges on Team
Extraverted Sensing (S_E) Experiencing	• Observant of all current data • Opportunistic and action-oriented • Now focused and quick thinking • Flexible • Resourceful • Ask questions to make abstract more concrete	• May be impatient with abstract data or what is perceived as not taking action • May change direction too frequently • Can get easily bored without sensory input • May not enjoy abstract planning process
Introverted Sensing (S_I) Recalling	• Has great reference store of past data • Brings historical perspective to new ideas • Has organized, sequential thought processes • Conserves traditions • Makes practical applications • Creates new ideas from previous experiences	• May appear impatient with abstract data or what is perceived to be impractical • May bring forward "old" failures • May appear inflexible and not respond positively to new ideas and change • Can appear laborious in providing detailed descriptions
Extraverted Intuition (N_E) Brainstorming	• Quick at creating possibilities • Sees lots of options with a future focus • Does not see limitations • Always has a fresh perspective • Will look at things from new angles • Able to identify trends and patterns	• Tends to be impractical; will not understand time constraints and may fail in implementation • May appear too flexible—will want to reinvent the wheel for the newness of it • May overload in taking on new projects • May seem impatient with practical details
Introverted Intuition (N_I) Visioning	• Will come up with completely new ways of approaching a subject or system of operating • Is insightful into the future • Has broad, long-range perspective • Able to extract the essence of a complex situation • Thinks independently • Has facility with theories and concepts	• Tends to be stubborn about own approaches and may find it hard to articulate the source of an idea or model • May miss practical application • May appear distanced from the events at hand • May try to integrate too many ideas in one

Table 2.12 Strengths and Challenges of Functions on a Team (cont'd)

First Function	Strengths on Team	Challenges on Team
Extraverted Thinking (T_E) Systematizing	• Takes quick, decisive action • Excellent at categorization and organization of data and plans in the external world • Emphasizes logic and fairness • Is great at logistics, making things happen • Able to critically analyze flaws and correct them	• May be viewed as harsh; may remain distant from people • May get impatient when there is a delay in making a decision; will push for closure • May appear too swift in making decisions • May not allow enough time for others to buy into the decision
Introverted Thinking (T_I) Analyzing	• Takes a logical and objective approach • Makes impersonal decisions no matter what the mood at the time • Able to create new frameworks or hypotheses to categorize existing data • Values accuracy and truth • Is clear and precise	• As decision making is internal, logic may not always be clear to others • May leave the external world relatively unstructured; annoying for those who like closure and structure • Critical analysis can be viewed as being uninterested in people • Critiquing may be mistaken for criticism
Extraverted Feeling (F_E) Harmonizing	• Has a warm and personal approach • Will ensure everyone on the team is feeling comfortable • Able to understand the team dynamic, who needs what • Excellent in building communication bridges between members of the team • Will help to create a positive working environment for the team	• Can show negative emotion too easily on their face and in body language • May not make clear, objective decisions because of the people focus • May avoid conflict • May take direct questioning personally
Introverted Feeling (F_I) Valuing	• Can act as the conscience for the team • Tolerates and understands different perspectives • Offers quiet, consistent support to others • Is passionately idealistic	• Others may not understand their decisions because of the private nature of the decision-making process • Will be suddenly rigid when confronted with a decision that contravenes internal values system • High moral standards may appear unrealistic in today's business world

CASE STUDY CONTINUED

In Chapter 1, we met a team of over eighty people responsible for delivering training to a large computer company. In this section we are going to revisit Kelly, Gwen, Eileen, and Suzanne so that we can assess the impact of their preferred functions on the team.

Team Overview

- Kelly is an Artisan: He primarily uses Experiencing and Valuing: S_E F_I.
- Gwen is a Guardian: She primarily uses Recalling and Systematizing: S_I T_E.
- Eileen is a Rational: She primarily uses Brainstorming and Analyzing: N_E T_I.
- Suzanne is an Idealist: She primarily uses Visioning and Harmonizing: N_I F_E.

As you can see, the team uses all eight functions with ease: S_E, S_I, N_E, N_I, T_E, T_I, F_E, F_I. The use of these functions became very obvious in their team performance.

Kelly is an Artisan: He uses Experiencing predominantly to gather information in the external world and then pulls inside to make decisions using Valuing against his internal belief system.

Kelly, the team leader, used Extraverted Sensing (S_E): Experiencing to constantly stay alert to what was happening in the company. As a fast-growing database manufacturer, the company had very little internal structure, so the rewards went to those who were the quickest to respond to what was happening. Kelly was able to turn on a dime many times and seize the opportunity rather than waiting for a formal change of position. He loved to make training programs more hands-on and fun. His desk would be piled high with paper, gadgets, new random facts, and data, but he could always find what he needed. Sometimes he overcommitted, "overdosing" himself with sensory stimuli, but he used his Introverted Feeling (F_I): Valuing to pull himself back to balance. His use of Valuing: F_I primarily to make decisions meant that he was incredibly protective of his people and his group. He believed in treating his entire team with respect and caring. He believed there was an appropriate way to lead—by walking the walk and talking the talk—and he did so. He also felt it was important for morale to organize regular planning and team meetings to ensure everyone remained committed to the group's purpose. When working with vendors whose tactical competence he valued, he would always look for opportunities to help them find other possibilities within the company. When a new vice president joined the group and made a decision to eliminate a series of jobs without consulting him, he felt she had unfairly compromised his internal values system and he found another job.

Gwen is a Guardian: She primarily uses Recalling to gather data, and then she comes into the outer world and uses Systematizing to make decisions.

Gwen, the operations manager, was able to use her Introverted Sensing (S_I): Recalling extensively when she came into Kelly's group. She used her prior experience in purchasing as a foundation for creating a complete logistical and financial system for the training group. Gwen's ability to start at the beginning and work through processes was critical in establishing a framework to grow the group from four people to seventy. The combination of Introverted Sensing (S_I): Recalling with Extraverted Thinking (T_E): Systematizing was crucial to structuring the group and the training delivery. Gwen would act as a balance to Kelly in introducing changes to systems or looking at new ways to operate. If she had no historical data, she would ask Kelly critical questions until she had gathered enough information to understand the change. This process curbed some of Kelly's impulsiveness but produced better results for the group as a whole. Once she had enough data, Gwen would take responsibility for the changes, and Kelly could move on to the next idea. She liked to push for closure using Systematizing: T_E so she could get on with implementation.

Eileen is a Rational: She predominantly uses Brainstorming to gather information in the external world, and then she evaluates decisions using her Analyzing function to create her own model and hypothesis.

Eileen, the field education manager, used dominant Extraverted Intuition (N_E): Brainstorming constantly to stimulate new ideas, create new possibilities, and formulate hypotheses. She was always the one to say "What if..." and look at a problem from a completely fresh perspective without getting bogged down in details or reality. In meetings her Extraverted Intuition (N_E): Brainstorming would appear as a constant stream of verbal consciousness while she encouraged the group to think "outside the box." No matter what was going on in the company, she always seemed optimistic about future possibilities. Eileen had a positive angle from which to view any situation and was resourceful in finding solutions. She appeared self-confident in her field and in applying new technologies. While using her Introverted Thinking (T_I): Analyzing to make decisions, she would brainstorm with the group but would withdraw to evaluate, prioritize, and analyze the situation. Even when a decision was made, she still wanted to consider other options. With her enthusiasm for new projects, she would occasionally overload herself because she did not pay enough detail to the practical realities. This would result in projects missing completion dates, or not meeting all commitments.

Suzanne is an Idealist: She gathers information from her internal world of future possibilities using Visioning and then uses Harmonizing to decide how these visions can be implemented while supporting the people on the team.

Suzanne, the technical training manager, used her dominant Introverted Intuition (N_I): Visioning to gain insights into training needed in the future. She gathered data and then quietly integrated it into her own mental model. She would then use this mental model as a basis for reshaping the environment. She refused to be hurried in this process. She reorganized her group and changed the reporting structure (having fewer people to report to her) because this model was more effective for her. Suzanne's auxiliary Extraverted Feeling (F_E): Harmonizing enabled her to be very sensitive to the group dynamic at all times. She would quietly observe the group process and give insights when appropriate. She was extremely loyal to the group. The director who headed up the group prior to Kelly advocated a culture of "creative conflict," and this was very unsettling for Suzanne.

As a team, whenever they took on a new project or worked in a specific area, they would rely on

- Kelly for his input into "What is happening in the organization right now?" (Experiencing)
- Gwen for "What has been done in the past that we might learn from and adapt for the future?" (Recalling)
- Eileen for her ability to think outside the box and ask, "What if we did this?" (Brainstorming)
- Suzanne for "What is the overall objective/result we wish to achieve?" (Visioning)
- Gwen for putting together a logical sequential action plan (Systematizing)
- Eileen for a new conceptual rationale or approach (Analyzing)
- Suzanne for understanding how others on the team might react to this approach (Harmonizing)
- Kelly for ensuring any decision was in alignment with team values (Valuing)

SUMMARY CHECKLIST

Understanding the functions you and your team members use to gather information and make decisions is the second step in analyzing your team profile and understanding your potential strengths as a team. The temperaments and functions are illustrated in Figure 2.2. Before moving on to the next chapter, answer the following questions:

1. Did you try on the information-gathering functions in Exercise 2.1 and assess which function was the easiest for you to use in Exercise 2.2?

2. Did you try on the decision-making functions in Exercise 2.3 and assess which function was the easiest for you to use in Exercise 2.4?

3. Did any of these functions remind you of a teammate? It can be difficult to recognize the functions you yourself use, but it will be helpful to you later on to try and generate some hypotheses for your team members, as you will use this information to create your team profile in Part 2. The grid below may help you make notes. Do keep in mind that a particular job or role may force someone to use a function more than he or she normally would. A person can even become quite adept with a function that is not naturally strong for them. While you can try to work with your hypotheses, they should be validated by the team member each pertains to. As noted in Chapter 1, all the personality profiling information in this chapter should be shared with everyone on your team.

Team Members and Functions

Function	Team Member Name(s)
S_E: Experiencing	
S_I: Recalling	
N_E: Brainstorming	
N_I: Visioning	
T_E: Systematizing	
T_I: Analyzing	
F_E: Harmonizing	
F_I: Valuing	

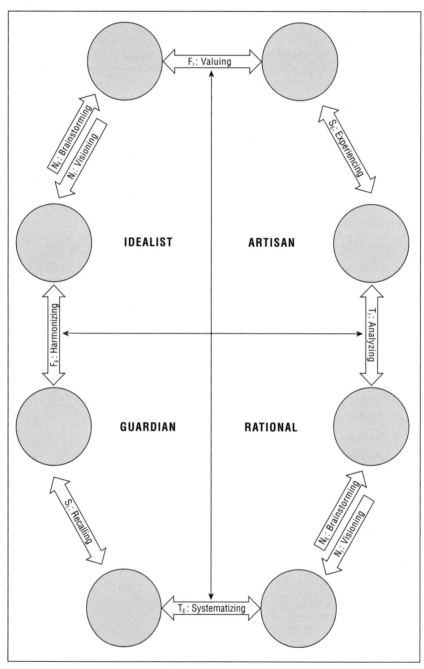

Figure 2.2 Temperaments and Functions

Understanding Type

HOW AM I WIRED?

*"One may understand the cosmos, but never the ego;
the self is more distant than any star"*
—G. K. Chesterton

The first two steps we used in creating our team profile focused on understanding temperament and functions for our different team members. In this third and final step we will integrate temperament and functions to determine type. The outcome of these discussions will be a four-letter code for you and your team members, often associated with the *Myers-Briggs Type Indicator* personality inventory. Type indicates your preferred functions, direction of energy flow, and orientation in the external world. This description will provide an objective framework to understand your own and other team members' preferred approach to their work. As with the other elements of personality, when you complete your team profile, you will also see that the team takes on a type of its own. Knowledge of type will help you better understand the preferred behavior of your team members, as well as that of your team as a whole. This chapter will complete Part 1, the team profiling section, and then we will be ready to move on to Part 2, where we will be able to diagnose our team performance against this profile and create an action plan to raise our team SCORE from the inside out.

THE *MYERS-BRIGGS TYPE INDICATOR*

The *Myers-Briggs Type Indicator* (MBTI) is one of the most widely used psychological assessments and a valuable tool in understanding personality. In this book we will use a method that allows you to arrive at a type through self-selection. If you have previously taken the MBTI, be aware that its accuracy on all four preferences simultaneously is between 65 and 85 percent and that any MBTI type code should be confirmed by self-validation. Numerous factors including stress, environment, and mood can affect an individual's results. Regardless of whether you are determining or validating your type, this chapter can guide you through the process.

Origin of the *Myers-Briggs Type Indicator*

Some years after Jung conducted his initial research, an American mother/daughter team, Katharine Briggs and Isabel Briggs Myers, were examining the question of why different kinds of people succeed or fail at different jobs. Jung's 1923 work *Psychological Types* resonated strongly with their own ideas on personality. Briggs and Myers began a twenty-year project of human observation and designed the *Myers-Briggs Type Indicator* to try to identify the functions that individuals innately use and in what sequence they come into play. They found that each individual could be distinguished by a four-letter type that indicates a preference for

Extraversion (E) or Introversion (I)
Sensing (S) or Intuition (N)
Thinking (T) or Feeling (F)
Judging (J) or Perceiving (P)

There are sixteen possible four-letter combinations of these eight preferences, which Myers and Briggs called personality types.

The *Myers-Briggs Type Indicator* was launched in 1962. Today it is the world's most widely used personality assessment tool, taken in 1997 by over 2.5 million people in the United States alone.

Integration of Type and Temperament

When Dr. David Keirsey, the psychologist who developed the modern perspective on temperament, came across the work of Myers and Briggs, he was amazed at the correlation between their work and his own. Their sixteen personality types matched his four temperaments almost perfectly, and he successfully synthesized the two theories into a holistic view of the human personality.

Myers, who continued the work her mother began, and Keirsey embraced each other's work, recognizing the validation and depth of perspective one brought to the other. Their combined work produces a deeper and more thoughtful understanding of the dynamics of personality: Temperament provides an insight into core needs and values, while type shows the typical approach individuals use to gather information and make decisions. In business, type and temperament have been adapted for valuable applications in team building, leadership, communication, career counseling, and management training in order to improve the effectiveness of individual and team performance.

While both Myers and Keirsey believed that temperament and type are innate, remember that there are other factors that affect character development, and other skills or aptitudes not in one's temperament/type code that can be acquired. For instance, upbringing, country of birth, native language, education, family values, cultural values, major life experiences, and other factors can cause many changes in the way we develop and the adapted style that we show the world. As you conduct your self-assessment, bear in mind the other factors that may have contributed to your character development.

DEFINING YOUR TYPE

The purpose of this process is not only to enable you to define your natural pattern of behavior but also to help you identify how other team members habitually respond to any given situation. Understanding this information will help you predict possible challenges and influence team behavior from the inside out. Use the steps outlined in Exercises 3.1 through 3.6 to define your type.

Exercise 3.1

SELECTING YOUR TEMPERAMENT

In Table 3.1 on page 68, circle in column one your best-fit temperament that you identified in Chapter 1.

Your Flow of Energy:
Extraversion–Introversion Preference

A critical set of differences, apart from functions, that was outlined by Jung is the preference for Introversion or Extraversion. Unfortunately, these words carry the baggage of a stereotypical set of behaviors. For instance, we often consider those with a preference for Extraversion

Table 3.1   Type Style Self-Asssessment Grid

Column One	Column Two	Column Three	Column Four	Column Five	Column Six
	Direction of Energy Flow	Information Gathering	Decision Making	External World	
Temperament	Extraversion(E) Introversion (I)	Sensing (S) Intuition (N)	Thinking (T) Feeling (F)	Judging (J) Perceiving (P)	Type
Artisan		S_E Experiencing	T_I Analyzing	P	E S T P I S T P
		S_E Experiencing	F_I Valuing	P	E S F P I S F P
Guardian		S_I Recalling	T_E Systematizing	J	E S T J I S T J
		S_I Recalling	F_E Harmonizing	J	E S F J I S F J
Rational		N_I Visioning	T_E Systematizing	J	E N T J I N T J
		N_E Brainstorming	T_I Analyzing	P	E N T P I N T P
Idealist		N_I Visioning	F_E Harmonizing	J	E N F J I N F J
		N_E Brainstorming	F_I Valuing	P	E N F P I N F P

to be gregarious, talkative, loud, and sociable. On the other hand, we often associate Introversion with those who are quiet, shy, unsociable, and reclusive. However, in reality you will find many gregarious Introverted types and many shy Extraverted types! People with both an Extraverting and an Introverting preference can be shy, as shyness is a form of anxiety in the presence of others probably linked to early life experiences. Gregariousness, on the other hand, is a learned behavior resulting from training and expectation (Pearman and Albritton, 1997). Our society encourages Extraversion as gregariousness and stigmatizes Introversion as antisocial. It is important to step away from these connotations in order to truly understand the meaning of Introversion and Extraversion in the sense we will be using them throughout this book.

In people with an Extraverting preference, energy naturally flows outward to the external world of people and events. More time is spent initiating and externally processing. In people with an Introverting preference, energy naturally flows inward to ideas and thoughts. Thus more time is spent in the inner world receiving and reflecting.

Many MBTI practitioners think of Extraversion and Introversion in terms of where you get your energy: from the outer world (Extraversion) or the inner world (Introversion). The common analogy is how you "charge your batteries." This definition, however, does not take temperament into account. An Idealist with a preference for Introversion may feel most energized when building a special relationship or getting involved in an organization that works to improve social conditions. In the same way, Artisans naturally seek sensory data, and therefore an Artisan with a preference for Introversion may still look like an Extravert. Individuals are most content and energized when their core needs are being met. It is more valuable to think of Extraversion and Introversion in terms of in what direction your energy flows—externally or internally—rather than its source.

Exercise 3.2

SELECTING YOUR
EXTRAVERSION–INTROVERSION PREFERENCE

There is no correlation between the direction of energy flow and temperament. For all temperaments there are those who prefer Extraversion and those who prefer Introversion. In Table 3.1 in column two alongside your temperament, write either E (Extraversion) or I (Introversion) based on the characteristics most like you in Table 3.2.

Table 3.2 Characteristics of Extraversion and Introversion

Extraversion	Introversion
Often draw out to interact	Often pulled in to reflect
Comfortable initiating relationships	Comfortable responding in relationships
Process information in the external world—talk everything over	Process information in the internal world—think everything over
Easier to "read": self-disclose readily	Harder to "read": share personal information with a few close people
Talk more than listen	Listen more than talk
Communicate with enthusiasm	May keep enthusiasm to self
Use more expressive body language	Use more reserved body language
Many diverse relationships	Smaller number of in-depth relationships
Need outer world validation	Trust self-validation and insights

To help you more fully comprehend the differences between Extraversion and Introversion, review the characteristic behaviors associated with using those preferences in Table 3.2.

Incorporating the Information-Gathering (Perceiving) Functions: (Sensing–Intuition)

The first of Jung's functions, as we discussed in Chapter 2, describes how each team member gathers information.

Extraverted Sensing (S_E): Experiencing is defined as moving outward for the acute uptake of sensory data (sight, sound, touch, taste, smell, and balance) in the immediate external world. Those who use Experiencing with ease approach life with a zealous hunger for experiences and adventure.

Introverted Sensing (S_I): Recalling is defined as moving inward to recall past experiences and compare the present information to a historical data bank of sensory data and internal thoughts, feelings, and sensations. Those who use Recalling with ease approach life with care, valuing the lessons they have learned in the past.

Extraverted Intuition (N_E): Brainstorming is defined as moving to the outer world for the unlimited creation and exploration of new ideas, new options, and the perceptions of patterns and meanings in the moment. Those who use Brainstorming with ease approach life with a constant enthusiasm for possibilities and a desire to create new options.

Introverted Intuition (N_I): Visioning is defined as moving inward for the unconscious correlation of conceptual ideas, possibilities, and symbols that enter consciousness as a whole system or idea. Those who use Visioning with ease approach life with intensity, seeking to understand the meaning of things and, through the perception of future implications, actualize their own intuitive insights.

Remember, all temperaments use all four information-gathering functions at different times. However, there is a link between the information-gathering functions they primarily use and their temperament.

- *Artisans* tend to use Extraverted Sensing (S_E): Experiencing first.

- *Guardians* tend to use Introverted Sensing (S_I): Recalling first.

- *Rationals* tend to use either Extraverted or Introverted Intuition (N_E or N_I): Brainstorming or Visioning first.

- *Idealists* tend to use either Extraverted or Introverted Intuition (N_E or N_I): Brainstorming or Visioning first.

Exercise 3.3

SELECTING AN INFORMATION-GATHERING FUNCTION

Go back to Exercise 2.5 on page 57 and make a note of which information-gathering function you selected. Then return to Table 3.1 on page 68, and in column three circle that information-gathering function. The goal of this process is to complete the table horizontally and finish a whole row.

All of the information-gathering functions are found in two places in column three. Circle both to facilitate this process. For instance, Experiencing is in the top and bottom boxes next to Artisan. Brainstorming is located in the bottom boxes next to Idealist and Rational.

Incorporating the Decision-Making (Judging) Functions: (Thinking–Feeling)

As we discussed in Chapter 2, the second of Jung's cognitive processes relates to how team members make decisions and come to conclusions.

Extraverted Thinking (T_E): Systematizing is defined as quickly making decisions using logical, objective criteria to organize, structure, and achieve goals in the external world. Those who use Systematizing with ease approach life with drive and assertiveness, looking to organize the environment against logical facts and data.

Introverted Thinking (T$_I$): Analyzing is defined as making decisions where information gathered is synergized into a model using internal logical criteria. Those who use Analyzing with ease approach life as objective observers, desiring to develop the rational principles by which they gain insight into the workings of the world.

Extraverted Feeling (F$_E$): Harmonizing is defined as making decisions using subjective criteria to optimize interpersonal harmony. Those who use Harmonizing with ease approach life as facilitators of group consensus, seeking connection with all those around them.

Introverted Feeling (F$_I$): Valuing is defined as making decisions based on subjective values and an internal belief system. Those who use Valuing with ease approach life wanting themselves and others to live in congruence with what is right.

Remember, all temperaments use all four decision-making functions at different times. However, there is a link between the decision-making functions they primarily use and their temperament (see Table 3.1).

- *Artisans* tend to use either Introverted Feeling (F$_I$): Valuing or Introverted Thinking (T$_I$): Analyzing first.

- *Guardians* tend to use either Extraverted Thinking (T$_E$): Systematizing or Extraverted Feeling (F$_E$): Harmonizing first.

- *Rationals* all use the Thinking preference. However, they will use Extraverted Thinking (T$_E$): Systematizing if they use Introverted Intuition (N$_I$): Visioning, or Introverted Thinking (T$_I$): Analyzing if they use Extraverted Intuition (N$_E$): Brainstorming.

- *Idealists* all use the Feeling preference. However, they will use Extraverted Feeling (F$_E$): Harmonizing if they use Introverted

---

Exercise 3.4

SELECTING A DECISION-MAKING FUNCTION

Go back to Exercise 2.5 on page 57 and make a note of which decision-making function you selected. Then return to Table 3.1 on page 68, and in column four, circle that decision-making function. The goal of this process is to complete the table horizontally and finish a whole row.

All decision-making functions are found in two positions in column four. Circle both to facilitate this process. For instance, Systematizing is next to Recalling in the Guardian row and next to Visioning in the Rational row. Valuing is next to Experiencing in the Artisan row and next to Brainstorming in the Idealist row.

Intuition (N_I): Visioning, or Introverted Feeling (F_I): Valuing if they use Extraverted Intuition (N_E): Brainstorming.

Your Orientation to the External World: Judging–Perceiving Preference

In developing the MBTI, Katharine Briggs and Isabel Briggs Myers added the Judging–Perceiving scale based on Jung's information-gathering (Perceiving) and decision-making (Judging) processes.

- If we have a Judging preference, we prefer to make decisions in the external world using our externally oriented judging functions—Extraverted Thinking (T_E): Systematizing or Extraverted Feeling (F_E): Harmonizing.

- Thus we will primarily gather information in our internal world with our internally oriented perceiving functions—Introverted Sensing (S_I): Recalling or Introverted Intuition (N_I): Visioning.

- If we have a Perceiving preference, we prefer to gather information in the external world using our externally oriented perceiving functions—Extraverted Sensing (S_E): Experiencing or Extraverted Intuition (N_E): Brainstorming.

- Thus we will primarily make decisions in our inner world using our internally oriented judging functions—Introverted Thinking (T_I): Analyzing or Introverted Feeling (F_I): Valuing.

- Using the Judging (decision-making) and Perceiving (information-gathering) functions in alternative worlds (external Extraversion and internal Introversion) provides balance for the personality. We could never operate successfully if we made decisions and gathered information in the outer world; we would never go inside to reflect. Or if we made decisions and gathered information internally, we would never emerge into the outer world!

To help you more fully comprehend the differences between Judging and Perceiving, review the characteristic behaviors associated with using those preferences in Table 3.3 on page 74.

Exercise 3.5

SELECTING YOUR JUDGING–PERCEIVING PREFERENCE

In column five of Table 3.1 on page 68, circle either the "J" or "P" letter code that might apply based on the characteristics most like you in Table 3.3.

Table 3.3 Characteristics of Judging and Perceiving

Judging	Perceiving
Most comfortable after decisions are made and then wish to adhere to them	Most comfortable leaving options open or quick to change decisions as additional information becomes available
Set goals and work toward achieving them on time	Change goals as information becomes available
Prefer knowing what events are coming up; less comfortable with the unexpected	Like adapting to new situations; more open to unexpected outcomes
Finish the task in a structured manner and find satisfaction in completion—push for closure	Finish the task in a random manner and find satisfaction in responding to the needs of the moment
Consider deadlines serious	Consider deadlines elastic
See time as a finite resource	See time as a renewable resource
Schedule time; plan and organize	Are spontaneous and flexible

---

Exercise 3.6

SELECTING YOUR TYPE

In Table 3.4 on pages 76 through 83 are descriptions of each type based on the four-letter combination of preferences, functions, and temperaments.

1. If the boxes you have circled or written in Table 3.1 are in one horizontal line—for example, you marked Artisan, Extraversion, Experiencing, Analyzing, and P—then your type in column six should be ESTP.

2. If the boxes you have circled or written are not in a horizontal line, then you may need to read multiple descriptions and see which seems to be the best fit.

3. As you read each description of type, think about how good a fit it seems. If you are not sure, go back to the grid and look at alternatives. If it really sounds like you, congratulations, you have identified your "true type." If it doesn't, keep reading until you find your "best fit" type. Artisans in particular can find themselves in multiple descriptions, as they adapt to the environment they are in. If you still are not sure, you may wish to see a professional counselor for a more complete assessment.

DESCRIPTIONS OF TYPES

Table 3.4 on pages 76 through 83 presents a description of each of the sixteen types. The descriptions are written in the following way:

- Four-letter code and temperament are in the heading.
- Core needs (related to temperament) are then listed.
- First function: the function that this profile uses first to either gather information or make decisions. This is the function that is smoothest, requires the least conscious thought, and appears most true to the descriptions in the tables (see Chapter 2).
- Second function: the function that this profile uses in a "support" role to balance the first function.
- The third and fourth functions: the functions that are the flip side of the most used functions and that will often appear as "jagged" or "awkward." These functions do not appear in the four-letter code, but the person does have limited access to them.
- General description: a few simple phrases describing the profile.

LINKING TEMPERAMENT, FUNCTIONS, AND TYPE

Artisans have a Perceiving (P) preference (see Table 3.1). They constantly gather information in the external world using Extraverted Sensing (S_E): Experiencing to pick up all current facts and data. Then they make internal decisions on how those facts relate either to their mental model using Introverted Thinking (T_I): Analyzing or to their internal values system using Introverted Feeling (F_I): Valuing. In later chapters we will refer to these two "versions" of Artisan as Thinking Artisan (STP) and Feeling Artisan (SFP).

Guardians have a Judging (J) preference. They constantly make decisions to either organize the external world using Extraverted Thinking (T_E): Systematizing or to create harmony and comply with group norms using Extraverted Feeling (F_E): Harmonizing. They gather data from their rich inner world of remembered experiences through Introverted Sensing (S_I): Recalling. In later chapters we will refer to these two "versions" of Guardian as Thinking Guardian (STJ) and Feeling Guardian (SFJ).

Rationals can have a Judging (J) or a Perceiving (P) preference. If they use Extraverted Thinking (T_E): Systematizing and Introverted Intuition (N_I): Visioning, they have a Judging (J) preference. As a result, they like to make quick, organizing decisions in the outer world using Extraverted Thinking (T_E): Systematizing. They also go

Table 3.4 Descriptions of the Sixteen Types

ISFP	ARTISAN
Core Needs	To act in the moment, be noticed, and produce concrete, tangible results.
First Function	F_I: Valuing—Make decisions quietly but firmly based on their own internal belief system. Guided by strong inner values and wish life to be in congruence with them.
Second Function	S_E: Experiencing—Rapid uptake of sensory data from the external world. Possess an acute awareness of specifics and realities.
Third Function	N_I: Visioning—May get flashes of insight that could be negative and slightly distorted. Will verify with sensory data.
Fourth Function	T_E: Systematizing—May appear sharply driven for closure in the external world. When used will appear "out of character" as boundaries are established and rigid plans are formed.
General Description "Composer"	Individuals with preferences for ISFP live in the present and prize the freedom to follow their own course. They are faithful at fulfilling obligations that are important to them. Often they appear as unassuming, easygoing, gentle, and soft-spoken. They will provide help in concrete, tangible ways and, with their observation skills, have a gift of expressing abstract things concretely. Their playful sense of humor may not be seen until they are comfortable with you. They will adapt well to new situations but may have trouble putting a plan in place and following through.

ESFP	ARTISAN
Core Needs	To act in the moment, be noticed, and produce concrete, tangible results.
First Function	S_E: Experiencing—Rapid uptake of sensory data from the external world. Posses an acute awareness of specifics and realities.
Second Function	F_I: Valuing—Make decisions firmly based on their own internal belief system. Guided by strong inner values and wish life to be in congruence with them.
Third Function	T_E: Systematizing—May appear sharply driven for closure in the external world. When used will appear "out of character" as boundaries are established and rigid plans are formed.
Fourth Function	N_I: Visioning—May get flashes of insight that could be negative and slightly distorted. Will verify with concrete data.
General Description "People Lover"	Individuals with preferences for ESFP are colorful, free spirited, and people focused. Using their acute sensory inputs, they make decisions based on what is in alignment with their internal values system. They are interested in people and new experiences, as they live in the moment. Generous of spirit, active, talkative, and flexible, their natural exuberance attracts others as they get the task done with maximum fun and minimum fuss. They find enjoyment in food, clothes, animals, the natural world, and activities, and work best in a flexible, unstructured environment.

Table 3.4 Descriptions of the Sixteen Types (cont'd)

ISTP	ARTISAN

Core Needs	To act in the moment, be noticed, and produce concrete, tangible results.
First Function	T_I: Analyzing—Make decisions using their internal logical criteria and principles. Evaluate how and why things work.
Second Function	S_E: Experiencing—Rapid uptake of sensory data from the external world. Possess an acute awareness of specifics and realities.
Third Function	N_I: Visioning—May get flashes of insight that could be negative and slightly distorted. Will verify with concrete data.
Fourth Function	F_E: Harmonizing—May show emotions inappropriately and appear excessively "loving" or "hateful." No clear understanding of societal norms or expectations.
General Description **"Instrumentor"**	Individuals with preferences for ISTP live in the present and act in the moment to get to the root cause of and solve problems. They are the most analytical of the Artisans, enjoying theoretical constructs with practical reasoning. They can absorb huge amounts of impersonal facts and have a high affiliation with numbers. Thriving on variety, they focus on doing what needs to be done with the least amount of fuss. They will change direction readily as additional information becomes available and maneuver systems to meet their ends. They are adept with tools and are able to reason impersonally and objectively.

ESTP	ARTISAN

Core Needs	To act in the moment, be noticed, and produce concrete, tangible results.
First Function	S_E: Experiencing—Rapid uptake of sensory data from the external world. Possess an acute awareness of specifics and realities.
Second Function	T_I: Analyzing—Make decisions using their internal logical criteria and principles. Ability to evaluate how and why things work.
Third Function	F_E: Harmonizing—May show emotions inappropriately and appear excessively "loving" or "hateful." No clear understanding of societal norms or expectations.
Fourth Function	N_I: Visioning—May get flashes of insight that could be negative and slightly distorted. Will verify with concrete data.
General Description **"Operator"**	Individuals with preferences for ESTP are action-oriented, quick-thinking, quick-moving, objective decision makers. Their focus on making things happen can make them appear impatient with slow-moving, theoretical discussion and concepts. They are direct and their word choice focuses on getting to the point. With intense observation skills, they can tune in to what's happening in the moment, are acutely aware of nonverbal cues, and then respond as needed. Their minds move so quickly that often their words are left behind, as they push on to closure. They constantly find new ways of doing things.

Table 3.4   Descriptions of the Sixteen Types (cont'd)

ISFJ	GUARDIAN
Core Needs	To be part of a group or team and fulfill responsibilities therein.
First Function	S_I: Recalling—Gather information by referring to a rich data bank of past sensory experiences and comparing and contrasting these to the present.
Second Function	F_E: Harmonizing—Make decisions using subjective criteria to optimize group interaction.
Third Function	T_I: Analyzing—May compare and contrast data against an internal model, but this will be superseded by appropriateness to the group.
Fourth Function	N_E: Brainstorming—May see patterns or connections that are not there.
General Description "Protector"	Individuals with preferences for ISFJ are stable, supportive, empathetic nurturers. Concrete and task focused, they value possessions and economy of resources. Also valuing traditions and historic experience, they make decisions that will meet the needs of the group. When communicating, they follow a detailed, sequential, step-by-step thought process and tend to establish orderly procedures. They enjoy helping others, are dependable and considerate, and gravitate to roles that involve service to others. Maintaining team cohesiveness and living up to their responsibilities are fundamental to the way they operate.

ESFJ	GUARDIAN
Core Needs	To be part of a group or team and fulfill responsibilities therein.
First Function	F_E: Harmonizing—Make decisions using subjective criteria to optimize group interaction.
Second Function	S_I: Recalling—Gather information by referring to a rich data bank of past sensory experiences and comparing and contrasting these to the present.
Third Function	N_E: Brainstorming—May see patterns or connections that are not there.
Fourth Function	T_I: Analyzing—May compare and contrast data against an internal model, but this will be superseded by appropriateness to the group.
General Description "Committee Member"	Individuals with preferences for ESFJ are warm, personable, and outgoing. They enjoy harmonious team environments, working within that structure to ensure organization is established and responsibilities are met. Conscientious and loyal, they value security and stability. They use information from their extensive data bank of past sensory experiences to apply in their concrete, task-focused work. Energized by being with others, they are genuinely interested in others' lives and concerns. Gregarious and talkative, they enjoy participating in groups and are good at organizing celebrations and preserving traditions.

Table 3.4 Descriptions of the Sixteen Types (cont'd)

ISTJ	GUARDIAN

Core Needs	To be part of a group or team and fulfill responsibilities therein.
First Function	S_I: Recalling—Gather information by referring to a rich data bank of past sensory experiences and comparing and contrasting these to the present.
Second Function	T_E: Systematizing—Make decisions using logical criteria to plan and organize logistics in the external world.
Third Function	F_I: Valuing—May consider their internal values and beliefs, but this decision will be subservient to logical criteria.
Fourth Function	N_E: Brainstorming—May see patterns or connections that are not there.
General Description "Creator of Procedures"	Individuals with preferences for ISTJ are logical, practical, deliberate organized, and thorough. They rely on historic experience from which to create concrete action plans. They will also create processes and procedures to smooth work flow, eliminate redundancy, and achieve economy of effort. Loyal and dutiful, they work with steady energy to ensure commitments are met on time. To work alone is often their preference, and they may appear as serious and orderly. They trust facts, are task oriented, and can manage extensive detail. Hard workers, once they have learned a skill, they perform it with competence.

ESTJ	GUARDIAN

Core Needs	To be part of a group or team and fulfill responsibilities therein.
First Function	T_E: Systematizing—Make decisions using logical criteria to plan and organize logistics in the external world.
Second Function	S_I: Recalling—Gather information by referring to a rich data bank of past sensory experiences and comparing and contrasting these to the present.
Third Function	N_E: Brainstorming—May see patterns or connections that are not there.
Fourth Function	F_I: Valuing—May consider their internal values and beliefs, but this decision will be subservient to logical criteria.
General Description "Take-Charge Organizer"	Individuals with preferences for ESTJ are detail-oriented, high-energy decision makers. They drive for closure with the aim of organizing, planning, and structuring the external environment. The most "driven" of the Guardians, they take action to get things done in a systematic and consistent way. With an objective approach to problem solving, they can be tough when the situation demands. They enjoy work that produces concrete, tangible results and are adept at creating systems that assign responsibilities and marshal resources. They enjoy interacting with others, especially around games and family activities.

Table 3.4   Descriptions of the Sixteen Types (cont'd)

INTJ	RATIONAL
Core Needs	To be competent and knowledgeable and to understand universal operating principles.
First Function	N_I: Visioning—Gather information by creating their own complete idea or future direction.
Second Function	T_E: Systematizing—Make decisions using logically proven data to categorize and organize the external world.
Third Function	F_I: Valuing—May consider their internal belief system, but will create a logical rationale for it.
Fourth Function	S_E: Experiencing—May appear bogged down in details and become obsessive about sensory data.
General Description "Life's Independent Thinker"	Individuals with preferences for INTJ approach life with an independent-minded, long-term vision coming from their internal world of possibilities. They make concrete, tangible action plans to achieve their overall objectives. They can always offer a detached, objective perspective with the propensity for original thought as they see patterns in external events. With their ability to categorize data, they are confident in their ideas and their ability to achieve their goals. They can appear skeptical and determined as they strive to achieve their high standards of performance.

ENTJ	RATIONAL
Core Needs	To be competent and knowledgeable and to understand universal operating principles.
First Function	T_E: Systematizing—Make decisions using logically proven data to categorize and organize events in the external world.
Second Function	N_I: Visioning—Gather information by creating their own complete idea or possibility.
Third Function	S_E: Experiencing—May appear bogged down in details and become obsessive about sensory data.
Fourth Function	F_I: Valuing—May consider their internal belief system, but will create a logical rationale for it.
General Description "Mobilizer"	Individuals with preferences for ENTJ are direct and organized and possess a strong desire to make their inner visions a reality. They are quick-thinking, strategic, logical decision makers with a drive for closure. They value intelligence or competence and abhor inefficiency. Able to conceptualize and theorize readily, they possess the innate ability to take charge and make things happen. They exude confidence and appear energetic and driven. They are aware of intricate connections, which they can explain with a logical model.

Table 3.4 Descriptions of the Sixteen Types (cont'd)

INTP	RATIONAL
Core Needs	To be competent and knowledgeable and to understand universal operating principles.
First Function	T_I: Analyzing—Constantly evaluate external logical data against internal mental criteria and model.
Second Function	N_E: Brainstorming—Constant external exploration of future possibilities, patterns, and meaning.
Third Function	S_I: Recalling—May go back to historic data, but may project negative past experiences into the future.
Fourth Function	F_E: Harmonizing—May demonstrate emotions inappropriately, or be unaware of behavioral norms.
General Description "Synthesizer"	Individuals with preferences for INTP spend their lives in a quest for logical purity. Using abstract data from ideas, future possibilities, and meanings, they analyze this information to align with their internal models. With insight into complex theories, they constantly search for patterns and systems to internally categorize data. They often function autonomously, absorbed in mastering and perfecting their theories. They possess a unique ability to dissect the complex and comprehend conceptual subtleties. Creating conceptual solutions are, to them, more enjoyable than putting the solutions into practical use.

ENTP	RATIONAL
Core Needs	To be competent and knowledgeable and to understand universal operating principles.
First Function	N_E: Brainstorming—Constant external exploration of future possibilities, patterns, and meaning.
Second Function	T_I: Analyzing—Constantly evaluate external logical data against internal mental criteria and model.
Third Function	F_E: Harmonizing—May demonstrate emotions inappropriately, or be unaware of behavioral norms.
Fourth Function	S_I: Recalling—May go back to historic data, but may project negative past experiences into the future.
General Description "Entrepreneur"	Individuals with preferences for ENTP are normally quick thinking, verbally expressive, and always focused on future opportunities. They thrive on looking at concepts and possibilities from multiple angles and then arguing their own philosophy or hypothesis. Optimistic, gregarious, and social, they enjoy debate and can be very persuasive. They naturally generate options and then are able to analyze them strategically, which makes them creative, abstract problem solvers. They are enterprising and resourceful in maneuvering systems to meet their ends.

Table 3.4   Descriptions of the Sixteen Types (cont'd)

ENFJ	IDEALIST

Core Needs	To have a purpose and make a meaningful contribution to the greater good.
First Function	F_E: Harmonizing—Make decisions using subjective criteria to optimize group interaction.
Second Function	N_I: Visioning—Gather information by envisioning their own complete idea or possibility.
Third Function	S_E: Experiencing—May appear bogged down in details and miss or become obsessive about sensory data.
Fourth Function	T_I: Analyzing—May compare and contrast data against an internal model, but this will be superseded by appropriateness to the group.
General Description "Mentor"	Individuals with preferences for ENFJ are outgoing, empathetic, expressive developers of people. They have a remarkable gift for seeing human potential and want to help others "be all that they can be." With their long-term focus, they like closure as they work to make their visions a reality. They are gifted communicators whether one on one, where they are able to get almost anyone to open up to them, or in front of a group, where they are able to stimulate enthusiasm. Highly attuned to the moods and emotions of those around them, they work to create a harmonious environment.

INFJ	IDEALIST

Core Needs	To have a purpose and make a meaningful contribution to the greater good.
First Function	N_I: Visioning—Gather information by envisioning their own complete idea or possibility.
Second Function	F_E: Harmonizing—Make decisions using subjective criteria to optimize group interaction.
Third Function	T_I: Analyzing—May compare and contrast data against an internal model, but this will be superseded by appropriateness to the group.
Fourth Function	S_E: Experiencing—May appear bogged down in details and miss or become obsessive about sensory data.
General Description "Counselor"	Individuals with preferences for INFJ are quietly insightful, constantly searching for deeper meanings and the coming into consciousness of their inner visions. Empathetically understanding the feelings and motivations of others, they are loyal to people and institutions. They are tactful, thoughtful, and concerned for the development of others. Very private people, they quietly exert an influence over others. Their language is full of imagery as they structure the external world to work toward their inner picture of the future.

Table 3.4 Descriptions of the Sixteen Types (cont'd)

ENFP	IDEALIST

Core Needs	To have a purpose and make a meaningful contribution to the greater good.
First Function	N_E: Brainstorming—Constant external exploration of future possibilities, patterns, and meaning.
Second Function	F_I: Valuing—Make decisions quietly but firmly based on their own internal belief system. Guided by strong inner values and wish life to be in congruence with them.
Third Function	T_E: Systematizing—May appear sharply driven for closure in the external world. When used will appear "out of character" as boundaries are established and rigid plans are formed.
Fourth Function	S_I: Recalling—May go back to historic data, but may project negative past experiences into the future.
General Description "Advocate"	Individuals with preferences for ENFP are energetic, spontaneous, and warm-hearted, and constantly generate creative, ingenious options for the future. They see endless possibilities that relate to the people around them. They love abstract concepts and are able to see beyond the obvious to hidden meanings and patterns. Their strong inner values guide their decision making, as they readily give appreciation and support to others. Empathetic and engaging, they are keenly perceptive and use their verbal fluency to persuade and influence those around them.

INFP	IDEALIST

Core Needs	To have a purpose and make a meaningful contribution to the greater good.
First Function	F_I: Valuing—Make decisions quietly but firmly based on their own internal belief system. Guided by strong inner values and wish life to be in congruence with them.
Second Function	N_E: Brainstorming—Constant external exploration of future possibilities, patterns, and meaning.
Third Function	S_I: Recalling—May go back to historic data, but may project negative past experiences into the future.
Fourth Function	T_E: Systematizing—May appear sharply driven for closure in the external world. When used will appear "out of character" as boundaries are established and rigid plans are formed.
General Description "Conciliator"	Individuals with preferences for INFP are quiet pursuers of their life's quest as they strive to live according to their strongly held internal values. Not wanting to take center stage, they can appear reserved and somewhat aloof until their internal belief system is "bumped up against," when they can react strongly in its defense. With a moral commitment to the fundamental worth of unique identity, they celebrate individual differences and want a purpose beyond a paycheck. They are adaptable and enjoy opportunities to explore the complexities of human personality. They value relationships based on authenticity and true connection.

back to their inner world to gather information from their own internal visions through Introverted Intuition (N_I). If Rationals have a Perceiving (P) preference, then they gather information in the external world, exploring ideas and possibilities through the use of Extraverted Intuition (N_E): Brainstorming. They also make decisions internally based on their principles and models using Introverted Thinking (T_I): Analyzing. In later chapters we will refer to these two "versions" of Rational as Structured Rational (NTJ) and Adaptable Rational (NTP).

Idealists can have a Judging (J) or a Perceiving preference (P). If they use Extraverted Feeling (F_E): Harmonizing and Introverted Intuition (N_I): Visioning, they have a Judging (J) preference. As a result, they like to make decisions in the outer world to ensure harmony and comfort (F_E). They also go back to their inner world to gather data from their own internal visions using Introverted Intuition (N_I). If Idealists have a Perceiving (P) preference, they gather ideas in the external world, exploring ideas and possibilities through the use of Extraverted Intuition (N_E): Brainstorming. They then make decisions internally based on their internal values system using Introverted Feeling (F_I): Valuing. In later chapters we will refer to these two "versions" of Idealist as Structured Idealist (NFJ) and Adaptable Idealist (NFP).

Temperament and Type

As shown in Table 3.5, there are four different types for each temperament, with similar core needs but using different information-gathering and decision-making functions. This begins to explain how team members sharing the same temperaments can look and act very different from one another. For each type the preferred information-gathering and decision-making functions are shown in the four-letter code.

For instance:

A *Guardian* with preferences for ESTJ uses Extraverted Thinking (T_E): Systematizing first and Introverted Sensing (S_I): Recalling second.

The other functions we use are not shown in the four-letter code. Remember, these are the functions that are harder to use, require more conscious effort, and are not as fluid.

Different Temperament/Same Functions

You might see very similar behavior from different temperaments as they use their first function, shown in Table 3.6 on page 86, but they will be trying to meet different needs.

Table 3.5 Temperament, Functions, and Type

Temperament	Type	Easily Used Functions
Artisan	E S_E T_I P E S_E F_I P I S_E T_I P I S_E F_I P	S_E T_I S_E F_I T_I S_E F_I S_E
Guardian	E S_I T_E J E S_I F_E J I S_I T_E J I S_I F_E J	T_E S_I F_E S_I S_I T_E S_I F_E
Rational	E N_I T_E J E N_E T_I P I N_I T_E J I N_E T_I P	T_E N_I N_E T_I N_I T_E T_I N_E
Idealist	E N_I F_E J E N_E F_I P I N_I F_E J I N_E F_I P	F_E N_I N_E F_I N_I F_E F_I N_E

For instance:

A *Guardian* with preferences for ESFJ uses Extraverted Feeling (F_E): Harmonizing first.

An *Idealist* with preferences for ENFJ also uses Extraverted Feeling (F_E): Harmonizing first.

Both will want to make decisions that bring harmony to the group and that are appropriate for the team. Idealists will want harmony for the group so that individuals can develop their potential. Guardians will want harmony for the group so that the team can be more focused.

Same Temperament/Different Functions

In addition, although two individuals may have the same temperament, the way they get their core needs met can be very different because they are accessing different functions.

For instance:

A *Guardian* with preferences for ESTJ who uses Extraverted Thinking (T_E): Systematizing first will want to organize the external world and take quick, logical, decisive action.

Table 3.6   First-Used Function

First Function	Type	Temperament
S_E: Experiencing	E S_E T_I P	Artisan
	E S_E F_I P	Artisan
S_I: Recalling	I S_I T_E J	Guardian
	I S_I F_E J	Guardian
N_E: Brainstorming	E N_E T_I P	Rational
	E N_E F_I P	Idealist
N_I: Visioning	I N_I T_E J	Rational
	I N_I F_E J	Idealist
T_E: Systematizing	E N_I T_E J	Rational
	E S_I T_E J	Guardian
T_I: Analyzing	I S_E T_I P	Artisan
	I N_E T_I P	Rational
F_E: Harmonizing	E N_I F_E J	Idealist
	E S_I F_E J	Guardian
F_I: Valuing	I N_E F_I P	Idealist
	I S_E F_I P	Artisan

A *Guardian* with preferences for ESFJ who uses Extraverted Feeling (F_E): Harmonizing first will want harmony in the external world, and to make the decision that is best for the group.

Figure 3.1 illustrates the interrelationships of temperament, functions, and type.

Connects and Conflicts

We will be using Figure 3.2, the Generic Connects and Conflicts diagram, repeatedly as we examine team interactions in later chapters.

- S_E F_I Ps (Artisans) will often connect or confuse themselves with N_E F_I Ps (Idealists) because of the common Valuing (F_I).
- S_E T_I Ps (Artisans) will often connect or confuse themselves with N_E T_I Ps (Rationals) because of the common Analyzing (T_I).
- S_I T_E Js (Guardians) will often connect or confuse themselves with N_I T_E Js (Rationals) because of the common Systematizing (T_E).
- S_I F_E Js (Guardians) will often connect or confuse themselves with N_I F_E Js (Idealists) because of the common Harmonizing (F_E).

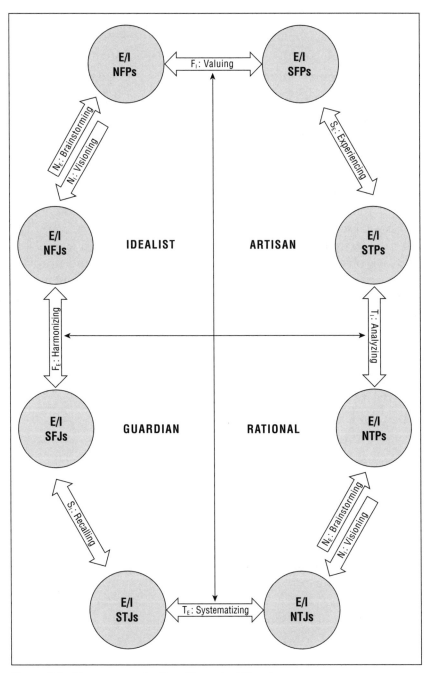

Figure 3.1 Temperaments, Functions, and Types

The greatest disconnections appear to happen as individuals have different temperaments and use different functions, for instance:

- $S_E F_I$ Ps (Artisans) will often conflict with $N_I T_E$ Js (Rationals).
- $S_E T_I$ Ps (Artisans) will often conflict with $N_I F_E$ Js (Idealists).
- $S_I F_E$ Js (Guardians) will often conflict with $N_E T_I$ Ps (Rationals).
- $N_E F_I$ Ps (Idealists) will often conflict with $S_I T_E$ Js (Guardians).

We will see how these differences manifest themselves in team behavior in the later chapters.

Type and Team Performance

Chapter 1 introduced you to the strengths and potential challenges each temperament brings to the team. Chapter 2 described the potential strengths and challenges of each function on a team. Now let's look broadly at the contributions of Extraversion and Introversion to team performance. Consider how these preferences impact your overall team performance, as well as the individual differences in team member approach.

Teams need the Extraverting preference to

- Keep up verbal communication
- Initiate activities
- Generate a sociable environment
- Develop a network of relationships

Teams need the Introverting preference to

- Focus the energy on the project and ideas at hand
- Encourage depth of consideration
- Provide a measured/reflective response
- Build in-depth relationships

As you can see in Table 3.7, each type also brings strengths and challenges to the team.

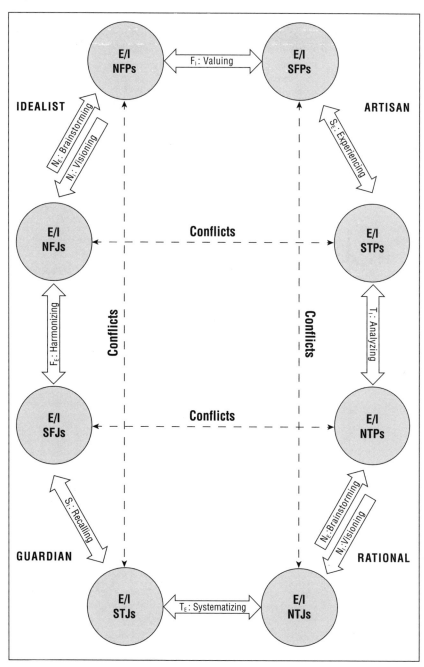

Figure 3.2   Generic Connects and Conflicts

Table 3.7   Strengths and Challenges of Type on a Team

Type	Strengths	Potential Challenges
ISFP **Artisan**	• Realistic, practical, concrete, and factual • Attune to the feelings and needs of others • Believe in contributing to others' happiness • Get the job done with the least amount of effort • Action oriented and know the right action for a particular situation • Curious and aesthetically aware	• May underestimate the time required to complete tasks and as a result miss deadlines • May withdraw from a situation if feeling unappreciated • May passively resist rules and structures • May appear aloof until comfortable • May lack long-term vision and understanding of the impact of their behavior on others
ESFP **Artisan**	• Realistic, practical, concrete, and fun loving • Generous with others, team focused • Bring energy, enthusiasm, and interest in people • Flexible and accepting of others • Make things happen • Learn well through group interaction	• May appear as class clown, lacking substance • May appear to be a "social butterfly" • May not look for the larger picture or see bigger patterns • May avoid conflict, have little patience for anxiety and interpersonal tensions
ISTP **Artisan**	• Realistic, hands-on implementers • Work around rules to complete tasks • Adaptable, action-oriented risk takers • Confident, independent, and self-determined • Believe in economy of effort • Concretely analytical • Naturally adept with numbers and systems	• May prefer to "do their own thing" and avoid team-focused planning • May appear indifferent to others' needs • May take the most expedient, not necessarily the best solution; may "shoot from the hip" • May lack long-term vision and an understanding of the impact of their behavior on others • May not enjoy tasks that appear "superfluous," such as meetings and strategic planning
ESTP **Artisan**	• Action-oriented implementers • Optimistic, can-do attitude • Excellent negotiators; play to win • Flexible and adaptable at finding new solutions • Realistic, hands-on, logical problem solvers • Change viewpoint as additional information becomes available	• May get bored easily if concrete, tangible progress is not made • May work around rules and not get to the root cause of a problem • May appear autonomous, "calling their own shots" • May be uncomfortable with the human element in teams • May appear overly cynical

Table 3.7 Strengths and Challenges of Type on a Team (cont'd)

Type	Strengths	Potential Challenges
ISFJ **Guardian**	• Conscientious—may pick up tasks that others have dropped • Look after others on the team—nurturers/caregivers • Strong, tactical implementers; use contingency planning • Work with steady energy • Inherently establish orderly procedures • Follow through using planning and organization skills	• May martyr themselves • May worry too much about possible negative events • May appear negative with new, untried methods • May not assert their own needs—blame and complain • May be uncomfortable with confrontation
ESFJ **Guardian**	• Organized, linear thought process; follow-through skills • Aware of and cater to others' needs • Energetic, enthusiastic, and warm • Like helping others who want to do likewise • Responsible; preserve the needs of the organization • Skilled with logistics	• May respond negatively to what they perceive as "breaking the rules" • May not consider the big picture • May avoid conflict • May make decisions on the group's needs and appear illogical at times • May seem too talkative
ISTJ **Guardian**	• Quiet, dedicated, and organized; great follow-through skills • Deliver on responsibilities if given clearly defined roles • Thorough, dependable, resourceful, and trustworthy • No-nonsense, hardworking team members • See tasks through to completion	• May appear rigid about time and schedules; go "by the book" • May not consider the people issues • May appear to have the "doom and gloom" syndrome • Instead of delegating, can get overloaded in details • May neglect the big picture
ESTJ **Guardian**	• Organized, logical, and systematic • Good with concrete, tangible data • Get things done quickly, in a logical, step-by-step manner with clarity of focus • Like to run things; will take control • Responsible and team focused • Matter-of-fact, decisive, and results driven	• May appear overpowering or task focused as they get the job done • May appear rigid and dogmatic, "know-it-alls" • May push for closure too quickly, without gathering enough data • May fail to respond to others' needs for support and connection

Table 3.7 Strengths and Challenges of Type on a Team (cont'd)

Type	Strengths	Potential Challenges
INTJ **Rational**	• Create general structures and devise strategies to achieve goals • Conceptual long-range thinkers • Readily able to relate the parts to the overall big picture • Provide an innovative and original perspective • Analytical and autonomous • Rational, detailed, and objectively critical	• May lock into ideas and not budge • May see outcomes so vividly they fail to understand how others might miss them • May insist on having their own way • May become aloof and abrupt while not giving enough information about their internal processing • May become impatient with those who do not see their vision quickly enough
ENTJ **Rational**	• Decisive, clear, and assertive • Organized and direct • Logical and objective • Create an organized, systematized approach to external order • Think in terms of systems and marshal resources to achieve an objective • Adept logisticians	• May be perceived as controlling • May be direct and to the point to the extent of being considered offensive • May be oblivious to social norms • May display reluctance to do anything but lead • May appear cold and impersonal
INTP **Rational**	• Contribute an alternative, detached, logical perspective • Use precision in communication • See possibilities and future meanings • Naturally create theoretical systems • Great researchers as they enjoy scientific, abstract subjects • Work alone or as part of the team	• May appear distanced as they either do not communicate or miss nonverbal cues • May have no concept of external time frames • May appear skeptical or overly analytical • May struggle with practical implementation • May confuse others with complex explanations
ENTP **Rational**	• Great at providing energy and thrust to new projects • Naturally optimistic and future focused; see opportunities • Creatively solve abstract problems • Self-confident and assertive • Can argue both sides of an issue • Engineer innovative solutions	• May need to be center stage; should learn to let go • May talk too much, externally processing without time for reflection • May appear arrogant • May lose track of details • May overextend as they explore the multiple possibilities

Table 3.7 Strengths and Challenges of Type on a Team (cont'd)

Type	Strengths	Potential Challenges
INFJ **Idealist**	• Believe in intuitive insights and future visions • See and develop potential in team members • Integrate people and systems effortlessly • Organized; good follow-through skills • Creative conceptual approach • Sensitive, compassionate, and empathetic	• May not be practical in implementation • May become single minded in pursuit of their vision and appear to make arbitrary decisions • May forget to apply reason to their insights • May not communicate important issues to the team • Can be unclear in articulating their vision
ENFJ **Idealist**	• Committed, enthusiastic team members if they believe in a cause • Fluent verbal skills in uniting disparate views • Create connections and warmth • Sell ideas to other team members and the organization • Create a positive, safe communication climate • Know what's appropriate behavior for the team or company	• May neglect logical choices for decisions based on personal values • Need frequent positive feedback or may become oversensitive to criticism and conflict • May show emotions under stress • May not work well alone; need relationships • May push for closure too quickly
INFP **Idealist**	• In-depth concentration and output when involved in a project • Reflect and produce intuitive insights particularly in written form • Loyal to other team members if they believe in the cause • Acutely sensitive to others' emotions and energies • Act as the conscience for the team • Dedicated to improving the world around them	• May find it difficult to do "meaningless" work • May find it difficult to follow through on detailed implementation plans • May not be aware of the "real" world and its tangible aspects • Disappointed when team members do not live up to potential • May react strongly when "hot buttons" are pushed
ENFP **Idealist**	• Generate creative options • Appreciate and support other team members • Quick thinking and verbally fluent when expressing ideas • Adapt to others' needs in order to build team process • Zest for life and enthusiasm for the cause, group, or team • Act as catalyst/crusader for new causes or ideas	• May appear scattered as they start lots of projects • May be reluctant to "close the door" on opportunities • Dislike routine and boring, repetitive tasks • May miss detailed implementation steps and fail to follow through • May be unaware of their physical needs when stressed

SUMMARY CHECKLIST

Chapter 3 completes the third step in creating a team profile through the combination of temperament, functions, and type. Before moving on to the next chapter, answer the following questions:

1. Did you define your four-letter type?

2. Did you read the descriptions of type in this chapter to verify your four-letter type?

3. Did you consider other team members as you read the descriptions of the sixteen types? Use the grid below to note your predictions. Be sure to share the information in this chapter, so that your team members can validate your ideas through self-selection.

Type Grid

ENFJ	INFJ	INTJ	ENTJ
INFP	ENFP	ENTP	INTP
ISFP	ESFP	ISFJ	ESFJ
ESTP	ISTP	ISTJ	ESTJ

PART TWO

Teams from the Inside Out

In Part 1 (Chapters 1, 2, and 3) we profiled our individual team members'
personalities through the study and use of temperament, functions, and
types. We are now ready to move to Part 2 in the Inside Out approach to
optimizing team performance, where you will not only examine the key prin-
ciples of high-performing teams but also learn how you can use the infor-
mation from your team profile to immediately improve team performance.
Chapter 4 will set the scene. The following chapters show how to achieve
results in each of the critical categories for high-performing teams:

- *Chapter 5 will cover setting a cohesive **strategy** (S).*
- *Chapter 6 will provide tools to define **clear roles and responsibilities** (C).*
- *Chapter 7 will provide insights on establishing **open communication** (O).*
- *Chapter 8 will show how to create a **rapid response** team (R).*
- *Chapter 9 will show the importance of **effective leadership** in raising*
  the level of team performance (E).

Finally Chapter 10 will give tools and techniques for maintaining a high-
scoring team.

4

Understanding Your Team Profile

HOW TO RAISE YOUR SCORE IN TEAM PERFORMANCE

"Coming together is a beginning; keeping together is progress; working together is success."
—**Henry Ford**

This chapter will help you develop your team profile and assess your team's performance. Here you will use all you have learned about yourself and your team members' temperament, functions, and type to build an insightful team profile. We will look at an example and walk you through the creation of your own profile. The team profile will be your tool throughout the remainder of the book for understanding and improving team performance. Using the Inside Out approach, you will be able to customize performance improvement strategies for your team to immediately impact team performance and raise your team's SCORE.

CHALLENGES WITH TEAMS

The old adage "two heads are better than one" explains why teamwork is an effective way to produce results. However, while teams are beneficial, there are numerous challenges to creating effective teams in the reality of today's business world. The challenges are seen in Table 4.1 on page 98.

Despite these barriers, teams can positively affect individuals by supporting an atmosphere of trust, fun, and ongoing relationships. Team benefits can be summarized as follows:

- Increased productivity
- Better problem solving and decision making
- Reduced costs
- Improved customer service
- Innovative approaches
- Higher morale
- More fun

Table 4.1   Barriers to Team Performance

Barriers	Explanation
Cultural Values	While many organizations preach teamwork, cultural values in the Western world are geared more toward competition than collaboration. Often collaboration is considered as "taking the edge" off performance.
Individual Approach	Individuals vary in the extent they like to work with others to achieve a goal and in their degree of competitiveness. Working in a team, individuals think that they have to suppress their individuality.
Different Styles	Teamwork necessitates working together to achieve a common goal. All of us have our own pattern of being, with different core needs and values (temperament) and our own style of operating in the world (functions and types). We can mean the same thing but disagree because we see an issue from different perspectives. One of teamwork's greatest challenges is to understand and value the differing perspectives we all bring to the team.
Politics	Politics are an inevitable part of business life, and when team members get caught up in political maneuvering, performance suffers.
Lack of Strategic Direction	Many teams are introduced with inadequate corporate support and no real commitment. The team's performance is inhibited by lack of authority to do what it needs to do.
Lack of Clear Performance Goals	Many teams are brought into existence to "fix something" and are unable to clarify that directive. Without a driving performance need, the team will simply not perform.
No Training	Establishing and building a team requires knowledge, skills, and techniques in order to establish good team habits. Training in areas such as goal setting, defining team purpose, facilitating meetings, coaching team members, defining team responsibilities, and monitoring performance will help give team members the tools they need to succeed.

If you think back to your best team experience that you described in Chapter 1, you will experience again the benefits of being part of a positive team. The rest of this book is dedicated to skills and techniques to make these benefits a reality, not an illusion.

STAGES OF TEAM DEVELOPMENT

As dynamic entities, teams move through different developmental stages. B. W. Tuckman (1965) described the four stages teams experience: Forming, Storming, Norming, and Performing. Each stage in this process presents a specific set of challenges. In working with a team, it is critical to know which stage the team is currently in, because different intervention strategies may be required in each phase.

Forming

Forming occurs when the team first comes together and each time a new member joins. In this stage, team members have little knowledge of each other, an incomplete understanding of the project, no clear goals, and no definition of responsibilities. Basically, everything is "up for grabs," which makes Forming a difficult yet fundamental step in achieving team performance.

Storming

Storming begins as the team starts to define roles and responsibilities. At this point, the barriers to teamwork surface: differences in power needs, clashes in working styles, conflicts between members, lack of trust, communication deterioration, and leadership blaming. Storming occurs when the polarity of collaboration meets the polarity of individual focus. It is a valuable stage in moving the team on to performance. If these issues do not arise at this point, they may affect team productivity at a later stage.

Norming

The Norming stage is the outcome of the Storming phase. At this stage, communication appears more open and honest, and roles and responsibilities are accepted. The team begins to develop an "identity" of its own separate from the individuals who are its members. This is where the team takes on its temperament and type.

Performing

In the Performing stage we see the benefits of team performance. The team is accomplishing its milestones, putting additional plans into place, and rotating leadership amongst team members depending on the workload. Performing is the stage at which we see high levels of commitment to the task and performance growth from individuals on the team

CHARACTERISTICS OF HIGH-PERFORMING TEAMS

Task and Group Process Elements

In team performance there is a task element and a group process element. The task element is defined as "doing the work" that the team is assigned. This includes setting objectives, deciding plans, and defining roles and responsibilities. The group process element is defined as helping the team to work together productively. It includes creating open and honest communication, establishing team values, and developing ground rules. A team needs to balance the task and group process elements in order to succeed. It is hard to work when there is in-fighting in the team, and it is hard to work together effectively if there are no tasks to complete!

Review the following five key elements found in high-performing teams and consider where your team stands in regard to these elements. Figure 4.1 on page 101 displays the characteristics in diagram form. Find your own team's SCORE using Exercise 4.1.

S: Strategy

- Shared purpose
- Clearly articulated values and ground rules
- Understanding of risks and opportunities facing the team
- Clear categorization of the overall responsibilities of the team

C: Clear Roles and Responsibilities

- Clear definition of roles and responsibilities
- Responsibility shared by all members
- Specific objectives to measure individual results

O: Open Communication

- Respect for individual differences
- Open and nonjudgmental communication environment among team members

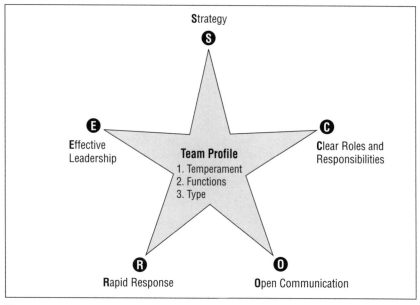

Figure 4.1 Characteristics of High-Performing Teams

R: Rapid Response

- Rapid response to the team's problems, as well as to customers' needs

- Effective management of and response to change in the internal and external environment

E: Effective Leadership

- Team leader able to help members achieve the objective and build the team

- Team leader who can draw out and free up the skills of all team members, develop individuals

USING THE REST OF THIS BOOK

Each of the characteristics of high-performing teams will be specifically addressed in the following chapters of the book. These in-depth sections are designed to aid you in improving team weak spots in order to raise your team SCORE and be successful. Once you have diagnosed your team's trouble areas, you may head directly to the appropriate chapter or chapters in order to get to work. For

Exercise 4.1

TEAM ASSESSMENT: WHAT IS YOUR TEAM SCORE?

1. In each of the sections below, review each question and indicate to what extent your team is meeting the prerequisites for a high-performing team.

2. Ask the other members of your team to also rate each characteristic in the same manner.

3. Create an average for each characteristic. Discuss each one in turn and identify why individuals have rated them as they have and what might be done to improve each rating.

4. Discuss any marked differences in rankings. For instance, if one person rated Open Communication as a 9 and another rated it as a 2, discuss the reasons for the disparity.

Rating: 1 = Very Clear/Successful   10 = Not Clear/Not Successful

Strategy

1. To what extent is your team purpose clear to you and your team?

2. To what extent is your team adhering to its values?

3. To what extent is your team sticking to the agreed-upon ground rules?

4. To what extent are the team's results clear and effective?

*Overall rating in this category*_____

Clear Roles and Responsibilities

1. To what extent is your team leader ensuring the team has the correct skill sets?

2. To what extent are team members clear about their individual expected outcomes?

3. How effective are the team's objectives?

4 To what extent are team members' workloads accurately reflected in their objectives?

5. To what extent are objectives regularly reviewed?

*Overall rating in this category*_____

Exercise 4.1 (cont'd)

Open Communication

1. To what extent do your team members communicate effectively among themselves?

2. To what extent do your team members communicate ideas?

3. To what extent do your team members communicate feelings?

4. To what extent do your team members try to adapt individual style when communicating with others?

*Overall rating in this category*_____

Rapid Response

1. To what extent does your team recognize, define, and analyze problems effectively?

2. To what extent does your team generate creative problem-solving options?

3. To what extent does your team objectively evaluate problem-solving options?

4. To what extent does consensus decision making take place?

5. To what extent does the team adapt to external changes?

*Overall rating in this category*_____

Effective Leadership

1. To what extent is your team leader constantly assessing team performance?

2. How successful is your team leader in "running interference" so that your team can complete its work?

3. To what extent is your team leader providing relevant feedback to team members?

4. To what extent is your team leader motivating team members?

5. To what extent is your team leader guiding the team through the stages of team development?

*Overall rating in this category*_____

What is your team SCORE? S ____ C ____ O ____ R ____ E ____

instance, if the numerical score for Open Communication is very high, you have rated it Not Clear or Not Successful, and you may want to go directly to Chapter 7 now. Alternatively, you can continue sequentially through the book, gathering information to improve your team's status in each of these imperative areas. However, before moving on be sure to complete the team profile section that follows. Understanding team members' temperaments, functions, and types provides key insights into the actions of the team, as behavior influences performance from the inside out.

SAMPLE TEAM PROFILE:
ACCOUNT MANAGEMENT TEAM

The case study on the following pages and summarized on page 106 provides a sample of the type of profiling you can do for your team, using the information on temperaments in teams (Chapter 1), functions in teams (Chapter 2), and types in teams (Chapter 3).

Background Information

This sales team works for a major computer company based in Silicon Valley. The company divides its sales force into global vertical organizations, one of which is responsible for business development in the industrial vertical sector. The sales team, part of this sector, is based in California and comprises a team of account managers who are responsible for many of the large corporate accounts in Silicon Valley. The team has been working together for a long time. It is highly productive and wishes to learn additional skills to enable it to partner more effectively with its customers. Off-site, team members have been introduced to team profiling as an objective framework for helping to build stronger customer relations. In addition, the team wishes to gain a greater understanding of its members so as to improve interpersonal communication and raise team spirit.

Connects and Conflicts

- As you can see from Figure 4.2 on page 106, the team is weighted toward the right side of the page: it has no Idealists.
- Potential conflicts exist between Alvin/Andy/Jim and Elizabeth. However, the team is subdivided (surprise!), with Alvin, Andy, Jim, and Mike on one subteam and Elizabeth, Laith, and Rob on the other.

SAMPLE TEAM PROFILE

Individual Analysis

Name	Temperament	1st/2nd Function		Type
Mark	Guardian	S_I	T_E	ISTJ
Alvin	Artisan	F_I	S_E	ISFP
Elizabeth	Rational	N_I	T_E	INTJ
Andy	Artisan	F_I	S_E	ISFP
Mike	Artisan	T_I	S_E	ISTP
Laith	Guardian	F_E	S_I	ESFJ
Rob	Rational	T_I	N_E	INTP
Jim	Artisan	F_I	S_E	ISFP
Karen	Guardian	S_I	F_E	ISFJ

Team Analysis

Temperaments: Guardians __3__   Artisans __4__

Idealists __0__   Rationals __2__

Team Temperament: __Artisan__

Team Leader Temperament: __Guardian__

Functions (First and Second Combined):

Perceiving S_E: __4__ S_I: __3__ N_E: __1__ N_I: __1__

Judging T_E: __2__ T_I: __2__ F_E: __2__ F_I: __3__

Preferences: E: __1__   I: __8__

S: __7__   N: __2__

T: __4__   F: __5__

J: __4__   P: __5__

First Function for the Team: F_I: Valuing

First Function for the Team Leader: S_I: Recalling

Team Type: __ISFP__

Team Leader Type: __ISTJ__

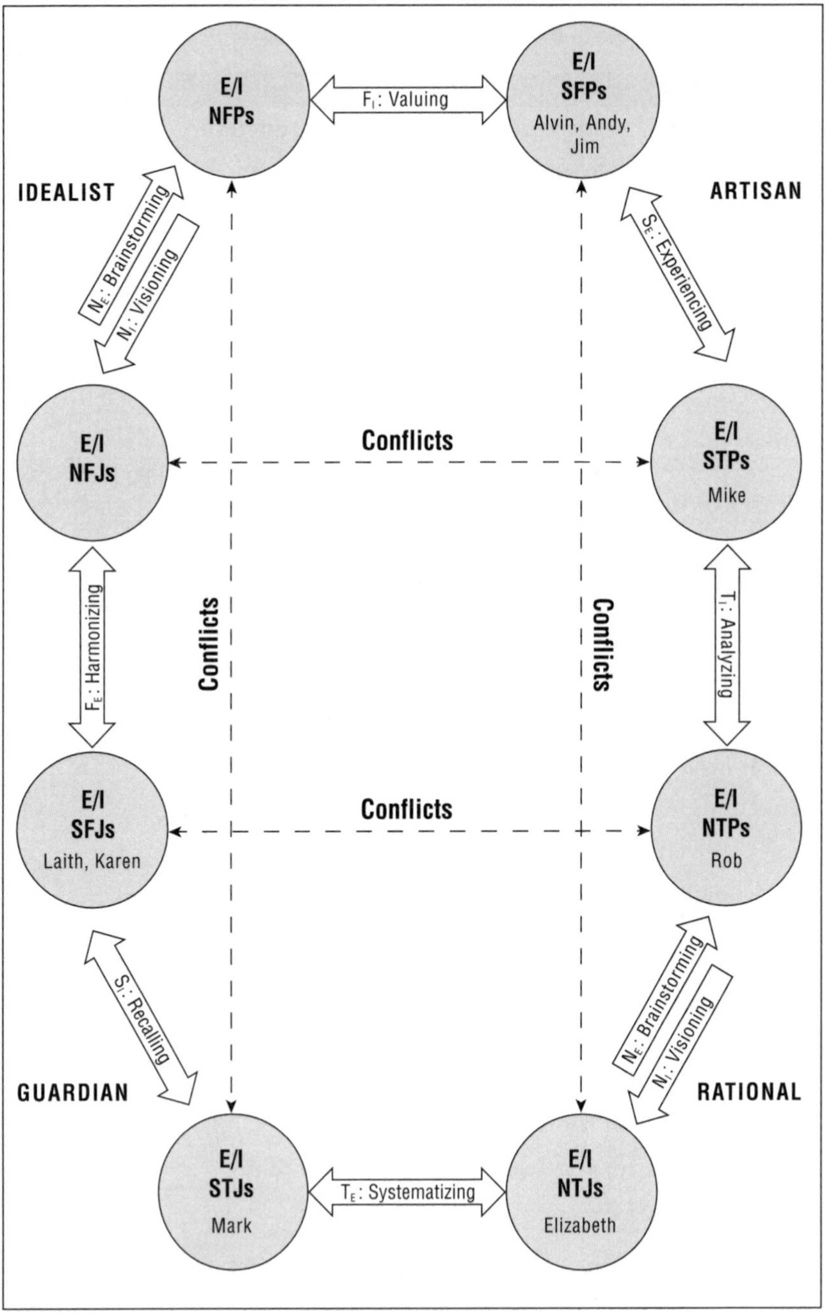

Figure 4.2 Sample Team Connects and Conflicts

- In the same way, there may be a potential conflict between Rob and Laith/Karen, but they also work on different teams (Karen is Mark's administrative assistant).

- Most teams are connected by one or two "bubbles" to those close to them. When one person is separated from (not directly connected to) the rest of the team, then this person is often seen as "different" by other team members.

Implications for the Team: Temperament

- There is no Idealist on the team, which, paired with the low number of Rationals, may mean a lack of long-term vision, particularly in relation to understanding and describing the impact on customers of introducing new technology. In addition, Idealists normally help with building communication bridges when team members disagree. This team has no disagreements currently (the company is doing well and making quota), but it may need to consider building a relationship with an Idealist for future reference.

- When discussing client interactions, team members could not identify any Idealist customers with whom they interacted. This could be for two reasons. First, there may be fewer than average Idealist decision makers within information technology departments in high-tech companies. Also, the team may be unconsciously filtering out Idealist customers.

- The team temperament is Artisan, which means that this is a very fast-moving, tactile team, which you would expect in a sales environment, particularly in Silicon Valley. The benefits of the team temperament are that the work environment will be fun, fast-paced, opportunistic, and strongly action oriented. Challenges associated with this team temperament might be lack of strategic approach and boredom.

- The team leader's temperament is Guardian. This means that he is likely to bring stability to the group, and building team cohesiveness will be an important focus for him.

Implications for the Team: Functions

- The first function in the group is F_I: Valuing, which means that the team members are likely to have a strong internal values system and be supportive of one another.

- Other first-used functions for team members are S_I: Recalling (2), F_E: Harmonizing (1), N_I: Visioning (1), and T_I: Analyzing (2). Therefore the team has members for whom it is easy to recall previous data (S_I), ensure harmony (F_E), have a strong internal vision (N_I), and analyze data to create their own model (T_I).

- The functions that are not being used first by any team member are S_E: Experiencing, N_E: Brainstorming, and T_E: Systematizing. Having four Artisans on the team, for whom Experiencing is a second function, compensates for its absence as a dominant function. Also, one person on the team has N_E: Brainstorming as a second function and one has T_E: Systematizing as a second function, so these viewpoints will be represented.

- The team leader's first function is S_I: Recalling, which ensures a sense of history and continuity to the group. The ability to review previous data and compare to current experience will be valuable for a sales team so that it does not continually reinvent the wheel and is able to learn from past successes.

- When the first- and second-used functions are combined, N_E: Brainstorming and N_I: Visioning are present only once. This may indicate an absence of exploring new patterns and seeing hidden meanings (N_E) and a lack of overall vision (N_I).

Implications for the Team: Type

- The team has far more members preferring Introversion (responding and reflecting) than Extraversion (initiating and outward processing). This may indicate that inward rather than outward processing occurs. However, with four Artisans, this effect will be diminished. Artisans, due to their need for concrete sensory data, often appear as Extraverted types.

- The team has a high representation of team members with a Sensing (practical and tangible data-gathering) preference rather than an Intuition (conceptual, abstract data-gathering) preference. This may indicate, as has already been discussed, a lack of big-picture thinking and a more concrete, practical approach. Both approaches can be beneficial in the sales cycle, but neglecting one may mean an overall loss of team productivity.

- There is a good balance between using subjective (Feeling) and objective (Thinking) decision-making approaches, and between using flexibility (Perceiving) and planning (Judging) in controlling the external environment.

- The team type is ISFP, which means that the team culture appears as fun, flexible, and opportunistic—a pretty good type for a sales group. The only factor that may detract from team performance is that one of the characteristics of ISFP types is easygoingness. A sales team can never afford to be easygoing!

- The team leader's type is ISTJ, which means that he brings a focused direction to the leadership. He will be more than able to balance the easygoing profile of the team!

Team Plan of Attack

Temperament
- With no Idealist among its members, the team could build an informal partnership with an outside Idealist in order to include this perspective in its positioning to clients. In case of conflicts, the team would benefit from establishing links with the human resources department or a neutral third party that might be able to help address any issues.

- In addition, the team can learn how to speak "Idealist" more fluently by studying the section on Idealist communication style in Chapter 7.

Functions
- As discussed previously, with only one team member using N_E: Brainstorming and only one using N_I: Visioning, the team could conduct brainstorming sessions as part of weekly meetings to ensure new ideas are explored. The other team members need to pay attention when these team members, who use N_E and N_I with ease, talk about hidden patterns or meanings that they perceive.

Type
- With the team members having predominantly preferences for Introversion, the team would benefit from face-to-face meetings, both one on one with the team leader and as an entire team.

- With the relatively low representation of team members expressing a preference for Intuition, the team could benefit from conducting a strategic planning session to clarify vision and purpose. Using the exercises in Chapter 5, the team could reaffirm its overall direction. In addition, the team needs to make sure that it listens to its members with an Intuition preference when they speak. What they say might seem impractical to team members with a Sensing preference, but it could be useful.

General
- Use Exercise 4.1 to clarify where the group feels it is and to open up communication.
- Individual interactions can also be examined on a one-on-one basis. More information is included in Chapter 7.

Now that the team has been profiled, the indicators discussed by this analysis can be matched against the criteria for high-performing teams, in order to assess strengths and areas of possible concern. How easy will it be for this team to SCORE? Table 4.2 on page 111 shows details for each of the SCORE categories.

CREATING A TEAM PROFILE

A team profile is a valuable tool that helps clarify how team members' temperaments and types affect team performance from the inside out. Any team's productivity is undoubtedly related to the types, temperaments, and functions of its members. Analyzing a team's profile not only can give a strong indication of the team's strengths and challenges but also can provide insights as to why certain areas are more difficult for the team than others. Using these data, it is possible to implement strategies and techniques almost instantly, customized to your specific team needs, to improve team performance. Table 4.3 on page 111 shows you how.

INTERPRETING YOUR TEAM PROFILE

Connects and Conflicts

Using the Connects and Conflicts diagram in the appendix, answer these questions:

1. Where are your team members located in the diagram?
2. What "bubbles" are not represented?
3. Which team members are grouped close to each other?
4. Which team members appear disconnected from the team?
5. Where are the potential conflicts in the team, if any? How do they correlate with the team members' types/locations on the diagram?
6. Where are the strong connections in the team?

Table 4.2 The Team SCORE

Team Element	Comment
<u>S</u>trategy	• Not having an Idealist in the team may mean less focus on purpose and long-term direction. • A team with most members expressing a Sensing preference may mean that the team focus will be more short-term/practical rather than long-term. • The absence of Idealist customers may mean that business opportunities are being missed because no team member "speaks that language."
<u>C</u>lear Roles and Responsibilities	• With three Guardians on the team, there will be a natural push to define roles and responsibilities. • Having four Artisans will ensure that these definitions will be flexible and will change according to the needs of the moment.
<u>O</u>pen Communication	• With a strong internal values system (F_I), there appears to be an open environment. • Team members are supportive of each other's differences. • With the majority of team members expressing a preference for Introversion, the team may need time to process internally and needs to ensure it meets frequently to maintain face-to-face communication. • Having four Artisans means a fun, flexible environment. • This is a supportive team (Feeling = 5) with a strong understanding of what it takes to build communication both internally and externally.
<u>R</u>apid Response	• With four Artisans, the team will appear very task focused and be able to respond quickly where necessary. With Artisans providing the dominant temperament, the group is adept at solving problems from a hands-on perspective. • When trying to solve problems, the team needs to capitalize on its two members with a preference for Intuition—Rob to brainstorm possible options (N_E: Brainstorming) and Elizabeth to identify new solutions (N_I: Visioning). • With most team members preferring Sensing, the team will be hands-on and tactical, getting the steps done to complete the plan. • If work becomes mundane, the Artisans may build "fires" to stimulate excitement. However, this is unlikely in a sales environment with ongoing regular challenges.
<u>E</u>ffective Leadership	• Mark, as an Introverted Thinking Guardian, brings these leadership strengths and possible challenges to the team: *Strengths* *Possible Challenges* Practical May lack long-term vision and Good historical knowledge direction of prior successes May allow past experience to Team focused influence future direction Excellent follow-through May be seen as inflexible Strong planning Organized and thorough

Table 4.3 Creating Your Team Profile

Profile Step	What It Involves	Tips
Team Background Information	• List background information pertaining to team performance.	• Think about the company. What changes have taken place recently that might affect team performance?
Individual Analysis	• Name • "Best fit" temperament • Functions used most easily • Type	• Use the information in Chapter 1 to help identify temperament. • For functions used for each temperament and type, see Chapter 3, Table 3.4. • For information about these functions, see Chapter 2, Tables 2.2–5, 7–10. • Use the information in Chapter 3 to identify type.
Team Analysis	• Number of each temperament • Team temperament • Team leader temperament • First and second functions • Number with each type: E–I. S–N, T–F, J–P (leads into type) • First function for the team • First function for the team leader • Team type • Team leader type	• Total number of team members of each temperament. • Largest number of a given temperament within the team. • From the individual analysis. • Look through the list of first and second functions and count the total number of times each function appears. • Count up numbers from the group. • Largest number of a given first function within the team. • From the individual analysis. • The four preferences with greatest representation (highest number). • From the individual analysis.
Connects and Conflicts	• Map the team names on the generic Conflicts and Connects diagram (see appendix).	• Refer to the individual analysis list and exclude the Extraversion–Introversion preferences.

Implications for the Team: Temperament

Refer to the information in Chapter 1.

Using the information in Table 1.1 (pages 24 and 25) it is possible to make some general conclusions about your team based on temperament analysis. Following are a few questions that could be used to discuss the results.

1. What temperaments are not represented in your team?

2. What could be the consequences of these temperaments not being represented?

3. What is the team temperament?

4. What are some general statements that you could make about the team based on the team temperament?

5. What is the team leader's temperament?

6. How is this different from or similar to the team temperament?

7. What might happen as a result?

8. What are the implications for decision making if all temperaments are represented? (Clue: speed of decision making)

9. What are the implications for team performance if only two temperaments are represented? (Clue: speed of decision making)

10. If your team does not possess a particular temperament, yet other teams you work with possess that temperament, what might happen? (Clue: miscommunication)

11. What are the benefits of all temperaments being represented on a team? (Clue: no stone left unturned)

Implications for the Team: Functions

Refer to the information in Chapter 2.

Using the information in Table 2.12 (pages 58 and 59), it is possible to make some general conclusions about your team. Below are a few questions that could be used to discuss the results:

1. What is the first function on the team, and what impact does this have on the team approach?

2. Which functions are used first by team members and which are missing? What types of information or data may be missed as a result?

3. What is the first function for the team leader, and what implications does this have for team performance?

4. Which functions are not represented in the team as first or second functions, and what could this mean?

5. What other comment can be made about the functions on the team?

Implications for the Team: Type

Refer to the information on type in Chapter 3.
1. What is the balance on the team between Extraversion and Introversion, and what does this mean for the team?
2. What is the balance between Sensing and Intuition, and what can you deduce from this?
3. What is the balance between Thinking and Feeling, and how could this impact team performance?
4. What is the balance between Judging and Perceiving, and what might happen as a result?
5. What is the team type?
6. What are some general statements you could make based on the team type?
7. What are the implications for decision making if all types are equally represented? (Clue: balance and time)
8. How is decision making in the team skewed if some types are overrepresented and some are underrepresented?
9. What is the team leader's type?
10. How is this different from or similar to the team type?
11. What are the implications of that difference or similarity?

Plan of Attack to Raise Your Team SCORE

1. How can your team compensate for "lacking a temperament?"
2. How can the team capitalize on the strengths of all its members' temperaments?
3. How can the team reap the benefits its temperament brings to its performance?
4. How can the team compensate for any potential challenges it faces based on its temperament?
5. If the team has a predominantly Extraverting preference, how can it ensure that reflection takes place before action and that those with an Introverting preference are heard?
6. If the team has a predominantly Introverting preference, how can it ensure that action takes place after reflection and enough face-to-face communication takes place in the team?
7. If the team has a predominantly Sensing preference, how can it ensure that abstract ideas and long-term possibilities and meanings are considered in gathering information?

8. If the team has a predominantly Intuition preference, how can it ensure that concrete reality and practical applications are considered in gathering information?

9. If the team has a predominantly Thinking preference, how can it ensure that subjective criteria and the impact on people are considered in making decisions?

10. If the team has a predominantly Feeling preference, how can it ensure that logical criteria and an objective perspective are also considered in making decisions?

11. If the team has a predominantly Judging preference, how can it ensure that the team remains flexible in times of change and open to new possibilities?

12. If the team has a predominantly Perceiving preference, how can it ensure that change is not being made merely for change's sake and that there is some sort of plan to follow?

13. Team members need to make sure that in any action they consider the following questions:

    - What is happening right now? (S_E: Experiencing)
    - What has happened in the past? (S_I: Recalling)
    - What are some possibilities and hidden meanings? (N_E: Brainstorming)
    - What is the overall vision/objective/goal? (N_I: Visioning)

14. Team members need to make sure that in any action, they consider the following questions in making decisions:

    - What do the published facts and data suggest and how do we make it happen? (T_E: Systematizing)
    - What other logical model could we use to make decisions? (T_I: Analyzing)
    - How are people involved in the decision going to feel? (F_E: Harmonizing)
    - How does the decision align with our team values? (F_I: Valuing)

ESTABLISHING YOUR TEAM PROFILE

Use the information in the previous section to create your own team profile. The case study on pages 103 through 109 will help you understand how to work through each section. Write down your team profile on a copy of the blank profile provided in the appendix. After you have completed your team profile, use Exercise 4.2 to assess your strengths and blind spots as a team member.

Exercise 4.2

TEAM MEMBER SELF-ASSESSMENT

In working within a team, your own approach is as critical as the team profile itself. Take a moment to reflect on the questions below and complete this self-assessment.

1. My temperament is _____.

Strengths to the Team   **Possible Blind Spots as a Team Member**

2. My first and second functions are _____.

Strengths to the Team   **Possible Blind Spots as a Team Member**

3. My type is _____ .

Strengths to the Team   **Possible Blind Spots as a Team Member**

SUMMARY CHECKLIST

This chapter lays the foundation for raising your SCORE in team performance, which we will examine in depth in the rest of the book. Before moving on to the next chapter, answer the following questions:

1. Have you assessed your current team using the SCORE checklist (Exercise 4.1)?

2. Have you used this checklist with other team members and discussed the results?

3. Have your conducted an initial profile of your team using type, functions, and temperament using the blank profile in the appendix?

4. Have you analyzed your team according to this preliminary profile and identified strengths and potential challenges to team performance based on this profile?

5. Have you assessed your own type and its implications for team performance (Exercise 4.2 above)?

6. Have you prioritized the chapters that your team needs to focus on most to improve team performance?

Strategy

WHAT'S OUR GAME PLAN?

"Our dreams come true if we have the courage to pursue them."
—**Walt Disney**

As we continue in Part 2, "Teams from the Inside Out," we will be studying in depth the characteristics of high-performing teams. In this chapter we will examine techniques and approaches teams can use to establish a clear strategy for themselves. In today's rapidly changing world, team purpose and direction are the factors that provide stability and focus to guide the team toward its goals. Included in this section is a series of exercises designed to help you in identifying and defining your team purpose, values, and ground rules. Worksheets for conducting a SWOT (Strengths, Weaknesses, Opportunities, Threats) analysis and documenting the overall responsibilities of the team (Key Result Areas) are also included. Individual team members' temperament, functions, and type also influence team strategy and direction from the inside out. To this end we will analyze another team looking at type and temperament as it defines its strategy and evaluates its ability to raise its SCORE in team performance.

The steps in aligning a team's strategy are listed in Table 5.1 on page 118.

DEFINING TEAM PURPOSE

A meaningful team purpose sets the tone and aspiration for the team. Teams develop direction, momentum, and commitment by working to shape a meaningful purpose. The team purpose needs to be applicable and desirable to everyone in the team; otherwise, individuals will

Table 5.1   Steps in Defining Strategy

Strategy	Definitions and Guidelines
Team Purpose	• Broad setting of the tone and inspiration for the team • Ask, Why are we here? What is our ultimate theme? Our overall direction?
Team Values	• Clear articulation of what is important to the team
Ground Rules	• General principles that guide day-to-day team operation • Cover such areas as meetings, communication channels, decision making, and role definition
SWOT Analysis	• Team internal Strengths and Weaknesses • External market/organizational Opportunities and Threats
Key Result Areas	• A tool to categorize a team's workload • Use nouns as headings/overview only

not support it. In addition, the purpose must raise the bar high enough to inspire performance, while not appearing too unrealistic. One example of a team purpose statement is: "To maximize sales productivity by stimulating and facilitating a learning culture leading to a sustainable competitive advantage." Use Exercise 5.1 to design your own team purpose statement.

Exercise 5.1

DEFINING YOUR TEAM PURPOSE

When time is invested in creating the team purpose, one or more broad aspirations or values often emerge that motivate team members and produce a fundamental reason for their extra effort. This exercise is to be conducted with all team members.

1. Provide basic information (from this chapter) to all team members.

2. Allow each person to individually write his or her own statement.

3. Facilitate a discussion with all team members to agree on the final team purpose statement.

Use the space below to create the team purpose for your team.

_____

_____

_____

DEFINING TEAM VALUES AND GROUND RULES

The team purpose gives direction and guides the team in achieving its objective. Teams also need to define their ground rules and values as a means of establishing the way group members are committed to treating each other. These values and ground rules provide the basis for group interaction. Combining these factors as you are establishing your team's direction can help raise your team's SCORE. Use Exercise 5.2 to determine the values held by your team.

Values

Building an understanding of team values is critical to establishing the culture of the team and acts as a starting point for developing team ground rules. Ground rules will not be effective if they go against the team's fundamental values system.

Examples of values are the following:

Achievement	Honesty
Commitment	Innovation/creativity
Communication	Loyalty
Cooperation	Participation
Empathy	Respect
Empowerment	Responsiveness
Encouragement	Sense of humor
Expertise	Service

Exercise 5.2

ESTABLISHING TEAM VALUES

1. Create several sets of cards listing values such as those shown above (one value per card). Feel free to add additional values.

2. Each member picks out his or her five top values or adds new ones.

3. Each team member shares with the team his or her choices and explains the reasons for his or her selection.

4. The team agrees on its top five to ten values through a facilitated group discussion.

Our Values Are: _____

_____

Ground Rules

Ground rules are the general principles the team agrees to in order to manage its interactions. Ground rules can be fairly obvious and easy to set but more difficult to maintain within day-to-day business challenges. Ground rules are normally set for team meetings, but they also can be set for other aspects of team interaction and communication. Time spent defining ground rules up front will save time later.

Examples of categories for ground rules include the following:

Parameters around holding meetings

Communicating away from meetings

Making decisions

Solving problems

Role of the team leader

Team roles

Team workload/performance

With your team, work to define the ground rules that can guide your team's interactions.

SWOT ANALYSIS

A SWOT analysis takes a probing look at the Strengths, Weaknesses, Opportunities, and Threats that face the team. Strengths and Weaknesses refer to the team's internal advantages and potential disadvantages. These factors are under the direct control of the team. Opportunities and Threats refer to aspects outside of the team's direct control that might open up potential or result in negative consequences. Opportunities and Threats can originate outside the organization in the market at large, in other organizations, or even in other departments within your own company.

The purpose of a SWOT analysis is to view from a macro perspective the world in which your team is performing. This vantage point ensures that the planned strategy and direction are possible, given the team's inherent Strengths and Weaknesses. It also assures that the strategy is geared toward capitalizing on Opportunities and minimizing Threats. Use Exercise 5.3 to perform a SWOT analysis for your team.

Exercise 5.3

CONDUCTING A SWOT ANALYSIS FOR YOUR TEAM

1. As a group, discuss and list answers to the following questions. Do not qualify your answers but list them as they are stated.

2. Review the list for its completeness using current project plans, objectives, and so on.

What are your team Strengths?

_____

_____

_____

_____

What are your team Weaknesses?

_____

_____

_____

_____

What are the Opportunities available to your team?

_____

_____

_____

_____

What are the Threats that might inhibit team performance?

_____

_____

_____

_____

ESTABLISHING KEY RESULT AREAS

Establishing Key Result Areas is a tool that categorizes the team's entire workload. While many teams set objectives for their members, often there is no direct link between the team purpose and the tasks the team has to complete on a day-to-day basis—project milestones. Establishing Key Result Areas is a valuable technique that links the overall direction and workload of the team with project goals and milestones. Key Result Areas reflect the most important areas of the team's responsibilities, the areas in which results have to be achieved. Key Result Areas do not describe the type of results to be achieved but rather categorize work into *headings*. Use Exercise 5.4 to determine your team's Key Result Areas.

Exercise 5.4

DEFINING YOUR TEAM'S KEY RESULT AREAS

List your Key Result Areas in the space provided below. Some sample categories are listed here. The list is by no means complete but is meant to serve as a support tool. For further information, see the case study at the end of this chapter.

Financial	Sales
Marketing	Team development
Customer service	Operations
Communication	Reporting
Projects	Quality
Research and development	Manufacturing
Vendor management	Purchasing
Process improvement	Problem identification

_____

_____

_____

_____

_____

_____

_____

_____

Now that we have introduced the theory and concepts behind setting the team's direction, we will discuss the ways in which team members' temperament, functions, and type contribute to or detract from this process. In later chapters, we will move from the high-level overview of the team's responsibilities to a more tactical breakdown in terms of who does what and when (in Chapter 6, "Clear Roles and Responsibilities").

TEAMS IN ACTION

While the approach to setting a team's strategy and direction is fairly straightforward, team members' personalities will affect this procedure from the inside out. Each temperament, function, and type contributes different facets to the process.

Temperament

Listed below are a few guidelines and considerations to keep in mind about temperament as you move through the strategic planning process. They are also detailed in Table 5.2 on pages 124 and 125.

- Each temperament brings some innate strengths to different areas critical to team performance. For instance, Rationals and Idealists bring a big-picture perspective to establishing purpose. Guardians bring a sequential thought process to defining roles and responsibilities. In each chapter we will summarize the innate strengths and potential challenges that each temperament "brings to the table" in helping the team SCORE and produce results.

- When setting strategy and direction, both Rationals and Idealists will begin with the big picture and then narrow down to details. Guardians will build up the purpose by using their linear, step-by-step thought process. Artisans will approach setting strategy in short time frames; rather like quarterbacks, they will call each play after they see the result of the previous play.

- Idealists will tend to express the team purpose and vision in impressionistic, flowing language. Rationals will want the statement to contain the precise words, where Guardians will want to respect tradition in their word choice; and if defining the statement takes too long, Artisans will want to "get to the point."

- When defining values and ground rules, those temperaments with a Feeling preference will innately value the process (Feeling Artisans, Feeling Guardians, and Idealists). The other

Table 5.2 Strengths and Challenges of Temperaments in Setting Strategy

Temperament	Strengths	Potential Challenges
Artisan *Coaching Suggestions:* • Encourage them to think long term, not just in terms of today. • Explain the results of the process and how positive the team will look. • Encourage them to slow down and take aim. • Help them to maintain focus during slower periods by encouraging their input and keeping their attention. • Explain that setting up ground rules allows smoother functioning later.	• Bring a realistic perspective of the current situation • Adapt naturally (if the team is new); energized by new challenge • Lighten up the process with humor • Know how purpose relates to current target audience • Won't let the process bog down • Help in keeping statements to the point • Contribute to SWOT analysis based on their observation of current data • Attune to what actions need to be taken; see lots of opportunities in the current situation • Like the prioritizing aspect of Key Result Areas—focus on producing results	• May be cynical during the process • May think more in terms of current tactics and details than long-range strategy • May want quick, tangible results • May not want the group process to be so defined (i.e., ground rules) • May get bored if process slows down • May have difficulty breaking work into categories • Feel confident about their ability to handle threats but may push for too many risks • Will push for doing "real work" instead of what they might perceive to be "fiddling around"
Guardian *Coaching Suggestions:* • Encourage them not to be too reality based at this point but to focus on ideals. • Clearly explain the practical benefits of determining a team purpose. • Take heed of their experience-based opinions, but don't let them get stuck in the past. • Encourage their questions and comments.	• Enjoy the process because it creates a stronger team culture and bond • Value ground rules • Keep the team in accordance with the company's traditions and culture • Seek clarity and practicality • Encourage realism, which can benefit (and limit) the process • Create reproducible processes that allow for continuation of the purpose • Refer to what they have done in the past as a source of data for Key Result Areas • Like the organizational and structural aspect of the process • Encourage team collaboration toward common goals	• May want to start from the details (tasks) in order to build up to the big picture • May get upset if ground rules are not adhered to • Want team purpose to be practical • May not want to challenge authority • Won't get excited if they haven't done it before • May want to push to the end result • May use past negative experiences to block future visioning • May want to focus on improving weaknesses rather than on opportunities • May not gather new information, just historic data

Table 5.2   Strengths and Challenges of Temperaments in Setting Strategy (cont'd)

Temperament	Strengths	Potential Challenges
Rational *Coaching Suggestions:* • Appreciate their search for precision, but encourage them not to get too caught up in wordsmithing. • Encourage them to be tactful when commenting on other people's ideas. • Explain how team values and ground rules are vital to achievement. • Encourage them to consult "experts" about realistic time frames.	• Naturally enjoy the strategic planning process • Can clearly categorize work • Critical thinking skills useful in defining team purpose • Enjoy the brainstorming element of SWOT analysis • Bring an excellent perspective on trends for the SWOT analysis • Notice possible threats, weaknesses, and opportunities in the future • Seek consistency in different statements and ideas • Appreciate the intellectual challenge and abstract nature of the process • May ask, "What is our vision and why?"	• Want just the right words for the team purpose; may wordsmith to death • May find team values exercise too "touchy feely"; focus more on pragmatism • May not value ground rules • May struggle with creating realistic time frames • May want to master all the projects • May not recognize and appreciate all the strengths of the team • May argue to make a theoretical point and be oblivious to team response
Idealist *Coaching Suggestions:* • Encourage them to be more realistic in terms of overall team workload and opportunities. • Appreciate their striving to attain the best for the team, but make sure they lower their standards a little. • Explain that team members not acting in alignment with team purpose and values is not a malicious choice.	• Want to ensure that the purpose is meaningful to all and show the team contribution to the organization • Place importance on the team values exercise if team input is genuine • Like to create an overview of work to see how all tasks are connected • May be able to facilitate group process • Will point out all the strengths of the team and its members • Will enjoy the creative aspect of the SWOT analysis and be optimistic about opportunities • Enjoy imagining the future and focusing the team in a specific direction • Want results to be inspirational • Enjoy exercises as an opportunity to learn and develop team potential	• May get offended if the team is flippant about the process of defining team values • May be unrealistic in defining what the team's overall mission should be • Will be disappointed when other team members don't perform in accordance with the purpose • May have a problem categorizing Key Result Areas as all work appears to be integrated • May not be realistic about potential threats • Despite great intentions, may not implement

temperaments may view some of these group process elements as too "soft." Neither viewpoint is right or wrong; each is just different.

- Most temperaments enjoy the process of conducting a SWOT analysis because it capitalizes on all temperaments' strengths. For instance, Artisans see the opportunity in the moment, Guardians bring their enormous data bank of historic sensory experiences to the table, and Rationals and Idealists are naturally future focused. This means that this step in the strategic planning process is often received well by all players.

- When defining Key Result Areas, Rationals and Idealists begin from the abstract perspective in categorizing the team's workload. Guardians often need to list the detailed milestones/projects and then build the categories from there. The categorization process is hardest for Artisans because of their preference for living in the present; they tend to want to do everything *now!*

- Each chapter includes coaching suggestions for each temperament to enable team members to capitalize on their strengths while minimizing their potential challenges. These coaching suggestions can also be used as ideas for optimizing overall team performance depending on the team temperament.

Functions

Here are some guidelines for considering functions.

- Each chapter includes brief details on how each function approaches each subject. Remember to look at all different functions when you are working in each chapter.

- As all temperaments can use all eight functions (with varying degrees of ease and proficiency), coaching suggestions for using functions are not included. Just remember where you are proficient (based in your first and second functions), and remember to consider all sources of possible data and different criteria in making decisions. Table 5.3 on pages 127 through 129 provides a detailed chart of the strengths and challenges of the different functions, and Figure 5.1 on page 130 shows how the different functions approach setting direction.

Table 5.3 Strengths and Challenges of Functions in Setting Strategy

Functions	Strengths	Potential Challenges
Extraverted Sensing (S_E): Experiencing	• Use all current data in the planning process • Now focused, action oriented, and quick thinking • Want purpose to be attention grabbing • Tactically focused; enjoy SWOT analysis and see lots of opportunities • Feel they can handle threats/risks • Ready for a challenge • Able to capitalize on opportunities provided by strengths and weaknesses of team members	• Focus only on the here and now • May change direction too frequently • May get bored talking about future • May jump ahead in the process • May not enjoy the abstract nature of the planning process
Introverted Sensing (S_I): Recalling	• Refer back to strategic planning, bringing a historical perspective • Bring an organized, sequential thought to strategic planning • Bring the memory of what worked/didn't work in the past to SWOT • Want to maintain any traditions from previous teams that have worked • Ability to organize what has to be done in an orderly manner • Will bring data and testimony (evidence) in regard to Threats and Opportunities • Want to plan for Threats and Weaknesses	• May get stuck on details • May appear to be cautious or negative with new ideas or projects or those they see as unrealistic • Want practical applications; may be impatient with the abstract • May bring forward old failures: "We can't do that because…" • May need to think of the details of their day in sequence in order to build Key Result Areas

Table 5.3 Strengths and Challenges of Functions in Setting Strategy (cont'd)

Functions	Strengths	Potential Challenges
Extraverted Intuition (N_E): Brainstorming	• See lots of options • Believe future focus and big-picture ability critical to strategic planning • Have a fresh perspective; will look at things from new angles • Quick at brainstorming possibilities in the SWOT analysis • Will investigate how to improve strengths and weaknesses • Able to identify trends and patterns • Flexible and encouraging of ideas	• May have difficulty focusing the purpose • Do not see limitations • May not be realistic in establishing Key Result Areas • Take on too many ideas and unable to prioritize among them • May not be grounded in reality or see downside when excited
Introverted Intuition (N_I): Visioning	• Develop new ways of approaching a subject or new operating systems • Have insightful vision of the future with a broad, long-range perspective • See the deeper meaning and implications • Bring an independent perspective • Able to extract the essence of a complex situation in setting Key Result Areas • Have awareness and understanding of future situations—aware of opportunities and threats • Have a complete picture of the team's potential output	• May be unable to articulate the vision • May not be willing to listen to other ideas not in agreement with their vision • May be rigid in attempting to achieve vision without compromise • Have limited awareness of concrete details • Have difficulty distinguishing a gap between criteria and current situation
Extraverted Thinking (T_E): Systematizing	• Emphasize logic and equality in establishing ground rules • Analyze data and use logical approach based on published data • Want process to be effective and serious • Provide detailed, logical support for all opinions • Gifted in categorization and definition of Key Result Areas • Offer quick, objective input in SWOT analysis • Want proven facts and data to support threats and opportunities	• May not perceive the values exercise to be useful • May be impatient with delayed decision making • Systematic approach may not take into consideration the people aspects • Point out inconsistencies and inaccuracies in reasoning; may appear critical • May want to implement before the team is ready

Table 5.3 Strengths and Challenges of Functions in Setting Strategy (cont'd)

Functions	Strengths	Potential Challenges
Introverted Thinking (T_I): Analyzing	• Logical and analytical approach to establishing purpose • Enjoy creating new hypotheses and frameworks for team functioning • Push for consistency in the whole result • Recognize weaknesses and threats; able to see what's missing as well as what's there • Will analyze data and be able to present an alternative viewpoint • Are able to evaluate and sort data to create new possibilities	• If information does not match their current model, will challenge data and approach • May question the team values exercise as to how much team values affect performance • Logic they give for Key Result Areas may be based on their own internal logic • May appear overly argumentative about specific data
Extraverted Feeling (F_E): Harmonizing	• Build communication bridges • Help create a positive working environment • Consider the human aspects in the SWOT analysis • Push for consensus on ideas • Place high importance on ground rules • Quick to point out strengths and make people feel good about themselves	• Feel uncomfortable when conflict erupts and may not want to move on without resolution • May want to obtain consensus in situations when there is not time, or it is not appropriate • Want to ensure that all team members agree with the Key Result Areas • May be disappointed when individuals do not follow the ground rules • Show emotion on face, which can be unproductive at times
Introverted Feeling (F_I): Valuing	• Have strong beliefs about the way the team should work together • Highly value different perspectives in the team • Place high import on team values exercise • Seek a team purpose that adheres to their beliefs • Will want to ensure that Key Result Areas are in alignment with team values • Will consider subjective and intangible components of SWOT analysis	• May adamantly oppose ideas that go against their internal values system • May refuse to compromise values to take advantage of opportunities or deal with threats • May be judgmental when values aren't in alignment • May appear unrealistic in their ideals • May not voice all their concerns

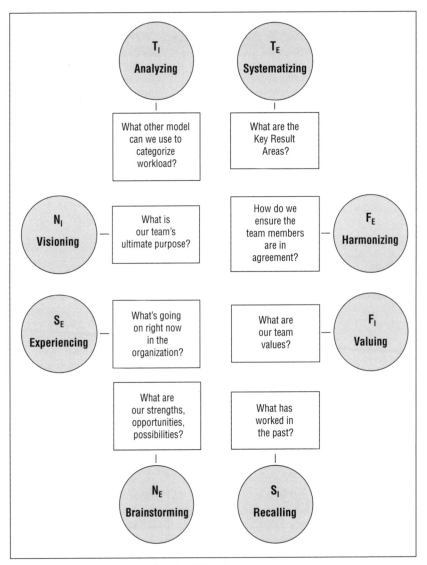

Figure 5.1 Functions and Setting Direction

Types

The Extraverting preference can help teams set direction by

- Maintaining verbal communication
- Initiating activities
- Generating a sociable environment
- Saying what they have to say

The Introverting preference can help teams set direction by

- Focusing the energy on the project and ideas at hand
- Encouraging depth of consideration
- Providing a measured/reflective response
- Building in-depth relationships

Here are some coaching suggestions:

Extraverting

- Encourage team members to pause and reflect on their ideas.
- Make sure they allow for those with a preference for Introversion to contribute.
- While allowing them to enjoy the interaction, focus them on the task at hand.

Introverting

- If possible, give them the information in advance, so that they have time to think it through.
- Encourage them to verbalize values and thoughts, but give them reflection time in order to do so.
- Be sure they are allowed to get their opinions into the discussion.

Strengths and challenges of the various types are shown in Table 5.4 on page 132.

SAMPLE TEAM PROFILE: MANAGEMENT TEAM

Background Information

This case study, summarized on page 134 describes the management team for a specific area of a large retailer of sports apparel and equipment. The company primarily distributes through dealers but also owns a small number of company retail and outlet stores. The company decided to act on a new initiative to create "stores within stores" as a cost-effective way of increasing brand recognition. These stores within stores are the area that our sample team manages.

The management team began with twenty stores and within a year expanded to over a hundred. The team had to grow rapidly, as did the team of regional merchandisers responsible for stocking the stores and training the dealers. The company decided to invest in the team profiling approach in order to provide all its team members with the tools to optimize team performance in their dynamic, expanding environment.

Table 5.4   Strengths and Challenges of Type: Setting Strategy and Direction

Type	Strengths	Potential Challenges
ESTP, ISTP (Thinking Artisan)	• See opportunities in the moment in SWOT analysis • Are skilled at tactical strategy and technique • Have logical models using their rich storehouse of facts and data	• May have short-term focus • May be distracted by immediate needs • May want to take a step and see where it leads
ESFP, ISFP (Feeling Artisan)	• Place high emphasis on alignment of team and organizational values • See opportunities for people in SWOT analysis • Will create more concrete purpose statements	• May get distracted by immediate short-term people needs • May obstruct creation of objective framework for the team's direction • May focus on short-term tactical strategy
ESTJ, ISTJ (Thinking Guardian)	• Use logical, sequential, concrete strategy • Take the past into the future • Grounded in reality with logical linear time lines and causal effect sequencing	• May focus on weaknesses and threats in SWOT analysis and disregard ideas that have not been tried before • May concentrate on what's missing rather on than what's there • May push for closure, thereby shortening consideration of strengths and opportunities
ESFJ, ISFJ (Feeling Guardian)	• Take step-by-step approach to build the parts into the end result or whole • Have concrete, realistic vision using team collaboration toward goals • Use traditional linear progress to logical end result and bottom line for the company	• May be too concrete, discount possibilities, and worry about consequences • While trying to achieve consensus, may take too long in reaching a decision • May discount out-of-the-box possibilities
ENTP, INTP (Adaptable Rational)	• Have big-picture focus with evolving mental models • Constantly incorporate new ideas into team's strategy and direction • Will see lots of opportunities and possibilities in the SWOT analysis; naturally optimistic	• May articulate too many ideas that other team members take literally and act on, when NTPs were really only hypothesizing • May be unrealistic; have infinite time orientation • May change model too frequently
ENTJ, INTJ (Structured Rational)	• Have logical, objective direction and able to clearly articulate strategy • Will take vision to action • Will abstractly categorize Key Result Areas	• May be perceived as inflexible • May always want to lead and not be open to alternatives • May be perceived to be rigid

Table 5.4   Strengths and Challenges of Type: Setting Strategy and Direction

Type	Strengths	Potential Challenges
ENFP, INFP (Adaptable Idealist)	• Will be passionate about the team's purpose and symbolize a vision for the team • Always see opportunities (Brainstorming) in SWOT analysis • Behavior will be supporting their internal and the team's values system	• May get excited about lots of different options and appear unable to settle on one vision • Vision may not be tethered in reality • Key Result Areas may lack an apparent structure
ENFJ, INFJ (Structured Idealist)	• Approach strategy from macro to micro focus • Will obtain closure around purpose and direction • Able to understand the team's entire workload and then categorize it	• If the work has no meaning, may be unable to set the direction • May be too people focused and unable to move on without consensus • Direction may not be realistic

Unlike many organizations, the company has taken a proactive approach to team building. Rather than wait until the team is suffering from severe conflicts before taking action, the company wanted team members to know how to work best with each other from the beginning. As a result, knowledge of type and temperament was able to produce considerable results for the team as it raised its SCORE in team performance using the Inside-Out methodology.

Connects and Conflicts

- As you can see from Figure 5.2 on page 136, two types are not represented in the team at all: the SFJs and NTJs, both of whom produce organization and structure (Guardian SFJ and Systematizing NTJ). This could mean lack of follow-through and planning.
- Most of the team members are "connected" in the top right-hand corner, which could explain the team cohesiveness.
- David is "disconnected" from the team by one "bubble." While this is beneficial for team diversity, it may make David feel like the odd one out.

Aligning on Strategy

Based on the approach advocated in this chapter, the team worked through the steps as follows:

SAMPLE TEAM PROFILE

Individual Analysis

Name	Temperament	1st/2nd Function		Type
Jackie	Rational	N_E	T_I	ENTP
Daniel	Artisan	S_E	F_I	ESFP
Debbie	Idealist	F_I	N_E	INFP
Anita	Idealist	N_I	F_E	INFJ
Mark	Idealist	N_E	F_I	ENFP
Liz	Idealist	F_I	N_E	INFP
Kathleen	Artisan	T_I	S_E	ISTP
Tracy	Artisan	T_I	S_E	ISTP
David	Guardian	T_E	S_I	ESTJ

Team Analysis

Temperaments: Guardians __1__   Artisans __3__

Idealists __4__   Rationals __1__

Team Temperament: __Idealist__

Team Leader Temperament: __Rational__

Functions (First and Second Combined):

Perceiving S_E: __3__ S_I: __1__ N_E: __4__ N_I: __1__

Judging T_E: __1__ T_I: __3__ F_E: __1__ F_I: __4__

Preferences: E: __4__   I: __5__

S: __4__   N: __5__

T: __4__   F: __5__

J: __2__   P: __7__

First Function for the Team: N_E: Brainstorming; F_I: Valuing

First Function for the Team Leader: N_E: Brainstorming

Team Type: __INFP__

Team Leader Type: __ENTP__

- Set a team purpose
- Decided values and ground rules
- Conducted a SWOT analysis
- Established Key Result Areas

For each step, we will describe the process the group used, the effect that the team profile had on the process, the end results, and the plan of attack they devised to raise their team SCORE.

Team Purpose

The team used Exercise 5.1 to define its team purpose. The members divided their department into two teams, and they worked on the project in parallel. There was an enthusiasm for the project, with several team members immediately taking advantage of props around the office with which to build their three-dimensional model. You could certainly see the influence of the three Artisans. Selecting the words for the definition seemed relatively painless, and the groups agreed easily. The Idealists felt that the spirit of the statements accurately reflected the unique contribution of the team, and that therefore they did not need "wordsmithing." The end result, when the two statements were combined, was "To create international brand awareness for the company."

With Idealist as the dominant temperament, the team agreed to the purpose and every team member was able to articulate it. Team members also exhibited enthusiasm and commitment to the purpose.

Values and Ground Rules

The team completed Exercise 5.2 to clarify ground rules and values for the team. With the presence of four members with F_I : Valuing, the team inherently had a cohesive set of values. The team members articulated similar values and agreed on the following:

- Respect
- Honesty
- Sense of humor
- Creativity
- Commitment

The team exhibited a high level of commitment to creating a comfortable work environment and building up support amongst members. This commitment was probably a result of the main temperament (Idealist) and the strong presence of F_I : Valuing and F_E : Harmonizing.

Strengths

- Creativity
- Quick thinking/flexibility
- Commitment/team spirit
- Lots of retail experience

Weaknesses

- Take on too many projects and change direction too frequently
- Follow-through sometimes lacking
- No systemized planning
- Overlap of roles

Opportunities

- Closer relationship with sales force
- Stores within stores in CEO's initiatives
- Adequate sustainable funding
- Huge worldwide market for product with clear brand identity

Threats

- Change in organizational direction; new CEO and other organizations also poised for growth with more funding
- Changing market trends: depression in Asia, one of new potential markets
- Utilization of new technologies

Key Result Areas

The team type (INFP) indicated a strong commitment to other individuals on the team, and also a future focus and willingness to consider new possibilities. As a result, the team tended to get overloaded and change strategy without considering the logical consequences of that change (Systematizing is the fourth function for INFP). This was probably the outcome of the team leader's preference for ENTP and the team type (INFP), both of which share N_E: Brainstorming as the main information-gathering function. New options were very appealing for the team and its leader.

As the team categorized its Key Result Areas, it was able to build a more complete overview of the extent of the team's responsibilities. With four Idealists and one Rational, the team tended to underestimate the time needed for tasks and overestimate its capability for completing projects. The team identified eight Key Result Areas where energy needed to be focused in order to be successful (see Table 5.5).

Table 5.5 Team Key Result Areas

Area	Explanation
Financial Management	The team had to pay for itself, meet budget requirements, and control its costs.
Merchandising	The success of the team was strongly influenced by the regional merchandisers, who visit the dealers regularly to ensure that layout and product mix are correct. This was an area in which team members already had objectives.
Purchasing	The purchase of products is a vital element in retail. This was an area in which team members already had objectives.
Dealer Communication	Team members recognized that much of their time was spent communicating with dealers, which had not been included in their goals. Creating a Key Result Area that reflected this time helped ensure that team members had a more realistic picture of their workload.
Shop Design	The design of the stores is a vital element in retail. This was an area in which team members already had objectives.
Internal Communication	Team members recognized that a lot of their time was also spent communicating with the direct sales force. Creating a Key Result Area that reflected this time helped ensure that team members had a more realistic picture of their workload.
Process and Procedures	A great deal of time was also absorbed fixing things that had gone wrong. The team decided it was necessary to establish consistent processes and procedures so that it could be proactive instead of reactive. With only one Guardian on the team, it was not surprising that the team had had limited success in this area. Verbalizing this work focus helped keep proactive process development in sight and in mind.
Strategic Direction	The team members felt that establishing a strategic direction was an important Key Result Area because they were creating and rolling out a relatively new concept for the company. This was another area that was taking time but that had not had specific objectives related to it.

Team Plan of Attack

- The team put in place a process to evaluate new ideas against current workload before jumping into new projects. The team invested in additional sessions where members defined Key Result Areas, set objectives, and more clearly defined roles and responsibilities. In addition they created a master project plan showing all tasks necessary to achieve team objectives.

- As there was only one Guardian on the team, the team found an internal partner (the operations manager) who could bring this perspective.

- The team committed to evaluate itself on a regular basis using Exercise 4.1 (see pages 101 and 102).

- The knowledge of type and temperament was used to enhance the team's already supportive culture, to increase the level of trust in the team.

- The team created a Process Improvement Task Force to evaluate opportunities for proactive problem resolution. This team comprised team members from the management team, the field, and other departments in the organization.

CREATING AND INTERPRETING YOUR TEAM PROFILE

Use the information in Table 4.3 on page 112 and the Team Profile form in the appendix to create your team profile. Use the information in this chapter and in the case study provided to evaluate your team and the strengths and challenges it might face in the process of setting strategy. In addition, consider what actions you could immediately take to raise proficiency and create a more cohesive strategy for your team. Then use the questions in Table 5.6 on page 142 as the basis for diagnosing your team's performance. Use the Connects and Conflicts diagram in the appendix to remind you of the interrelationships of temperament, functions, and type.

Once you have assessed your team strengths and diagnosed any potential challenges your team might face in setting direction, it is time to decide what you can do, as a team, to raise your team SCORE in this arena. It is not possible to recommend specific actions for each team because no two profiles are exactly the same. Instead, we will use the same approach as we did in diagnosing your team, providing a list of questions you can discuss with your team to act as a stimulus in formulating your own plan of attack in Table 5.7 on page 143.

General Data		
Temperament	Table 1.1	Pages 24–25
Functions	Tables 2.2–2.5	Pages 41–44
	Tables 2.7–2.10	Pages 51–54
Type	Table 3.4	Pages 76–83
Specific Data on Setting Strategy and Direction		
Temperament	Table 5.2	Pages 124–125
Functions	Table 5.3	Pages 127–129
Type	Table 5.4	Pages 132–133

Table 5.6   Implications for Your Team: Strategy

Temperament/Connects & Conflicts	Function/Preferences
What is the team temperament?	What is the balance of Extraversion and Introversion on our team? What are the implications of this breakdown in terms of discussions to define our purpose and values? (For instance, if the team predominantly uses the Introverted preference, there will be a need to allow reflection before moving on to the next subject.)
Looking at the temperament charts (Table 5.2), what does this tell us about this team's approach to setting strategy and direction?	
What might be our team's strengths? What might be some potential team challenges?	
What temperaments are not present in the team?	What is the first function on the team, and what does this mean to the strategic planning process? (For instance, if N_E: Brainstorming is first, this would mean the ability to generate lots of ideas in the SWOT analysis, but it might also signify a reluctance to limit the direction to a few options.) (Remember to use Table 5.3 in this chapter and the general tables in Chapter 2.)
What factors might we miss in setting strategy and direction? (Remember to use Table 5.2 in this chapter and the information in Chapter 1.)	
What temperaments are there in the team and what is their approach to defining purpose, defining team values and ground rules, conducting the SWOT analysis, and categorizing Key Result Areas?	
	What is the first function for the team leader, and what implications does this have in terms of establishing a cohesive direction?
What is the team leader's temperament?	
Using the temperament tables, what are the strengths of the team leader in setting strategy and direction? (For instance, if he or she is a Guardian, there might be less focus on future possibilities that have not been tried before.)	What functions are not represented in the team as first or second used, and what impact could this have on the team, considering all options for the team direction? (For instance, if S_I: Recalling is not represented, the team may reinvent the wheel but will not be held back by historic perspectives.)
What is the difference between the team leader's temperament and the team temperament? How might this affect our strategic planning process?	What is the team type, and what does this indicate about the team's approach to setting direction? (Use the descriptions of type in Chapter 3 and the information in Table 5.4 for ideas.)
Where are the team members located in the diagram? What "bubbles" are not represented?	
	What is the team leader's type? What are the team leader's strengths in getting the team aligned on a purpose? What are the potential challenges in this arena?
Which team members are grouped "close" to each other? Which team members appear "disconnected" from the team?	

Table 5.7 Plan of Attack: Strategy

Temperament/Connects & Conflicts	Function/Preferences
What implications does this have for discussions on setting strategy and direction?	How can we ensure that those with an Extraverting preference do not dominate the discussions? How do we ensure that input from those with an Introverting preference is included in the mix?
How can we compensate for "lacking a temperament" as we establish our purpose, values, and Key Result Areas?	
How can we ensure we capitalize on the strengths of all temperaments in our team in setting strategy? Is there one temperament that naturally has talents in a specific area?	If the team has a predominantly Sensing preference, how can the team ensure that its strategic direction is long-term focused and not "too practical"?
How can we ensure we reap the benefits of our team temperament in setting team strategy and direction?	If the team has a predominantly Intuition preference, how can the team ensure that the strategic direction is realistic?
How can we compensate for potential challenges in setting direction based on team temperament?	If the team has a predominantly Thinking preference, how can the team ensure that the process of setting team values is given the credence it warrants?
How can we ensure that we do not overuse one temperament in defining future direction?	If the team has a predominantly Feeling preference, how can the team ensure that the long-term direction is objective and logical?
Looking at the Connects and Conflicts diagram for our team and the table on type (Table 5.4), what can we do to improve communication?	If the team has a predominantly Judging preference, how can we ensure that the team remains flexible in changing its strategy and direction?
How can we ensure that team members are heard?	If the team has a predominantly Perceiving preference, how can the team ensure that the strategy and directions stay somewhat consistent?
What ground rules could we institute to reinforce this approach?	

SUMMARY CHECKLIST

Before leaving this chapter, answer the following questions:

1. Have you completed the team purpose exercise with your team members (Exercise 5.1)?

2. Have you defined your team values with your team members (Exercise 5.2)?

3. Have you conducted a SWOT analysis to understand the broader business perspective for your group (Exercise 5.3)?

4. Have you established Key Result Areas for your team (Exercise 5.4)?

5. Have you analyzed your team in terms of its profile and approach to this planning process?

6. Have you created a plan of attack to raise your team SCORE in setting strategy?

6

Clear Roles and Responsibilities

WHAT ARE WE SUPPOSED
TO BE DOING?

"A straight path never leads anywhere except to the objective."
—André Gide

Chapter 5 addressed how to establish a clear strategy for the team. Now we need to link the responsibilities of the team with day-to-day tasks and activities. Overall team workload is allocated to members through the establishment of Key Result Areas for every person on the team. It is important to set specific objectives so that members completely understand their deliverables and their contribution to overall team achievement. To aid in this process, we will explore how to set roles and responsibilities from the inside out. By assigning duties reflective of individual preferences and needs, we ensure that team members are not only capable of doing the work but also motivated to do their best. Taking time in this area will enable team members to produce better team results and raise the team SCORE. Figure 6.1 on page 148 illustrates this planning process.

DEFINING MEMBERS' RESPONSIBILITIES

The simplest, most common way to determine team member responsibilities is to evaluate the individuals' proficiencies and apportion team tasks accordingly.

However, rather than merely divvying up duties, team performance will once again benefit if the Inside Out approach is taken. Though seldom considered, team member likes and dislikes are a critical part of the mix. One of the central reasons teams get stuck is because team members aren't doing enough work that they take

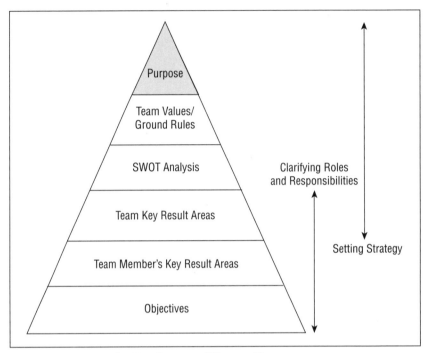

**Figure 6.1   Linking Setting Strategy (Chapter 5)
with Clarifying Roles and Responsibilities (Chapter 6)**

pleasure in. Rather than allocate responsibilities randomly, why not assign them appropriately? Use Exercise 6.1 to determine the individual preferences of your team members.

If team members have a say, they will feel better about the work they do, not to mention enjoy the benefit of doing more of what they like. Compiling a list of team member likes and dislikes is the obvious and effective way to address this issue. While it is impossible for members to do only the tasks that they enjoy, considering individual preferences in determining workloads provides a valuable point of reference so that individuals are not totally submerged in responsibilities they disfavor.

DEFINING TEAM MEMBERS' KEY RESULT AREAS

While considering team member preferences in assigning responsibilities positively affects team performance, optimum productivity will still not be reached if individual roles are not effectively defined. Team member productivity means completing objectives and achieving results. If team members are to accomplish the team goals, they need

Exercise 6.1

WHAT WE LIKE/WHAT WE DON'T LIKE

In order to determine individual preferences, ask team members to list the tasks they like and dislike. This exercise can be used to define roles with a new team or to redefine roles with an existing team.

Your team is: _____

Team Member	**Like**	**Dislike**

Team Member	**Like**	**Dislike**

Team Member	**Like**	**Dislike**

Team Member	**Like**	**Dislike**

to clearly visualize their deliverables and spend time on the right things, their Key Result Areas. Just as team Key Result Areas are the most important work categories in which the team must produce results, individual Key Result Areas are the main facets of a team member's duties. High-performing team members focus their time and resources on these functions.

There are various approaches to identifying Key Result Areas for team members. The team can start by identifying the team Key Result Areas (Exercise 5.4, page 122) and use this information to help categorize each team member's workload. Team members can also use other sources such as these:

- Their job description
- Discussions with other team members
- Overall direction of the company
- Customer requirements

The Key Result Area framework enables the team to unify its overall direction, while providing a common language and approach for understanding team roles. Use Exercise 6.2 to determine your own and your team members' Key Result Areas. The case study at the end of the chapter shows clearly how individual Key Result Areas link in with team Key Result Areas.

Exercise 6.2

DEFINING INDIVIDUAL KEY RESULT AREAS

1. Revisit the team Key Result Areas you identified in Exercise 5.4.

2. Brainstorm the complete list of tasks that you have on your to-do lists and in any written goal information available.

3. Categorize this workload into no more than seven individual Key Result Areas.

4. List your Key Result Areas in the space provided below.

5. Get your team members to use the same process to create their Key Result Areas.

Your Key Result Areas

_____

_____

_____

Team Member Key Result Areas

_____

_____

_____

DEFINING OBJECTIVES

Having defined Key Result Areas, the next step is to create concrete, tangible objectives to define and measure work output. Spending time in the areas that count can make or break a team. The objectives show the actual outcomes expected within each of the Key Result Areas. They take the heading and add substance and depth to it.

Objectives are concrete, tangible, measurable results or outcomes, not just roles or activities. An effective objective meets the SMART criteria:

S: Specific—Does it hone in on a particular performance component?

M: Measurable—What is the quantity, quality specifications, cost and revenue, and so on?

A: Aligned—Is it aligned with the team purpose?

R: Results Focused—Does it lead to a tangible result?

T: Time Based—Does it have a specific due date?

Too often we confuse tasks with objectives. A task is the action we must take in order to reach an objective. To differentiate between tasks and objectives, we must ask ourselves, What are we trying to achieve by completing this task? What is the benefit of accomplishing this task?

Use Exercise 6.3 to define objectives for your team. Make sure you use words in your objective statements such as *ensure, increase, reduce, obtain, achieve, attain, and raise.* Examples of Key Result Areas linked to objectives are shown in the case study on pages 158 through 167.

Now that we have established individual Key Result Areas and objectives, let's take a look at how temperament, functions, and type influence team performance in this area from the Inside Out.

TEAMS IN ACTION:
TEMPERAMENT, FUNCTIONS, AND TYPE

Type and temperament influence our propensity to clearly define roles and responsibilities. Rationals and Idealists tend to start with the big picture/overall goal of their position, then create the categories and build (perhaps) the list of tasks: the top-down approach. Artisans and Guardians tend to start with the tasks they have to complete and build up (possibly) to the categories: the bottom-up approach. Neither approach is right or wrong; each is just different. Of all the temperaments, Guardians excel at clearly defining roles and responsibilities; knowing what they are responsible for and helping to clarify responsibilities for others is one of the ways they meet their

Exercise 6.3

ESTABLISHING YOUR TEAM'S KEY RESULT AREAS
AND OBJECTIVES

For each of the Key Result Areas you identified, try to write one objective in the grid below. Remember to make sure each objective is SMART—Specific, Measurable, Aligned, Results Focused, and Time Based.

Overall Goal Key Result Area	Objective(s)

core needs. Conversely, of all the temperaments, Guardians are the most uncomfortable, and get quickly demotivated, without a clear role definition.

In addition, each individual has roles and responsibilities he or she likes or dislikes depending on temperament. The statement "One person's meat is another person's poison" is certainly true in the area of allocating workloads to team members. While every team member can potentially fulfill every role, each temperament is motivated differently. Recognizing these differences and then trying to allocate workloads to ensure team members meet their core needs can positively affect the way the team performs.

Artisans enjoy roles where their contribution is visible and there is lots of flexibility. They want to see short-term, concrete results. The worst thing you can do for Artisans is put them on a long-term project with no immediate tangible results, and then cancel the project! When Artisans' core needs are not being met in their role, they may take action in other areas at work so that they get noticed. For instance, they may appear to act friviolously, or say something inappropriate to provoke a response.

Guardians enjoy roles where there is a concrete, tangible result and they are fulfilling their role as part of the team. They excel at writing clear SMART objectives, and they enjoy consistency both in direction and in their role. When their core needs are not being met, or when other team members don't fulfill their responsibilities adequately, they may become negative and blame and complain to others on the team.

Rationals enjoy roles where there is an opportunity to create long-term future strategy and solve abstract problems. They excel at analytical thinking and can see long-term ramifications that others might not expect. When their core needs are not being met, or if they perceive themselves to have been incompetent, they may become preoccupied and overanalyze situations.

Idealists enjoy roles where there is an opportunity to create or reinforce their own identity and where there is some greater meaning to the work. They excel at roles where they need to build communication between disparate viewpoints. When their core needs are not being met, or if they perceive that someone has betrayed them, they may appear to disconnect from the team.

Table 6.1 shows the types of responsibilities each temperament likes and dislikes. The purpose of presenting this information is to highlight the types of roles to which each temperament is best suited; therefore we have not included coaching suggestions. Obviously team roles will possess many diverse elements; helping to ensure the role meets the core needs and possesses some of the elements each temperament enjoys, while minimizing elements that the temperament does not enjoy, will help ensure a productive team.

Table 6.2 on pages 154 and 155 shows, for each function, the types of roles that are complementary to those for whom this is a first or second function (column one) and the types of roles that are not (column two). By reviewing Table 3.4 (see pages 76 through 83), you can see the functions that you use most easily. As we have previously discussed, every individual can use all eight functions; the differences are in the ease and fluency with which we use them. When we are in roles that rely on using functions that are not easy for us, several things can happen. First, we can feel more tired: using less-easy functions requires more conscious thought. Second, when we use these functions, they are not as smooth as the first and second functions, so we may perceive individuals who use these functions to be acting out of character or "in the grip" (Quenk, 1996). As we continue to use these functions, we may develop some degree of fluency in them, but under stress we still tend to go back to our first and second functions. Table 6.2 shows how functions relate to team role likes and dislikes. Figure 6.2 on page 156 summarizes what each function most wants in a role. Table 6.3 explores what each type brings to a role.

Consider the following when you are clarifying roles and responsibilities for team members with an Extraverting preference:

- Make sure they are not in a cubicle working on solitary projects all day—because they won't! They will come out to socialize.

- Give them roles that require initiating interaction with others. For instance, salespeople and trainers often have an Extraverting preference.

- Remember, when talking about roles and responsibilities, that those with an Extraverting preference will tend to process out loud, so you will know their views.

Consider the following when you are clarifying roles and responsibilities for team members with an Introverting preference:

- Make sure their roles allow time for in-depth solitary consideration, so that they have the time they require to internally process and to provide input.

- Don't use them entirely in roles where they have to initiate interaction with people. They are normally most comfortable responding to others' first moves.

Table 6.1 **Temperaments and Team Roles**

Temperament	Responsibilities They Like	Responsibilities They Dislike
Artisan	• Hands-on problem-solving opportunities in a fast-paced environment • Constant concrete, tangible results from their efforts • A certain amount of freedom and flexibility • Opportunities to negotiate and maneuver to achieve results • Opportunities to make an impression	• Dealing with abstract data not directly linked to results • Long-term projects with no visible milestones • Repetitive, boring, and heavily detailed jobs • Jobs controlled by processes, procedures, and rules
Guardian	• Implementing processes and procedures in a step-by-step manner • Responsibilities clearly defined; they know who is in charge • Concrete results from their sequential approach • The chance to be involved with the team, look after team members, and feel a sense of belonging • Stable roles where any change can be managed	• Constant change but no apparent reason for it • No clear role definition, many people "wasting time and resources" by doing the same thing • Dealing with abstract data with no practical application • Team environment competitive and political, no clear hierarchy
Rational	• Work dealing with abstract data • Roles complementary to their intellectual competence • Opportunity to apply theoretical principles and systems on the cutting edge • Working with other experts and continuing to learn • Analyzing, strategizing, designing	• Practical jobs with lots of concrete details • Boring, repetitive tasks that do not play to their areas of expertise • Intellectually uninteresting work, no opportunity to analyze and categorize data • No opportunity to change operating procedures and affect end results
Idealist	• Connections with others on the team, and unified under a cohesive purpose • Work that is conceptual, makes a difference • Helping individuals develop their potential • Roles where their unique contribution is recognized • People-focused work, communicating with others	• Meaningless work with no obvious contributions to the team, organization, or greater good • Highly detailed work, with no conceptual elements • Being viewed as the same as everybody else • Roles involving a high degree of conflict or questionable ethics

Table 6.2 Functions and Team Roles

Function	Responsibilities They Like	Responsibilities They Dislike
Extraverted Sensing (S_E): Experiencing	• Having constant access to current sensory data; being able to use the newest fun tools and gimmicks • Being able to act in the moment as they receive new data • Using their quick-thinking, tactical, problem-solving ability • Seeing the concrete outcome of their work	• Dealing with abstract data, no sensory frame of reference • Slow-moving roles, no practical outcome • Roles where they are supposed to lead but aren't able to do so • Boring, repetitive work; lack of change
Introverted Sensing (S_I): Recalling	• Jobs that require step-by-step implementation • Work where they can use their previous experience • Creating and implementing processes and procedures to produce tangible, consistent results • Consistency with group norms and historical beliefs	• Dealing with purely theoretical or abstract data • No historical perspective, job has to start from scratch • Work where there is constant change without a proven need • Lots of risks and quick decision making
Extraverted Intuition (N_E): Brainstorming	• Future-focused jobs that require optimism • Lots of variety in terms of project assignments • "Thinking outside the box," devising new enterprises and approaches • Opportunity to think of new projects	• Repetitive, detail-oriented, sequential work • No set ways of doing things and no opportunity to improve the situation • Attention needs to be focused on practical data • Their ideas being constantly shot down, unused, or unappreciated
Introverted Intuition (N_I): Visioning	• Opportunity to develop their own vision • Long-term perspective valued • Independent, fresh perspective appreciated • Dealing in concepts and distilling meaning	• Practical and mundane work • Constantly managing sensory data • No opportunity to build a future vision • Large amount of detailed systematic knowledge required

Table 6.2 Functions and Team Roles (cont'd)

Function	Responsibilities They Like	Responsibilities They Dislike
Extraverted Thinking (T_E): Systematizing	• Implementing a plan • Authority to take quick, decisive action to achieve team goals • Access to data; able to conduct logical pros and cons analysis on information • Their direct communication style benefits team	• Extensive analysis and time delays before arriving at decisions • No authority to make a decision; being unable to take charge • Dealing with extensive people issues without an objective framework • Dealing with systems that are not cause/effect based
Introverted Thinking (T_I): Analyzing	• Creating their own models • Researching, predicting, and theorizing possible alternative philosophies • Objectively analyzing abstract data into their own theory • Providing independent, objective feedback; observing and analyzing	• No opportunity to create their own models; essentially practical work • Dealing with subjective data; not allowed to question and critique • Asked to use an approach that does not fit with their mental model • Dealing with imprecision
Extraverted Feeling (F_E): Harmonizing	• Helping to create a harmonious, diplomatic environment • Sharing information with others, making information relevant to all • Interacting with a wide range of people in a nonconfrontational atmosphere • Creating a safe environment	• Conflict frequently arising between individuals or in the process of getting the work done • Forced to argue and to manage difficult people • Have to make decisions that don't meet the needs of others • Non-people-focused work
Introverted Feeling (F_I): Valuing	• Individual differences and perspectives are valued • Personal feedback is valid • Work in alignment with their personal values • Clarifying their personal values	• Work not in alignment with personal values • Unethical work, or not linked to organization's values • Work that goes against individual rights • Decisions made that compromise their beliefs

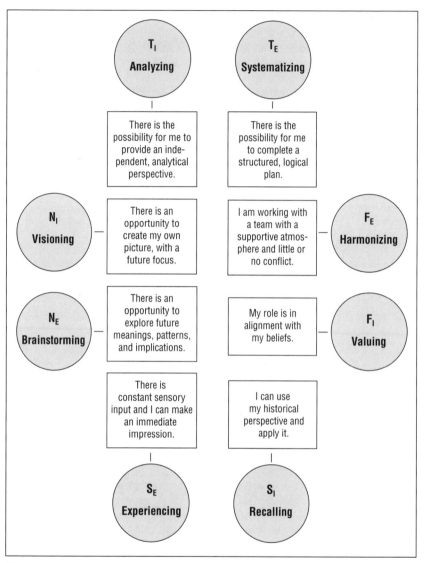

Figure 6.2 What Each Function Desires in a Role

SAMPLE TEAM PROFILE: MERCHANDISING TEAM

Background Information

This case study, summarized in the sample team profile on page 161, revisits the team we studied in Chapter 5. This time we will be analyzing the team of regional merchandisers who are responsible for

Table 6.3 Strengths and Challenges of Type: Clarifying Roles and Responsibilities

Type	Strengths	Potential Challenges
ESTP, ISTP (Thinking Artisan)	• Able to define and deliver on objectives • Will do what needs to be done • Will build Key Result Areas from specific to general	• May not want to stick to what could be perceived as a rigid structure • May shift objectives midstream • May push others to go into action before they are ready
ESFP, ISFP (Feeling Artisan)	• Will put right people on team and understand what is important to them • Will allow flexibility in roles • Will focus on short-term objectives and results	• May want flexibility at the expense of structure • May not hold people to task • May not take the time to define specific roles and responsibilities
ESTJ, ISTJ (Thinking Guardian)	• Can logically categorize Key Result Areas with SMART objectives with concrete implementation plans • Will provide detailed, written information on contracts and plans • Have clear boundaries, know who does what	• May be reluctant to change the plan when it is completed • May implement standard operating procedures to the extreme • May find it difficult to tolerate those who do not live up to their responsibilities
ESFJ, ISFJ (Feeling Guardian)	• Assign clear responsibilities on a task-specific basis • Start from the bottom up and categorize Key Result Areas with SMART objectives with concrete bottom-line deliverables • Will live up to their responsibilities even if that means working additional time	• May be passive-aggressive when others do not live up to their responsibilities • May pick up slack for other team members and then resent it • May need structure to be productive and appear inflexible with changes in structure
ENTP, INTP (Adaptable Rational)	• Hire the right people who can complement them on the team • Adept at categorizing workload and defining objectives • Good at defining a predetermined end result and convincing others to follow them	• May assign roles but not want to be bothered about details • May not understand the detailed steps required to get the job done • May change objectives too frequently as they see new opportunities and possibilities
ENTJ, INTJ (Structured Rational)	• Clearly define roles and responsibilities • Assign tasks at hand and put together logical, detailed plan of action • Design conceptual process for achieving end goals	• May be reluctant to change once roles have been decided • May be unable to see different possibilities for individuals • May not change goals as additional information becomes available

Table 6.3 Strengths and Challenges of Type:
Clarifying Roles and Responsibilities (cont'd)

Type	Strengths	Potential Challenges
ENFP, INFP (Adaptable Idealist)	• Geared toward individual potential • Able to persuade and motivate others to complete workload • Will establish training to gain skills	• May misread potential for currently demonstrated skills • May provide broad role definition with indistinct categories • May tend to be fluid in roles
ENFJ, INFJ (Structured Idealist)	• Allocate workload according to knowledge, skills, and interests • Able to define objectives • Willing to reshuffle team and put it back together	• May be unclear about boundaries and specific responsibilities • May want to do it all • May hire to potential based on subjective criteria and be disappointed

maintaining the shops within the dealer stores, training internal staff on graphics and display requirements, and acting as a liaison between the dealers and the sales reps.

Connects and Conflicts

• As you can see from Figure 6.3 on page 160, the team was "centered" in three "bubbles," which means that there again was a cohesive team but that broader perspectives were missed.

• The team had only one representative (Jessica) who was able to do any type of structuring. This sometimes brought her into conflict with the Artisans on the team.

• Jessica often felt that she was "speaking a different language."

Establishing Roles and Responsibilities

Based on the approach advocated in this chapter, the team leader worked through the steps as follows:

• She started the team.

• She asked the team members what they liked and did not like.

• She established Key Result Areas for the team members.

• She began to establish objectives for each team member.

SAMPLE TEAM PROFILE

Individual Analysis

Name	Temperament	1st/2nd Function		Type
Liz	Idealist	F_I	N_E	INFP
Lisa	Artisan	S_E	F_I	ESFP
Lollie	Artisan	S_E	T_I	ESTP
Colleen	Artisan	S_E	T_I	ESTP
Zoe	Artisan	T_I	S_E	ISTP
Jessica	Rational	T_E	N_I	ENTJ
Kevin	Idealist	F_I	N_E	INFP
Marisa	Artisan	S_E	F_I	ESFP

Team Analysis

Temperaments: Guardians   0   Artisans   5

                            Idealists   2   Rationals   1

Team Temperament: Artisan

Team Leader Temperament: Idealist

Functions (First and Second Combined):

     Perceiving S_E: 5 S_I: 0 N_E: 2 N_I: 1

     Judging T_E: 1 T_I: 3 F_E: 0 F_I: 4

Preferences: E: 5   I: 3

                  S: 5   N: 3

                  T: 4   F: 4

                  J: 1   P: 7

First Function for the Team: S_I: Experiencing

First Function for the Team Leader: F_I: Valuing

Team Type: ESTP/ESFP

Team Leader Type: INFP

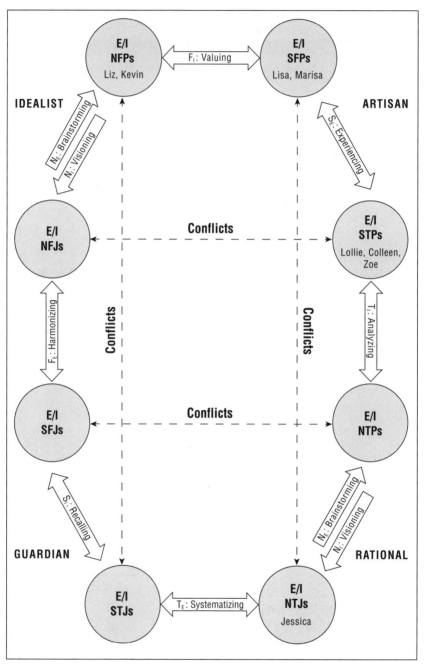

Figure 6.3 Sample Team Connects and Conflicts

Selecting Team Members

Liz began the team from scratch and therefore was able to define the Key Result Areas for the team. She also defined the ideal critical job requirements for the role of regional merchandiser.

Major Responsibilities (from Key Result Areas)

- Dealer and corporate communication
- Visual and product merchandising
- Administration
- Travel
- Training
- Product knowledge

Team Responsibilities

Technical Skills and Knowledge

- High school diploma, merchandising and retail background (required)
- Some sales knowledge, conducted training programs (desired)

Communication Skills

- Ability to write reports
- Listening and oral skills

Interpersonal Abilities

- Sensitivity to the needs of others
- Ability to build rapport with a wide range of people
- Ability to sell ideas

Personality Characteristics

- Flexiblility
- Independence
- Responsiveness

Management Skills

- Ability to plan and organize workload
- Proficiency in monitoring performance

Problem-Solving/Decision-Making Abilities

- Resourcefulness and creativity
- Ability to develop alternative courses of action
- Sensitivity to the needs of the organization

Motivational Qualities

- Attention to detail
- High energy
- Self-organization

Evaluating Your Team

When Liz later assessed the team against the criteria, she deduced the following:

- *Technical Skills and Knowledge:* She had focused too much on retail and merchandising experience and was missing balance in some traits.
- *Communication Skills:* The team tended to be enthusiastic, but sometimes the direct, to-the-point communication style associated with Artisans alienated clients.
- *Interpersonal Abilities:* The team had good persuasive skills.
- *Personality Characteristics:* While Artisans thrived on the flexibility of the environment and got the job done, there were tendencies to not follow through.
- *Management Skills:* Although the job really appealed to Artisans with its flexibility, travel, and aesthetic elements, the team was somewhat one-dimensional and Liz felt like the mother figure.
- *Problem-Solving/Decision-Making Abilities:* The team was effective at tactical problem solving but tended to change decisions frequently, sometimes without letting the corporation or the dealer know.
- *Motivational Qualities:* The team members were highly committed to their roles.

What We Like and Don't Like

Next Liz completed Exercise 6.1 with her team. Not surprisingly, the insights were very much in alignment with Liz's evaluation and with what one would have expected based on the team's temperaments, functions, and types. Lollie's list, which was surprisingly similar to that of other team members, included the following:

What I Like	*What I Don't Like*
Travel	Paperwork
Flexibility	Detail
Variety	Planning
Laying out stores	Follow-up

This posed a problem for Liz. She knew it was against her ethics to look for a Guardian for the team, and she wasn't sure that a Guardian would enjoy the work. The fact that a Guardian had not been attracted to the position implied that there was a self-selection process at work anyway.

Instead of complaining about the team's inability to do paperwork, stick to the process, and adhere to a plan, she decided to reorganize the team and create a new position, a logistics manager. This person would be responsible for instituting processes to simplify and reduce the paperwork required and would be available as a resource to the team. The Key Result Areas for the regional merchandisers are listed in Table 6.4 on page 164.

The job description for the regional merchandiser's role could have been written for an Artisan—an ESFP or ESTP. The role was constantly changing and the merchandisers were at a different location each day. The role required aesthetic and sensory awareness and lots of interaction with dealers, dealers' staffs, the head office, and the sales reps. Unfortunately, with such a relatively homogeneous team the team leader occasionally got overwhelmed in trying to institute administrative procedures. In addition, there were some viewpoints that were not represented on the team. Regional merchandisers were actually given slightly larger districts, as there was no possibility of adding to the head count. But because the workload was allocated more effectively, the team as a whole was more productive. The Key Result Areas for the logistics manager are shown in Table 6.5 on page 165.

Objectives

Once the new role of logistics manager had been assimilated into the team, Liz began the process of defining specific objectives for each regional merchandiser and for the logistics manager. Samples of these objectives are listed below.

Regional Merchandisers

- To raise the product knowledge of the dealer's staff by running at least two training clinics

Table 6.4 Regional Merchandiser Key Result Areas

Areas	Explanation
Dealer Communication	Merchandisers have to communicate extensively with dealers about layout, product availability, store staff, and other issues.
Visual Merchandising	When regional merchandisers are at stores, they are responsible for maintaining visual and merchandising displays.
Product Purchasing	Merchandisers are responsible for obtaining product and stimulating demand for new products.
Corporate and Sales Rep Communication	Merchandisers have to communicate extensively with corporate office, buyers, and sales reps.
Travel	Regional merchandisers travel extensively to the ten to twenty stores in their geographic area. Planning and managing this travel takes much time.
Training	Merchandisers often are required to run training programs for dealers' staffs on products and merchandising approaches.
Product Knowledge	Team is required to have excellent interpersonal skills, with a high standard of aesthetic awareness and detailed product knowledge.

- To achieve a 98 percent customer satisfaction rating
- To increase sales in your stores by 10 percent over last year's figures
- To meet all visual merchandising standards as assessed by the visual merchandising manager

Logistics Manager

- To improve operational effectiveness by creating an operations manual and implementing standardized processes for reporting and paperwork
- To meet the yearly budget figures by tracking and eliminating wasted costs

Other General Actions of the Team

- With no Guardians on the team, they found an internal partner who could bring this perspective to the team.

Table 6.5 Logistics Manager Key Result Areas

Areas	Explanation
Merchandiser Communication	The logistics manager became the central point of contact for the team.
Administration	The logistics manager managed the administrative elements of the work and saved time through centralization of effort.
Process Improvement	Often problems were solved in the immediate term (reactive), but there had been little root-cause analysis. The logistics manager was able to identify several factors that were creating multiple problems, change the process, and eliminate the problems.
Financial Management	The logistics manager took control of the financial side of the team's responsibilities.
Training Support Materials	Whenever the merchandisers ran a training program, they had to prepare some of the materials themselves, above and beyond actually running the program. The logistics manager took over this role, resulting in standardized, consistent training materials.
Internal Communication	The logistics manager helped coordinate all information coming from the field.
Product Knowledge Support Materials	The logistics manager centralized product information for easier access.

- They completed the team purpose exercise in Chapter 5 (Exercise 5.1).
- They used the senior manager, Jackie, in some of the decision making to bring the objective future focus.
- They began to standardize some ground rules around logistics, planning, and administration to ensure there was closure and the team stuck to its plans.
- They recognized and used Jessica's ability in logistical planning.

CREATING AND INTERPRETING YOUR TEAM PROFILE

Use the information in Table 4.3 on page 112 and the Team Profile form in the appendix to create your team profile. Use the information in this chapter and in the case study provided to evaluate your team and the strengths and challenges it might face in the process of defining its roles and responsibilities. In addition, think of what actions you could take to ensure that team members' strengths and challenges are considered in the allocation of tasks and activities. Then use the questions in Table 6.6 on page 167 as the basis for diagnosing your team's performance in this category. Use the Connects and Conflicts diagram in the appendix to remind you of the interrelationships of temperament, functions, and type.

Once you have assessed your team strengths and diagnosed any potential challenges your team might face in clarifying roles and responsibilities, it is time to decide what you can do as a team to raise your team SCORE in this arena. Table 6.7 on page 168 provides a list of questions you can discuss with your team to act as a stimulus in formulating your own plan of attack.

General Data		
Temperament	Table 1.1	Pages 24–25
Functions	Tables 2.2–2.5	Pages 41–44
	Tables 2.7–2.10	Pages 51–54
Type	Table 3.4	Pages 76–83
Specific Data on Roles and Responsibilities		
Temperament	Table 6.1	Page 153
Functions	Table 6.2	Pages 154–155
Type	Table 6.3	Pages 157–158

Table 6.6   Implications for Your Team: Clarity of Roles and Responsibilities

Temperament/Connects & Conflicts	Function/Preferences
What temperaments are present on the team? What types of roles do they like and dislike? Use the tables in this chapter and the general tables in Chapter 1.	What is the first function on the team, and what implications does this have for establishing Key Result Areas and defining objectives? (For instance, if T_I: Analyzing is first, this would mean fairly simple categorization of Key Results Areas.)
To what extent can Artisans on the team, within the structure of their role, meet their core needs of making an impact and acting in the moment?	What functions are missing on the team as a first or second function? How could this impact team performance? (For instance, if no one on the team used T_E: Systematizing, it could mean that the team as a whole will lack a clear plan. Remember to use the information in Chapter 2 and in this chapter.)
To what extent can Guardians on the team, within the structure of their role, meet their core needs of being part of the team and living up to their responsibilities?	
To what extent can Rationals on the team, within the structure of their role, meet their core needs of creating their own mental frameworks and demonstrating their competence?	Look at the work of each team member: What are the opportunities for team members to use their first and second functions at work? Remember to use the detailed descriptions of the functions in Chapter 2.
To what extent can Idealists on the team, within the structure of their role, meet their core needs of making a difference and being valued for their own unique contribution?	What team members have to use functions extensively in their role that are not listed as first or second for their type? What could this mean?
What is the team temperament?	What is the balance between Extraversion and Introversion on the team? What could this mean in defining roles and responsibilities?
Using the temperament tables, what are the strengths of this team temperament in establishing clear roles and responsibilities? What are the potential challenges? (For instance, if the team temperament is Guardian, this might indicate that the team will define and live up to its responsibilities, but be inflexible.)	What is the balance between Sensing and Intuition on the team, and what implications does this have for defining roles and responsibilities? (If the majority of team members have an Intuition preference, there may be a tendency to miss the practical implementation on possible projects.)
What temperaments are not represented on the team? What implications does this absence have in clarifying roles and responsibilities? (For instance, if there are no Rationals, this might indicate a lack of clear categorization of individual workload.)	What is the balance between Thinking and Feeling on the team and how easy will it be for the group to establish logical objectives?
What is the team leader's temperament? What implications does this have for defining roles and responsibilities?	What is the team type and what does this indicate about the team's approach to clarifying roles and responsibilities? Use the descriptions of type in Chapter 3 and the information in the relevant tables for ideas.
Where are the team members located in the diagram? What "bubbles" are not represented?	What is the team leader's type? What are the team leader's strengths in defining roles and responsibilities? What are the potential challenges in this arena?
Which team members are grouped "close" to each other? Which team members appear "disconnected" from the team?	
What implications does this have for discussions on roles and responsibilities?	

Table 6.7 Plan of Attack: Roles and Responsibilities

Temperament/Connects & Conflicts	Function/Preferences
How can you ensure that Artisans on the team can, within the structure of their role, meet their core needs of making an impact and acting in the moment?	Based on the functions we use in the team, how can we make sure we gather all possible information by using the four information-gathering functions (Experiencing, Recalling, Brainstorming, and Visioning—see Figure 6.2) when collating ideas for Key Result Areas and objectives?
How can you ensure that Guardians on the team can, within the structure of their role, meet their core needs of being part of the team and living up to their responsibilities?	
How can you ensure that Rationals on the team can, within the structure of their role, meet their core needs of creating their own mental frameworks and demonstrating their competence?	Based on the functions we use in the team, how can we make sure we consider all relevant criteria when deciding Key Result Areas and objectives, and use the four decision-making functions (Systematizing, Analyzing, Harmonizing, and Valuing—see Figure 6.2)?
How can you ensure that Idealists on the team can, within the structure of their role, meet their core needs of making a difference and being valued for their own unique contribution?	How can we ensure that those with an Extraverting preference get their needs for external processing met within their role? How do we ensure that those with an Introverting preference get their needs for internal reflection met within their role?
How can we compensate for "lacking a temperament" as we define our Key Result Areas and set objectives?	
How can we ensure we capitalize on the strengths of all temperaments on our team in defining roles?	If the team has a predominantly Sensing preference, how can we ensure that the Key Result Areas are categorized effectively?
Could we totally reorganize the team roles to better capitalize on team members' temperaments? Could we bring in a new role to play to strengths and minimize team challenges?	If the team has a predominantly Intuition preference, how can we ensure that the objectives are achievable?
How can we ensure we reap the benefits our team temperament brings to clarifying roles and responsibilities?	If the team has a predominantly Thinking preference, how can we ensure that there is consensus in defining roles?
How can we compensate for any potential challenges our team faces in defining Key Result Areas and setting objectives based on its temperament?	If the team has a predominantly Feeling preference, how can we ensure that the objectives are clearly and specifically defined?
Based on the Connects and Conflicts diagram, who should be working with whom?	If the team has a predominantly Judging preference, how can we ensure that the team remain flexible in redefining roles and responsibilities as required?
How else could we reorganize the group to better capitalize on working relationships?	If the team has a predominantly Perceiving preference, how can we ensure that the team makes some commitment to adhering to a consistent definition of roles and objectives?

SUMMARY CHECKLIST

Before leaving this chapter, answer the following questions:

1. Have you asked your team members what they like and don't like to do (Exercise 6.1)?

2. Have you defined the Key Result Areas for your role and for your team members?

3. Have you established SMART objectives for these Key Result Areas?

4. Have you established Key Result Areas for your team (Exercise 5.4)?

5. Have you analyzed your team in terms of roles and temperament?

6. Have you reevaluated how you could reallocate workload based on temperaments, functions, and types?

7

Open Communication

GETTING TO KNOW EACH OTHER

"The entire population of the universe,
with one trifling exception, is composed of others."
—John Andrew Holmes

In this chapter we will discuss a fundamental building block of exceptional team performance: open and honest communication among members. By revealing the complexity of the communication process and undertaking exercises in this arena, we will become aware of all that goes into properly sending and receiving a message. We will also explore the different levels of interaction a team must pass through in order to achieve open communication.

As our temperament, functions, and type are all core to us, they always influence our behavior. However, our communication style is our most direct projection of who we are. Others must sharpen this image to see us with clarity, and we must project ourselves clearly for others to understand us. A great deal of interteam conflict and frustration can be avoided if we can eliminate the filtering factor that often occurs on both sides. When it seems as though we are speaking different languages, it is probably because we are! Aside from the various cultural idioms, there are also four "languages" of temperament, and this chapter will provide the basic skills for fluency in each one. While our types and functions do add an element to communication (the way accent and enunciation add nuances to what we say), the focus of this chapter will be on understanding these languages of temperament.

SETTING THE SCENE: TEAM COMMUNICATION

When teams assess their current performance level, they usually feel that communication could be improved. We spend the majority of our time communicating, and the effectiveness of interpersonal communication among team members and others in the organization can affect not only the team results but also how the rest of the organization views the team. The number one rule in business seems to be communicate, communicate, communicate! Team members have so many communication channels to manage that they cannot afford to communicate unproductively. In fact, improving communication will most likely reduce the unnecessary interaction that distracts members from the task, not to mention drastically increase the quality of team productivity. However, creating open communication involves more than just an effective transfer of information. Team members must build trust and be willing to take what at first seem like risks, in order to reach a level of interaction where everyone is sharing opinions and insights openly.

THE COMMUNICATION PROCESS

Communication is the exchange of information and ideas between sender and receiver. In order for communication to be effective, the message must be clear, and the receiver must understand it, believe it, and act on it. Too often we view communication as simply the process of sending a message. However, without feedback we have not completed the communication loop. Sending an e-mail without receiving a reply is not communicating! Complete Exercise 7.1 to identify any communication issues or barriers experienced within your team and to highlight successes.

Identifying the Process

When people are asked to identify the beginning of the communication process, they typically say it begins with words or with getting the other person's attention. In reality the communication process begins when the sender has an idea, a thought, or information that he or she wishes to communicate. The sender then must organize or "encode" the information, considering not only who will be the receiver but what are the desired results of sending this message. When the information has been mentally prepared, it is ready to be conveyed.

Exercise 7.1

COMMUNICATION BARRIERS AND SUCCESSES

1. List below any barriers that you believe are inhibiting communication in the team.

2. List any recent conflicts that have occurred in the team. What happened? What was the result?

3. List any relationships that are positive. What are the characteristics of these positive relationships?

Barriers

_____

_____

Conflicts, sources, and results

_____

_____

Positive relationships and their characteristics

_____

_____

When we are communicating with people face to face for the first time, we use both verbal and nonverbal communication. Verbal communication comprises *the words we use* and *the way we say them* (tone, pitch, and volume). *Body language,* our expressions, gestures, and posture, is the major component of nonverbal communication. Additionally, when we are meeting with someone with whom we have an ongoing relationship, a factor called *credibility* also plays a role in the process. Credibility is defined individually but usually derives from the amount of connection, knowledge, or reliability we recognize in the communicator. As illustrated in Figure 7.1, on a first meeting body language is the main component. When we have known someone for a while, credibility becomes more important.

When we have sent the message, if we are lucky, the other person will receive it. However, too often filters such as bias, insufficient interest, lack of understanding, and distraction prevent the listener from receiving the information. If the listeners do receive the message, then they process it against their own reference bank and decode it appropriately in order to take action or provide a response.

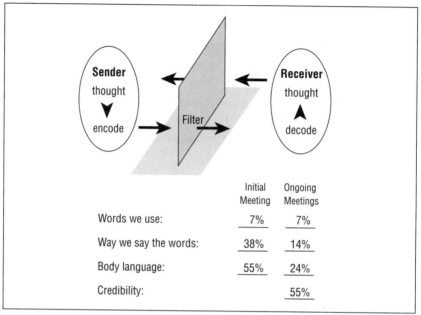

Figure 7.1 **Communication Process**

Complexity of the Process

Figure 7.1 is a simple model of the communication process. All the steps happen simultaneously. As the sender is thinking of an idea, she is formulating a sentence and possibly already sending the message. On the other end, the receiver is sending back a complex combination of responses during the transmission, while he processes and decodes the information.

Lots of things can go wrong with the communication process. The sender might have a stupid idea, communicate incorrect data, or formulate the information erroneously. By using the wrong words (too complex, too simple, jargon, slang), the sender might also offend, confuse, irritate, or bore the receiver. In addition, she might not deliver the words effectively (for example, by using unclear enunciation or inappropriate body language). The receiver might filter out the message or interpret it incorrectly because of his own personal frame of reference. The receiver might also provide a completely inappropriate response to the sender. The process is so complex that it is amazing anything is communicated accurately at all!

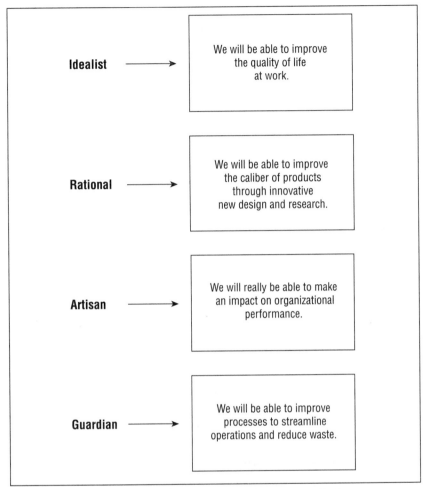

Figure 7.2 Interpretation of "You Have Been Selected to Be Part of Our Quality Improvement Team" in Four Languages

To complicate the process even more, cultural diversity and personality differences also drastically affect the communication process. Figure 7.2 illustrates how temperament affects understanding and interpretation of even a simple declarative statement—"You have been selected to be part of our quality improvement team." Each temperament values distinct ideas, organizes data in particular ways, selects unique words, and uses different intonations and body language cues. We all need to speak all four temperament languages, but often we speak only our own temperament's language proficiently, resulting in miscommunication among team members. The Four

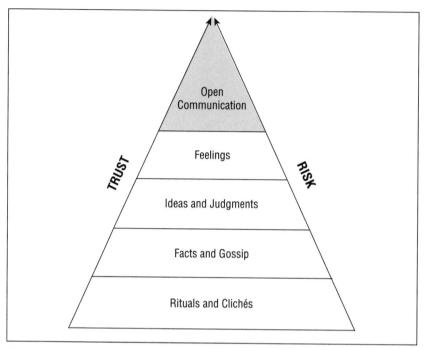

Figure 7.3 The Communication Pyramid

Languages of Temperament section beginning on page 177 will help us handle these types of communication barriers. First we will further explore the process of building open communication.

Building Open Communication

There are five levels in the "communication pyramid" shown in Figure 7.3. We move up the pyramid as we build trust with our team members or as we take a risk in the communication process. The base level of communication comprises rituals and clichés. This phase includes such interactions as "How are you?" or "How was your weekend?" No risk is taken and there may be very little trust. Facts and gossip characterize the next stage: "Sales last quarter were . . . " or "Did you hear that we may be buying . . . Company?" There is a marginal increase in trust and a little more risk taking, but overall communication is not meaningful. Teamwork will not be very productive if team members stay at this level in the pyramid. The next level of communication consists of ideas and judgments. Team members express ways of doing things differently and assert different perspectives on team activity at this point. With increased trust and risk taking, team members begin to share their feelings. This does not mean that "venting" takes place but rather that team members express emotions such as anger, concern, and frustration in a nonthreatening way. The team leader's ability to facilitate this stage will ultimately affect how well team members communicate. The final level in the communication pyramid is called open communication. At this stage one person is sending the message and the other person is receiving it in its entirety, hearing the words and responding to the intention and meaning. Team members finally feel that they can be open and honest with each other, as trust is strong and risk seems minimal. At this level all team members communicate their opinions, feelings, ideas, and concerns, knowing that the rest of the team will respond in a supportive and appropriate manner. Teams that can achieve this peak level of communication are more likely to produce exceptional results.

To improve communication among members, many teams use outdoor, experiential exercises and team-building sessions. While the tangible benefits may be hard to prove, any activity that forces team members to deepen their interpersonal communication will indirectly affect team productivity. In addition, there are many books on the market with excellent team-building activities. Any of these exercises will help in improving trust and team cohesiveness.

THE FOUR LANGUAGES OF TEMPERAMENT

On top of the complexity of the communication process lie the elements of temperament and type. As the four patterns of personality approach the communication process from fundamentally different perspectives, we say there are four languages of temperament. Each temperament has its own pattern of varying topics, ways of organizing information, vocabulary, delivery style, and body language. Our attention in this section will center on temperament because of this language phenomenon. While there are obvious themes in terms of temperament, functions, and type, it is important to remember that our communication style will also be influenced by the environment we are in, what is expected of us, our education, our background, and other factors. Therefore, assessing other individuals and adapting our style is a very complex process. Often it is better to simply practice speaking all four languages as much as possible and later try to adapt to one specific person when you get to know that person better.

In this section we will review each temperament, give examples of the language it speaks in three different types of situations, and then provide some general guidelines for interacting more effectively with each one. We will also provide an overview of the way each function and type might manifest itself in the communication process. While trying to determine what language others speak in order to communicate more effectively, remember these guidelines:

- Don't guess people's temperaments too quickly on the basis of their professional behavior. You are most likely seeing their adapted style.

- Learn more about temperament and functions by reading more.

- Observe behavior consistently and try out different ideas for adjusting. Then observe the results.

Artisan Communication Style

Ideas and Information
- Like practical, tangible data and information that they can use immediately.

- Talk about actions and get frustrated if forced to talk for too long about something with no action associated with it.

- Like to talk about what is exciting and current.

Organization of Data
- Organize data in a way that may not be immediately obvious because they often either go straight to the point or weave a story around a theme.

- Often organize their message around a concrete object, such as a piece of equipment with cooking, or a demo if displaying software, and use it to "facilitate thinking."

Types of Words
- Use jargon or colloquial language to make their point: *cool, stuff, bummer, trash and trinkets* (for giveaways at courses such as T-shirts and cards).

- Adapt to the group and easily pick up the current jargon.

- Use concise language and choose to get to the point in the communication process; communication style can appear terse, direct, and abbreviated.

- Use colorful words that paint a picture.

- Often use sports metaphors ("Teamwork is not a contact sport") to make a point.

- Use key words such as *fun, risk, excitement, luck, deals,* and *adventure;* talk about what is happening now.

Delivery/Body Language
- Body language and delivery style tend to be fast paced, upbeat, and expressive, yet also graceful.
- Enjoy using tools and gimmicks to support their point and will sometimes fiddle with objects when talking.
- Happy-go-lucky, relaxed, and somewhat carefree demeanor; when bored, body language becomes fidgety; often get up in the middle of a conversation and walk around.
- Being tuned into sensory stimuli, may create a unique, stylish look for themselves, or may dress more casually for comfort.

Building Involvement
- Build involvement through allowing others to experience their message; make others feel they are part of the interaction through descriptive stories and anecdotes; bring situation to the active, three-dimensional here-and-now versus the conceptual level.
- Observe and mirror language, which allows them to connect with others; love to see people's eyes light up as they pick up a topic of the person's interest; able to connect and consider the desires of all involved, which is at the core of their persuasive skills.
- Can read others' motives easily but have to be careful about pressing others' "hot buttons" in interaction; what is fun to them can alienate other temperaments.

Sense of Humor
- Can be outrageous on purpose. Immediately seeing objects in context, they will be able to relate another item in context to create humor. They are also good physical comics.
- May tell jokes and lighten things up. Although entertaining, they may have to watch their propensity to be flippant when communicating with others and must remember to use humor appropriately.
- Have a wonderful comedic sense of timing—Robin Williams offers an outstanding example of Artisan humor: in-the-moment, fast-paced, constant, and effortless.

Written Communication Style
- Communicate informally, directly, and to the point.

Guardian Communication Style

Ideas and Information

- Like practical, tangible ideas and information that can produce results and that are related to concrete, discernible outcomes.
- Want to talk about what is tried and true and proven effective.
- Talk about saving and wasting money, as this is tied to their economic values; don't want to waste time or resources.
- Ask for information and talk about role definition and clarification: "Who is responsible for what and when?"
- Talk about the process for getting things done: "How did we do this last time?" and "How can we ensure consistency in outcome?"

Organization of Data

- Organize data sequentially when communicating. They start at the beginning and move through the information in a step-by-step manner.
- Like data grouped into sections and subsections. In notes and reports they often use numbers and bulleting.
- Like to present lots of data and background information.

Types of Words

- Relate data to past experiences. They say things such as, "In my experience," "Last time I . . . ," "What's this person's experience?" They also listen carefully when anyone is speaking of past success or failure and talk about what is tried and true, proven.
- Use traditional language in regard to protocol and politeness.
- May use quantitative language.
- Compare and contrast things regularly, using such terms as *better than* and *worse than* to show where components are located on their internal ratings scale.

Delivery/Body Language

- Tend to use body language that is less expressive with a deliberate, methodical mode of delivery.
- May sometimes go into lecture mode, especially when conveying information to a group, in order to express the seriousness of the material and establish their authority as the instructor.
- Speak in a clear and deliberate manner, so that others can easily understand.

- Demeanor may appear no-nonsense, cautious, and respectful. They can come across as straightforward and responsible and seem to epitomize common sense. Sometimes they seem burdened by all the responsibilities they take on.

- Tend to dress appropriately in relation to their peers and are well coordinated, with attention to details such as matching accessories and polished shoes. In business settings they tend to be more conventional. Generally they look after their clothing and have a very "put together" look.

Building Involvement

- Like to build involvement by creating a group culture and observing group traditions.

- May be reluctant to build two-way communication when in the role of expert and may appear authoritative and directing.

- Listen carefully to historical data when others share it, but may discount what appears to them as overly abstract or unrealistic.

Sense of Humor

- Often use a dry, tongue-in-cheek humor.

- May have a store of "oldies but goodies" that they always seem to make funny again.

- May tease others warmly about lapses in common sense.

- May joke about Murphy's law, as they tend to think luck is never on their side.

Written Communication Style

- Write detailed memos and e-mails, clearly stating the necessary information. However, sometimes these communications seem like an instruction manual to other temperaments.

Rational Communication Style

Ideas and Information

- Gravitate to concepts and abstract data in their search for the operating principles of the universe.

- Enjoy talking about concepts without practical application and will philosophize about these concepts for extended periods of time.

- Enjoy debating issues and pride themselves on their intellectual rigor.

- Talk about logic, systems, and principles and will always ask "What and why?" However, in their examination of possibilities, they will often ignore or be unaware of physical time and resource constraints.

- Use their critical questioning skills to highlight what is missed. With this innate ability to see what is present and what is not, may forget to give positive feedback.

Organization of Data

- Categorize data in order to communicate, although the extent to which this is obvious varies between NTJs and NTPs.

- Like to use diagrams and models to illustrate their ideas.

- Are reluctant to state what they see as obvious because they don't want to be redundant.

- Organize information based on reasoning and use patterns of statements and conclusions to explain their point.

Types of Words

- Use words as tools and normally have extensive vocabularies. They tend to be extremely selective, often too esoteric, in their word choice, often correcting others and arguing over the most accurate word to use; will react negatively to words and information they feel are illogical. Also become frustrated when they cannot think of the precise word they want.

- Use complex language and sentences that are long and compound, and that address several different ideas. They can sometimes appear long-winded to other temperaments.

- Use conditionals. When they say "If x, then y," people don't always understand that they are conjecturing and believe that they want something done. (Sometimes they don't even bother to say "if.")

- May draw their ideas to a close with conclusive words such as *thus* and *therefore*.

- Use analogies and metaphors to make their points. They take all the facts of the situation and drop them into another scenario in order to point out the flaws of the argument or prove a theory.

Delivery/Body Language

- May appear confident in demeanor (sometimes to the point of arrogance) when they are sure of their competence. Sometimes they can be construed as self-doubting because of their qualified language: "If this, then this."

- Tend to use their appearance to demonstrate their status, wearing designer clothes and coordinating clothing appropriately, or can appear unconcerned about the way they look, the "absent-minded professor" type.

Building Involvement

- Can build involvement through their ability or will to stimulate a following. Their knowledge and confidence inspire trust and admiration in others.
- May use critical questioning skills when interacting with others. As a result, the receiver may feel criticized.
- Show genuine interest and connect easily with those whom they consider experts. They are eager to gather as much data from experts as they can in order to build their own store of knowledge.
- Can appear competitive as they argue principles or try to establish their competence.

Sense of Humor

- Create a cerebral humor, using such things as double meanings, puns, and plays on words to induce laughter.

Written Communication Style

- Categorize data and use elegant sentences and paragraphs with complex language.

Idealist Communication Style

Ideas and Information

- Naturally gravitate to conceptual data that allow individuals to build their identity and fulfill their potential, such as psychology and self-help.
- Talk a lot about relationships. Empathy and intimate communication are important to them. They will instinctively reject conversations that are nonauthentic, and will try to establish genuine, meaningful interaction.
- May discuss the problems of the world and conceptualize about what must be done. Their passion for meaning and purpose in their lives may come out in safe and comfortable environments.

- Often discuss what is meant or intended. They have a particular interest in understanding interactions and appreciate the symbolic significance behind everything.

- Recognize others' unique qualities and provide genuine, often spontaneous, positive feedback on these qualities.

Organization of Data

- Integrate information from various sources around a unified theme. They are integrative thinkers and see the connections between what seem like disparate categories.

- Organize information more sequentially if they are NFJs, whereas NFPs tend to organize the information around patterns. They are concerned with the natural flow of information.

- May appear to jump from one point to another, and some of their comments may seem to come out at random with no logical connection. However, the theme on which they are focusing is often just not apparent to others.

Types of Words

- Often use flowing, dramatic language, full of exaggerated words such as *epiphany, fabulous,* and *everyone.* They can speak in global language—the feeling or the big picture without concrete details. They will talk about their impressions of a specific situation but may have difficulty and become frustrated when trying to articulate the specific data behind an impression.

- Use metaphors as a teaching tool and to bridge communication barriers between individuals. They bring everyone to the same understanding by bringing up a common experience they can all relate to.

- Have a verbal fluency but may use general, imprecise language or too many words.

- Use phrases such as "connect with . . . ," "What's the purpose?" or "What's the meaning of . . . ?"

Delivery/Body Language

- Use flowing gestures and expressive body language when they talk about something meaningful or personal to them. They can also be quite intense when talking from the heart.

- Are usually very warm and welcoming, tending to stand close to others, as they desire an intimate communication style if they are

Extraverted types. Introverted types will seek the same intimacy but hold back, and may even come across as cold and aloof, until they know and like a person.

- Are absorbed in the world of people and ideas, and may appear clumsy and struggle with using tools and equipment.
- Don't show any uniformity in their dress—not surprising since unique identity is a core value for them.

Building Involvement
- Ask open-ended questions to identify what is important to other people. Coupled with their ability to listen empathetically and put themselves in the other person's shoes, this tendency often results in finding out lots of personal information about the other person while self-disclosing less about themselves.
- Instinctively recognize and value the uniqueness in others. They want to encourage everyone to actualize his or her potential.

Sense of Humor
- Sense of humor tends to be somewhat self-deprecating, and they will share funny personal examples when connecting with others.

Written Communication Style
- Flowing, dramatic, and metaphorical. NFJs will sequence their written words more, while NFPs will ensure smoothness.

Table 7.1 on page 186 is a simplified chart of the previously detailed information; it is designed to help you recognize the differences between the four languages of temperament.

SPEAKING IN FOUR LANGUAGES

When introducing a topic of conversation, we have to adapt our style, body language, and word choice so that each temperament receives the message, otherwise we will be heard clearly only by our own. In Table 7.2 are a few examples of speaking in four languages. The first column is an example of how a cooking school changed the wording in a marketing brochure to appeal to all four temperaments. The second column is an example of how you could sell the idea of an on-site company health club to all four temperaments. The third column shows how an engineering company sold its services to the different temperaments.

Table 7.1 Languages of Temperament

Area	Artisan	Guardian	Rational	Idealist
Subjects	Practical and tangible: action	Practical and tangible: process	Conceptual: theories and systems	Conceptual: people
Structure	To the point: 1, 2, 3, . . .	Sequential: 1, 1.1, 1.2, . . .	Series of statements followed by a logical conclusion	Integrated and unified theme
Words	Short and to the point; examples, stories, and similes	Specific and considered; examples from experience	Sophisticated and long; analogies and metaphors	Flowing and dramatic; analogies and metaphors
Feedback	Colloquial	Developmental and constructive	Critical	Positive
Humor	Outrageous or physical	Dry: tongue in cheek, sarcasm	Cerebral: double meanings, plays on words, and puns	Personal examples and self-deprecating jokes
Questioning Style	Questioning on motives	Questioning to identify relevant experience	Questioning of theories and competence	Questioning to find what's important to the other person
Body Language	May appear casual and flighty	May appear deliberate and uptight	May appear arrogant and cold	May appear "touchy-feely"
Clothes	Dress for comfort or to create a distinct "look"	Conforming, put-together, conservative	Use appearance as status symbol	No pattern
Approach	Pragmatic: get the job done expediently and move on; competitive	Relationship based: what about the people?	Pragmatic: get the job done; competitive	Relationship based: what about the people?

LEARNING NEW LANGUAGES

Speaking all four languages can be quite a challenge. The lists below provide helpful hints on improving your "language proficiency." Exercise 7.2 on page 190 is designed to raise your awareness of your own communication style and, if every team member completes the exercise, to show how each person on your team communicates differently. Use Exercise 7.3 on page 191 to try out all four languages.

Table 7.2 Speaking in the Four Temperament Languages

Temperament	Cooking School	On-Site Health Club	Selling Services
Artisan	• You can look good when you throw great dinner parties for family and friends. • You can change the recipes and create your own version. • The classes are fun!	• This will provide an immediate outlet for frustration. • There are lots of cool features with tons of exercise equipment. • This is a place at work to "hang out," maybe get a group together to play competitive games.	• We'll give you time to do other important stuff. • You'll be one of the first to use this approach—you'll make an impression. • We provide quick turn-around, lots of options. and a one-stop shop.
Guardian	• The cooking school has been in existence for twenty-five years. • You will receive structured, step-by-step recipes that are guaranteed to produce excellent, consistent results. • There are many courses: the introductory (essential series) starts you at the basics and then you can move into advanced courses.	• You will receive a step-by-step plan to progress to better health. • The company will ensure that there are both a safety and dress code and clearly defined policies for using the club. • You will be able to include exercise in your regular schedule.	• The service will include controls to ensure reliability, quality, and the repeatability of the process. • The company has been a leader in the industry since 1986 and has a great record of on-time delivery. • The company is ISO certified, complies with EPA regulations and other government standards.
Rational	• You will learn the chemistry of cooking. • You will know the whats and whys. • You will understand the universal principles of categorizing a menu and creating a meal.	• There will be the latest high-tech equipment. • There is a generalized trend for organizations to have in-house health clubs. • You will be able to design a scientifically based workout to improve fitness in all critical areas.	• We offer leading-edge technology providing a new way of solving old problems. • You will have an innovative way of collecting, analyzing, and distributing data. • You will have access to flexible knowledge for the future.
Idealist	• Learning to cook fresh and healthy foods will improve your quality of life. • Relationships are built over a good meal. • You will be able to create unique meals for the important people in your life.	• Healthy, happy employees mean higher retention. • It allows individuals to develop themselves physically, and that will help them feel better about themselves. • It's the right thing to do.	• Here is an individualized solution using environmentally safe chemicals. • We offer a collaborative, partnership approach. • You can trust us; we are an ethical company.

Communicating with Artisans

- Use brief and direct communication.
- Remember, less is more.
- Talk about concrete realities.
- Get to the point quickly and keep moving.
- Give feedback on their tactical competence.
- Tell them the required end result and turn them loose.
- Expect cynicism and stories.
- Adapt to their colloquial language.
- Use tools and hands-on experiences when explaining approaches.
- Talk about impact, end results, and variety.
- Remember, they read body language very accurately, so watch your body language cues.

Communicating with Guardians

- Talk about what was done in the past.
- Use a concrete, practical implementation approach.
- Be specific about who is responsible for what in terms of roles and responsibilities.
- Explain steps sequentially, starting at the beginning and using numbering.
- Be specific about the expected results.
- Expect questions about rules, what can be done, and what cannot be done.
- Use conservative body language.
- Talk about your prior experience.
- Focus on efficiencies and process improvements.
- Provide lots of data and background information.
- Give practical examples.

Communicating with Rationals

- Start with the big picture.
- Use precise language when explaining concepts and ideas.
- Give them an opportunity to analyze information and create new problem-solving approaches.

- Be sure of your facts and present theoretical information where possible; don't bluff!
- Don't take critical questioning personally.
- Recognize their intellectual competence.
- Define the end goal, but give them the freedom to develop the model.
- Talk about your expertise in a specific field.
- Use analogies to make points.
- Attend to conditional language: "If this, then . . . "
- Always explain what and why.
- Be prepared to debate possible approaches.

Communicating with Idealists

- Talk about the purpose of an approach.
- Offer positive, genuine feedback.
- Be authentic when communicating—they recognize fake conversation.
- Focus on the big picture and conceptual ideas.
- Use metaphors and analogies.
- Talk about the benefits of actions: ability to develop potential and the "greater good."
- Don't discount global language, and listen for the underlying meaning.
- Don't provide too much practical detail.
- Listen to their insights on people, which are usually accurate.
- Build an empathetic relationship.

FUNCTIONS AND COMMUNICATION

Our type and functions also affect our communication, but not to the same extent as temperament. Our functions will produce some characteristic communication approaches that vary in the moment according to the function we are using. Table 7.3 on page 192 details some of these contributions. In addition, the types will have different patterns of communication based on the differing first and second functions they use. Key information about their style and communication is listed in Table 7.4 on pages 193 and 194.

Exercise 7.2

YOUR COMMUNICATION STYLE:
AWARENESS BUILDING

1. Have everyone on the team complete the questions below.

2. Compare your answers with the information provided on your temperament's communication style.

3. Individually, have each member of the team share and/or discuss his or her answers to the questions.

4. Discuss how we can consider these differences in creating open and honest communication.

How do you like tasks explained to you?

_____

_____

_____

For what types of activities do you like to receive praise?

_____

_____

_____

For what types of accomplishments and activities do you provide positive feedback?

_____

_____

_____

How do you like to receive directions for projects?

_____

_____

_____

What words do you use to promote self-esteem in subordinates?

_____

_____

_____

Exercise 7.3

SPEAKING THE FOUR LANGUAGES

Think of an idea that you are trying to introduce to your team. Devise a communication strategy in order to express your wants from each temperament's perspective. Address the objections each temperament might have and list the benefits each would enjoy based on its core values and needs. Then check your ideas with someone of that temperament. We often think we are speaking another language but find we are not!

Artisan

_____

_____

Guardian

_____

_____

Rational

_____

_____

Idealist

_____

_____

EXTRAVERSION/INTROVERSION AND COMMUNICATION

The Extraverting and Introverting preferences will affect the degree to which we communicate with others externally (Extraversion) or within ourselves internally (Introversion). In Table 7.5 are some characteristics associated with each way of processing and some simple ideas to adapt in order to optimize communication effectiveness. Complete Exercise 7.4 to analyze the communication between two people.

SAMPLE TEAM PROFILE: PERFORMANCE TECHNOLOGY TEAM

Background Information

The technology team, profiled on page 196 and in Figure 7.4 on page 197, is located in the human resources group. The team is responsible

Table 7.3 Functions and Communication

Function	Characteristics in Communication
Extraverted Sensing (S$_E$): Experiencing	• Talk about the experience • Respond to all sensory data • Tell stories • Like concrete details • Expressive and active body language
Introverted Sensing (S$_I$): Recalling	• Refer to past data and compare • Describe past experiences in vivid detail • Talk about facts and details • Need time to reflect and go back to past experience • Reserved body language
Extraverted Intuition (N$_E$): Brainstorming	• Talk quickly • Talk about possibilities • Verbal brainstorming • Enthusiastic body language • Express enthusiasm
Introverted Intuition (N$_I$): Visioning	• Reserved body language until the ideas come to them • Want time to reflect on concepts • Describe picture or idea as a whole • May justify with "I just know" • May have difficulty articulating the vision (particularly Idealists)
Extraverted Thinking (T$_E$): Systematizing	• May verbosely explain rationale • Verbal pros and cons list • Talk through the decision out loud • Assertive and direct in tone and body language
Introverted Thinking (T$_I$): Analyzing	• Will not communicate reasons or rationale unless challenged • Will argue when external data do not match with internal criteria • Talk about models, theories, and ideas • Talk about their blueprint
Extraverted Feeling (F$_E$): Harmonizing	• Show emotions on face and in body language • Pick up emotions and feelings from others and reflect them • Talk about personal details and self-disclose to connect • Talk about what's appropriate and not appropriate to the team
Introverted Feeling (F$_I$): Valuing	• Expressive about values when pushed or when beliefs are compromised • Talk about what's right or what's wrong • Values and beliefs are important • May appear easygoing or indifferent until beliefs are challenged

Table 7.4 Strengths and Challenges of Type in Communication

Type	Strengths	Potential Challenges
ESTP, ISTP (Thinking Artisan)	• Direct, succinct, to the point • Tell stories and give practical examples to make a point clear • Say what's going on as they see it	• May say things that are viewed as inappropriate by and offend others • May not frame the communication before delivering the message • May have some discomfort with emotional issues
ESFP, ISFP (Feeling Artisan)	• Persuasive, empathetic, enthusiastic • Quick-witted humor that is appropriate in the moment • "Life's a party" to them; great at getting the team to participate	• May not tell the truth in order to avoid conflict • May appear frivolous as they attempt to lighten things up • May not communicate accomplishments in businesslike terms
ESTJ, ISTJ (Thinking Guardian)	• Direct, crisp, objective, data oriented • Organized, logical • Talk of productivity, output, results, tried-and-true methods	• Can appear insensitive to others' needs; "know-it-alls" • May discount others' opinions if they appear illogical • May use only logical, black-and-white data
ESFJ, ISFJ (Feeling Guardian)	• Sequential, step-by-step explanation of processes and actions • Make decisions with the team and ensure everyone is heard • Gentle and empathetic	• Under stress, word choice includes *should* and *ought to;* may blame and complain • May be challenged by constructive conflict • May avoid conflict but when challenged defend their position with vigor
ENTP, INTP (Adaptable Rational)	• Flowing verbal banter, fluid conversations, make intuitive leaps from one subject to another • Can appear empathetic and sociable (ENTPs) • If they judge receiver as competent, will be forthcoming and seek out experts	• May dominate a conversation (ENTPs) or become too pedantic (INTPs) • May get frustrated when others do not follow their thought process • May change their mind when presented with a new expert opinion
ENTJ, INTJ (Structured Rational)	• Possess an arsenal of words • Able to put abstract thoughts into concrete, actionable language • Articulate and precise	• May only see things from their own perspective • Perceived as cold if they are unable to incorporate the people focus • May not realize the impact that their direct, objective communication has on others

Table 7.4   Strengths and Challenges of Type in Communication (cont'd)

Type	Strengths	Potential Challenges
ENFP, INFP (Adaptable Idealist)	• Naturally empathetic; others self-disclose readily to them • Use dramatic, flowing language and metaphors; may appear to speak in non sequiturs • Attuned to hidden meanings; will instinctively adapt their communication style to others	• Under stress, may read patterns or implications that are not there • May be reluctant to engage in inauthentic interaction • Do not self-disclose readily
ENFJ, INFJ (Structured Idealist)	• Direct; will initiate empathetic relationships with others while intensely aware of interpersonal dynamics • Able to self-disclose to communicate with different team members • Able to reframe existing concepts to be comprehensible to others	• May be unable to distance themselves from others' "negative energy" • Under stress, may show inappropriate emotion • Global language may appear imprecise

for creating alternative models for delivering training using technology. Conflict has arisen within the team, particularly between two members, and they wanted to use the team-profiling approach in order to create more effective strategies for working together.

Table 7.5   Extraversion and Introversion in Communication

Preference	Characteristics	Communication Ideas
Extraversion	• Verbal processing out loud • Expressive body language • Vivid facial expression • Take the initiative or act, then reflect later (maybe)	• Listen more carefully • Give those with an Introverting preference time to respond to ideas and answer questions • Manage tendency to talk rather than listen
Introversion	• Mental processing: pausing before response • More reserved body language • Harder-to-read facial expression • Reflect first then take action later (maybe)	• Prepare ahead of time, if possible, and ask for additional time to reflect • Use alternative channels to communicate in different situations: memos, e-mail. • Give them feedback if they dominate the conversation

Exercise 7.4

ANALYZING A TWO-PERSON INTERACTION

1. List in the grid below the two people's names, temperaments, types, and first and second functions.

2. Using the information in this chapter, highlight the implications of any differences or similarities in temperament.

3. Using the information in this chapter, highlight the possible impact of any differences or similarities in preference for Extravertsion or Introversion.

4. Using the information in this chapter, highlight what the differences or similarities in functions might mean.

5. Using the information in this chapter, brainstorm ideas that could improve communication between the two individuals.

Name		
Temperament		
Differences/Similarities		
Actions		
External/Internal Processing		
Temperament		
Differences/Similarities		
Actions		
First and Second Functions		
Differences/Similarities		
Actions		

Connects and Conflicts

- The natural grouping of "team factions" was showing in the team interaction: Rob, Peter, and Kathy seemed to "speak the same language," as did Kathleen, David, and Lisa.

- Before the profiling, Rob could not understand what was happening to the team dynamic. Against the objective backdrop of personality profiling, he was better able to lead the team through difficult interactions.

- Lisa and Rob (assistant and manager) were able to bridge some of these communication difficulties.

SAMPLE TEAM PROFILE

Individual Analysis

Name	Temperament	1st/2nd Function		Type
Rob	Rational	T_I	N_E	INTP
Peter	Rational	T_E	N_I	ENTJ
Lisa	Guardian	F_E	S_I	ESFJ
Kathy	Rational	N_I	T_E	INTJ
Kathleen	Idealist	F_E	N_I	ENFJ
David	Idealist	N_I	F_E	INFJ

Team Analysis

Temperaments: Guardians __1__   Artisans   __0__

Idealists __2__   Rationals __3__

Team Temperament: __Rational__

Team Leader Temperament: __Rational__

Functions (First and Second Combined):

Perceiving S_E: __0__ S_I: __1__ N_E: __1__ N_I: __4__

Judging T_E: __2__ T_I: __1__ F_E: __3__ F_I: __0__

Preferences: E: __3__   I: __3__

S: __1__   N: __5__

T: __3__   F: __3__

J: __5__   P: __1__

First Function for the Team: N_I: Visioning

First Function for the Team Leader: T_I: Analyzing

Team Type: __I/ENF/TJ__

Team Leader Type: __INTP__

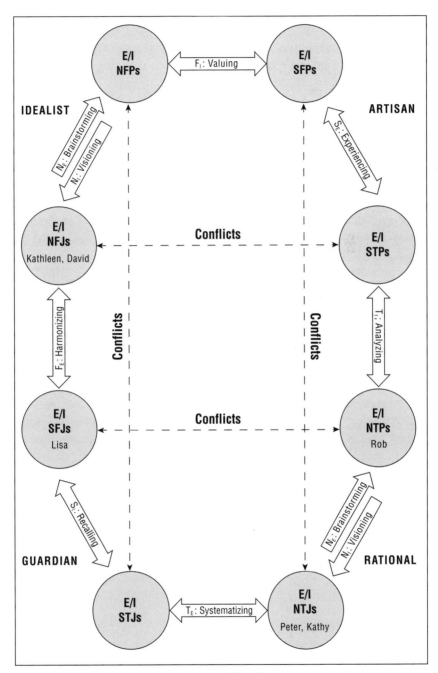

Figure 7.4   Sample Team Connects and Conflicts

Creating Open Communication

Based on the approach advocated in this chapter, the team leader and the team discussed the various issues raised in this chapter:

- They spent some time reviewing the key components of communication.
- They used some of the exercises to move the team up the communication pyramid.
- They identified and tried to resolve the communication issues in the team.

In other chapters, such as "Strategy" (Chapter 5) and "Roles and Responsibilities" (Chapter 6), the team was able to move through a step-by-step process to raise performance in a specific area. Creating open communication is related to group process, so it is not possible to move step by step through an implementation plan. Instead we have analyzed the communication climate in the team only from a temperament and type perspective.

Communication Climate

The team was small and relatively new (twelve months). David was the most recent addition, having joined two months prior to this session. Like all new members, he had attended a brief introductory profiling seminar to provide him with insights into his potential, individual strengths, and weaknesses. The team communication tended to focus around ideas and judgments (the third level on the communication pyramid), with some unproductive surfacing of issues and emotions, particularly between Kathy, whose type is INTJ, and David, whose type is INFJ. In discussions about the future direction for the group, Kathy and David often took different perspectives. Even when it seemed that the issue was resolved in the meeting, David would visit the team leader, Rob, later to rehash the decision and restate his perspective. Rob could not understand the dynamic and decided to spend time analyzing the team and individual profiles in order to gain insight.

You might assume that a conflict between Kathy and David would be unexpected, based on only one letter difference between their types. However, a closer analysis showed that there could be several sources of contention.

First, Kathy was a Rational and David an Idealist. While these are both future-focused temperaments, there are some key contrasts in their core needs. Kathy wanted to create her own destiny using the conceptual systems she had modeled, whereas David looked to the greater purpose in fulfilling his role.

While both Kathy and David share the same first function, N_I: Visioning, the second function for each is different: Kathy T_E: Systematizing and David F_E: Harmonizing. Kathy would develop an insight into a future possibility, logically articulate it (Rational: precise language), and see immediately how to put an action plan into place. David, on the other hand, was also creating his own insight into the future but had more difficulty articulating it clearly (Idealist: impressionistic, flowing language). In addition, with Harmonizing as his decision-making style not only would David want an appropriate solution for the team and the company but also what he perceived as criticizing would be uncomfortable for him. Kathy tended to view his approach as "wishy-washy" and imprecise, whereas David viewed Kathy's approach as too directing and inconsiderate.

As both Kathy and David had Introverting preferences, they both required time to process, and the differences festered without allowing reflection time and discussion. Kathy, with her second function Systematizing, was able however to suggest quick, decisive action in the external world and would push for premature closure around issues in meetings.

To adapt to David's and the team's style in order to improve communication effectiveness, Kathy tried to be more sensitive to what she perceived as nonlogical information. In addition, she listened more to David's ideas instead of rushing to a conclusion. She learned to realize that not everyone could see the outcomes as vividly as she could, and that patience in the short term meant that her ideas would receive more consideration and acceptance in the long term. One of the challenges she realized she faced, with first function N_I: Visioning, was that she was not allowing people to see or hear her thought processes soon enough. So she began to talk about her ideas a little earlier, and tried to be clearer as to their source. Her T_E: Systematizing: second function, combined with her Introverting preference, also meant that she tended to enjoy completing team projects on her own. While Rob was comfortable with this approach, the rest of the team felt excluded. But as they developed an understanding of Kathy's type, functions, and temperament, they were able to take her approach less personally.

With David's preference for INFJ, his Idealist temperament, his first function N_I: Visioning: and secondary function F_E: Harmonizing,

David was quietly convinced of his viewpoint, yet remained concerned for the harmony of the group. He possessed a single-minded concentration, which he used when working alone on projects. In his interactions with Kathy, he felt she was steamrolling over his ideas. In addition, when he needed support from other team members, he was not good at asking for it. As David adapted to Kathy's style in order to improve communication effectiveness, he started to seriously consider ideas other than his own. He began asking for help more, and also being assertive when he felt he was not being listened to. He realized that Kathy's style was not a personal attack, and this helped him to be more objective in listening to feedback and considering other ideas. When the hurt feelings were reduced, he realized that often he and Kathy were actually on the same track. In addition, he took more time to articulate his ideas clearly and tried to avoid the impressionistic language that turned Kathy off. He realized that Kathy's push for closure in the external world was similar to his, only her criteria tended to be published facts and data rather than consensus and group harmony.

As the team continued to work on its communication style, it moved up the communication pyramid, using this theoretical backdrop to discuss ideas that were important to the team. The members began to really value the different individual contributions to the team instead of simply responding to them. As they became more proficient in speaking and understanding different languages and functions, they found they were more adept at considering different perspectives, and overall team productivity increased.

Other General Actions for the Team

- With no Artisans on the team, they found an internal partner who could bring this perspective to the team.
- The team made a commitment to produce some short-term tangible results that would be visible to the rest of the organization.

CREATING AND INTERPRETING
YOUR TEAM PROFILE

Use the information in Table 4.3 on page 112 and the Team Profile form in the appendix to create your team profile. Use the information in this chapter and in the case study provided to evaluate your team and the strengths and challenges it might face in the process of building open communication. Then use the questions in Table 7.6 on page 202 as the basis for diagnosing your team's performance. Use the Connects and Conflicts diagram in the appendix to remind you of the interrelationships of temperament, functions, and type.

Once you have assessed your team strengths and diagnosed any potential conflicts within your team, it is time to decide what you can do, as a team, to raise your team SCORE in this arena. Table 7.7 on page 203 provides a list of questions you can discuss with your team to act as a stimulus in formulating your own plan of attack.

General Data		
Temperament	Table 1.1	Pages 24–25
Functions	Tables 2.2–2.5	Pages 41–44
	Tables 2.7–2.10	Pages 51–54
Type	Table 3.4	Pages 76–83
Specific Data on Communication		
Temperament	Table 7.1	Pages 178–186
		Pages 188–189
Functions	Table 7.3	Page 192
Type	Table 7.4	Pages 193–194
	Table 7.5	Page 194

Table 7.6 Implications for Your Team: Open Communication

Temperament/Connects & Conflicts	Functions/Preferences
What temperaments are present on the team? What is their usual communication style? Remember to use the tables in this chapter and the general tables in Chapter 1.	What is the first function on the team, and what implications does this have for communication? (For instance, if F_E: Harmonizing is first, this could mean that the team culture is supportive and warm.)
What are some potential conflicts among team members?	What functions are missing on the team (as a first or second function)? How might this affect team communication? (For instance, if no one on the team used S_E: Experiencing, it could mean that the team as a whole might not notice what's going on in the here and now.) Remember to use the information in Chapter 2 and in this chapter.
What is the team temperament? What does this say to us about the team culture?	
What temperaments are not represented on the team? What implications does this absence have in communicating internally and externally? (For instance, if there are no Artisans, this might indicate that there is no one to sell your services.)	What is the balance between Extraversion and Introversion? What might this say about the communication climate in the team?
What is the team leader's temperament? What implications does this have for his or her communication style?	What is the balance between Sensing and Intuition, and what type of information do team members focus on? (If the majority of team members have a Sensing preference, there may be a tendency to use more concrete, literal language.)
Where are the team members located in the Connects and Conflicts diagram? What "bubbles" are not represented?	
Which team members are grouped close to each other? Which team members appear disconnected from the team?	What is the balance between Thinking and Feeling, and therefore how supportive is the team culture?
What implications does this have for team cohesiveness?	What is the team type and what might this show about team communication? (Use the descriptions of type in Chapter 3 and the information in the relevant tables for ideas.)
	What is the team leader's type? What are some potential strengths and challenges in the team leader's style when communicating?

Table 7.7 Plan of Attack: Open Communication

Temperament/Connects & Conflicts	Functions/Preferences
Devise a strategy for communicating among different temperament groups about an important subject for your team. (Look at Artisan to Guardian, Artisan to Idealist, Artisan to Rational, and so on.)	Based on the functions we use in the team, how can we make sure we gather all possible information by using the four information-gathering functions when communicating (Experiencing, Recalling, Brainstorming, and Visioning)
For any conflicts, use the worksheet in Exercise 7.4 on page 195 to plan a more positive interaction.	Based on the functions we use in the team, how can we make sure we consider all relevant criteria when making team decisions and use the four Judging functions (System-atizing, Analyzing, Harmonizing, and Valuing)?
How can we compensate for lacking a partic-ular temperament as we communicate inter-nally and externally?	
How can we capitalize on the strengths of all temperaments when communicating with one another?	How can we ensure that those with an Extraverting preference do not dominate the conversation? How do we ensure that those with an Introverting preference are heard?
How can we reap the benefits and manage the challenges our team temperament brings to communication?	

SUMMARY CHECKLIST

Before leaving this chapter, answer the following questions:

1. Have you identified any communication issues in the team using Exercise 7.1?

2. Have you determined where in the communication process breakdowns are occurring?

3. Where is your team on the communication pyramid?

4. Have you used any exercises to raise the levels of trust and risk taking in the team?

5. Have you tried speaking all four temperament languages for a project you want to complete?

6. Have you seen evidence of the four languages at work in your team inter-action?

7. Have you evaluated your team for communication effectiveness?

8. Have you evaluated any possible conflicts in the team, against the models of type and temperament (Exercise 7.4)?

8

Rapid Response

HOW DO WE TURN ON A DIME?

"A problem well stated is a problem half solved."
—Charles F. Kettering

In this chapter we will focus on issues around a team's ability to adapt quickly to environmental events. There appear to be two main occurrences that set off an alarm and require a rapid team response: when problems arise from the team's responsibilities and when change occurs in either the organization or the general market. After looking at these topics generally, we will identify how change can be introduced effectively to the temperaments. By considering these differences from the inside out, we can optimize the ability of the team to respond positively to change and reduce negative consequences that can hinder the team's ability to SCORE. In this chapter's case study we will look at a team in which a change was made, focusing on what didn't work and what could have been done differently.

TEAM FLEXIBILITY

Often teams have to change direction because inadequate time or energy has been spent on ensuring that the qualities for high-performing teams are present. For example, the team may have an unclear strategy (S), unclear responsibilities (C), internal communication problems (O), slow response (R), or ineffective leadership (E). This entire book is devoted to helping teams raise their SCORE in these areas. This chapter will focus on the need to respond rapidly to environmental change. Flexibility in approach is essential for a team: even when there is a clear direction, external events often force teams to reevaluate their plan, solve problems, adapt quickly, make new decisions, and change their approach. But change, while conceptually easy, is behaviorally difficult. Many teams struggle with changing direction and having their team members support a new plan. This chapter will provide ideas and skills to help teams become more flexible in their approach.

PROBLEM SOLVING

No matter how organized and focused a team might be, because we live in a rapidly changing world and humans are capable of errors, problems often occur. Problems can be major, such as system faults, missed shipping deadlines, and shortfalls in sales, or more minor, such as incorrect data entry and communication issues. When a problem occurs, there is a tendency to want to fix it, but sometimes it is the symptom that gets fixed, not the root cause. Successful problem resolution involves identifying the source of the problem and then using proactive strategies to prevent the problem from recurring. Teams that adopt proactive problem-solving approaches will save time in the long run and be more productive in responding rapidly to the environment.

Proactive problem solving involves the following steps:

1. Perceive the problem.

2. Define the problem.

3. Analyze the problem.

4. Generate alternatives.

5. Evaluate alternatives.

6. Make a decision and implement it.

Table 8.1 provides some questions to ask and guidelines for approaching each step in the problem-solving process. An example of this process in action is included in the case study at the end of the chapter. Exercise 8.1 on page 208 lets you analyze step by step a current problem facing your team and identify some possible solutions.

CHANGE AND TRANSITION

Change is the second factor demanding a rapid response from the team. Whether it comes banging at the door or insidiously creeps in through the cracks, change is a fact of life in any organization. It is

Table 8.1 Problem-Solving Steps

Steps	Questions	Guidelines
Perceive the Problem	• Is there a problem? • What does it look like? • Where is it?	• Don't assume a problem is bad. • Look for the real problem.
Define the Problem	• What are the facets of the problem? • Is it a tangible problem (missing deadlines, sales targets)? • Is it an intangible problem (conflicts)?	• Avoid assumptions. • Create a problem definition that is specific and measurable. • Show how the problem relates to the organization.
Analyze the Problem	• What is the problem and what are its symptoms? • What is the root cause?	• Don't jump to resolution too quickly. • Use an analysis tool such as a fishbone diagram.
Generate Alternatives	• How could we approach this problem differently? • What are some new ideas? • What are some ideas we have tried before that we could adapt?	• Generate as many ideas as possible. • Record all ideas. • Allow no criticizing. • Be sure everyone participates. • Combine and build on ideas.
Evaluate Alternatives	• What criteria shall we use? • How will we weigh options? • How will we balance objective and subjective criteria?	• Make sure the criteria are verbalized. • Listen to all team members' input. • Be aware of win-lose tactics.
Make a Decision and Implement It	• To what extent is this solution satisfactory to all? • Do we have time to care?	• Try for a win-win solution. • Consider other restraints such as time and resources.

constant and can take place in any number of areas including leadership, team direction, team membership, company policy, and company ownership. These types of shifts are situational and take place in the external world. It is easy to discuss such changes objectively and to understand them intellectually because they are external to us.

However, when we try to change our behavior or mind-set to adjust to the external change, we react very differently. The psychological process we go through in order to come to terms with a new situation and change our behavior is called a transition. To experience the difference between change and transition, talk about folding your arms opposite from the way you normally do. Now try actually doing it. That's much more difficult! That's the difference between a change

---

Exercise 8.1

PROBLEM SOLVING

Think carefully about the underlying root cause of a current problem facing your team.

1. *Perceive the problem:* What is the problem?

_____

_____

2. *Define the problem:* Be specific. Make sure you find the root cause.

_____

_____

3. *Analyze the problem:* What are the components of the problem?

_____

_____

4. *Generate alternatives:* What are some possibilities, both conventional and unconventional?

_____

_____

5. *Evaluate alternatives:* What criteria will you use to decide on a solution?

_____

_____

6. *Make a decision and implement it:* Who is going to do what by when?

_____

_____

---

and a transition. Helping individuals and teams optimize transitions is one of the major challenges facing organizations today.

Managing Transitions by William Bridges (1992) provides practical, step-by-step ideas for implementing transitions and reducing psychological barriers to change. According to Bridges, a transition is an internal process with three distinct phases: the ending, the neutral zone, and the beginning. For instance, if a team reorganizes and members have to change teams, they would pass through each stage of the transition.

The Ending Zone. In the ending phase team members might experience emotional reactions (regret, sadness, anger, and so on). While the reason for the change can be completely valid, the ending of any experience produces an emotional grieving process. If teams can understand who is losing what specifically, they can help to ensure that these responses are kept in proportion and alternative avenues for getting these factors replaced are created in the new beginning. The reason for the change will need to be communicated again and again.

The Neutral Zone. The neutral zone is the most difficult yet creative stage. As André Gide said, "One doesn't discover new lands without consenting to lose sight of the shore for a very long time." The neutral zone is uncomfortable for individuals and teams because, although the change has taken place externally, team members have not internally made the transition. There will be many stress indicators in the neutral zone, such as a rise in anxiety, increased absenteeism, emergence of old complaints, more sick time taken, and dysfunctional information flow/ communication.

The Beginning Zone. The beginning phase is often characterized by ambivalence, as team members come to terms with the transition and try to understand the specifics of their situation. Teams will require a picture (of where they are going), a purpose (why they are going there), a part (what will they contribute), and a path (plan to achieve the goal). In this stage you will have to begin again with building the characteristics of high-performing teams by establishing a clear purpose, defining roles and responsibilities, establishing objectives, and putting plans in place. The team leader may need to revert back to a more directing style as a new Forming stage begins (see Chapter 4 for a discussion of team stages).

Even more challenging is the fact that we must deal with multiple transitions at the same time. A person is often unable to complete one transition before beginning another. An organization in Silicon Valley acquired four companies in thirteen months and was surprised when conflicts arose among team members! Each acquisition was one transition. Combining five transitions at once was guaranteed to create chaos. Now think about the changes before your team and those within your organization to complete Exercise 8.2. You will complete the second part of this exercise later in the chapter.

The addition of temperament differences as teams experience transitions adds another level of complexity to responding rapidly. Each temperament approaches change differently.

Exercise 8.2

CHANGES FACING YOUR TEAM: PART ONE

1. Identify what changes are occurring now in the organization that are affecting your team.

_____

_____

2. Identify what future changes may affect your team.

_____

_____

3. Identify what changes you could postpone.

_____

_____

Now let's look at how we can use our knowledge of temperament and functions to influence our team's rapid response from the inside out.

TEAMS IN ACTION

Temperament and Problem Solving/Decision Making

Each temperament brings unique strengths and challenges to teams in the problem-solving and decision-making processes. Understanding what each temperament innately does well can help make the problem-solving process more effective. See the data in Table 8.2. In addition, using differing information-gathering and decision-making functions will provide valuable perspectives in the problem-solving process. It is important that all types of data and varying decision-making criteria are used.

Temperament and Change

Let's look now at how temperament influences the transition process from the inside out, as illustrated in Table 8.3 on pages 214 and 215.

While every temperament approaches problem solving and transitions differently, the use of the information-gathering and decision-making functions will also affect a team's ability to respond rapidly in

Table 8.2 Temperament and Problem Solving

Temperament	Strengths	Potential Challenges
Artisan *Coaching Suggestions:* • When a problem recurs, look for a root cause. • Slow down in the problem-solving process. • Make sure you don't miss steps; even if you think you know the solution, be patient!	• Quick to see current problems • Quickly recognize the most expedient, tactical solution • Will want to implement it—now • Understand what each solution means for individual members • See creative contextual options for fixing problems • Excellent at "selling" the solution to differing perspectives	• May forget to consider future implications of solutions • May need help in slowing down to analyze the problem completely • May solve the same problem multiple times in the excitement of the moment • May get impatient with what appear to be unnecessary discussions around problem analysis and consensus decision making • May alienate others as they push to get on with it
Guardian *Coaching Suggestions:* • Be open to problem-solving approaches that lack proven data. • It's okay to drop a couple of steps in the problem-solving process. • Recognize when external pressures force non-consensus decision-making approaches.	• Conduct thorough analyses of previous data and build an understanding of what happened • Compare and contrast suggested approaches with prior experience • Identify processes that are creating the problem or that could be changed to eliminate the problem • Approach problem solving in a step-by-step, structured, and methodical way • Gravitate to solutions that respect rules and existing procedures • Strive for consensus decision making	• May have difficulty seeing beyond what has been done before • May slow down the response with their cautious approach • May not want to try completely new approaches • May appear too slow moving in problem solving and decision making as they strive for consensus • May appear too cautious and reluctant to take risks

different situations. Use Exercise 8.3 on page 215 to further explore how your team handles transition. Figure 8.1 on page 213 and Table 8.4 on pages 216 and 217 provide an overview of each function's strengths and challenges as it contributes to creating a flexible team. Each of the characteristics, except where noted, is how the function would appear as a first or second function.

Table 8.2 Temperament and Problem Solving (cont'd)

Temperament	Strengths	Potential Challenges
Rational *Coaching Suggestions:* • Make sure people considerations are included in the decision-making criteria. • Consult with a Guardian or Artisan about practical implementation. • Recognize the tendency to overanalyze in specific situations.	• Use critical thinking to perceive problems quickly; naturally consider what's missing • Able to use analytical skills to categorize problems • Approach problem solving from an abstract, conceptual perspective • Pay less attention to past or current experience and focus instead on patterns and possibilities • Identify many different options when generating alternatives • Able to create logical criteria as a basis for decisions	• May have difficulty understanding the practicality behind a solution • May not value the consensus decision-making process • May overanalyze a problem, slowing down response time • May not consider the people issues sufficiently • With infinite time orientation, may not allow sufficient time for implementation of new plans
Idealist *Coaching Suggestions:* • Make sure logical criteria are considered when making decisions. • Consult with a Guardian or Artisan about practical implementation. • Recognize the tendency to be unrealistic in your expectations.	• Identify many options, are future focused in solving problems • Understand and are able to articulate all team members' perspectives when evaluating options • Ensure that the people perspective is considered in the problem-solving process • Gravitate toward consensus decision-making processes • Able to build bridges between differing perspectives • Able to generate options and possibilities when trying to solve problems	• May not consider practical options • May want to "oversolve" the problem—go for a difficult and distant ideal • May not pay enough attention to logical, objective criteria • May find it difficult to disconnect from team members when they are not in agreement with a decision • With the future time orientation, may not allow enough time for implementation of plans

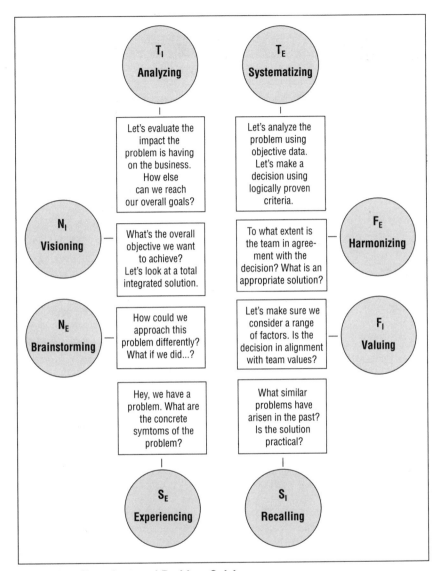

Figure 8.1 Functions and Problem Solving

We have also included the strengths and challenges each type brings to the team in responding rapidly to the environment (Table 8.5 on pages 218 and 219). This table is a further extension of the temperaments and functions tables but is used to highlight the unique components for each type.

Table 8.3 Temperaments and Change

Temperament	Beliefs	Managing Through Transition
Artisan	• Anything new and different is a positive change. • Transitions provide lots of new, exciting, and different tasks. • What's happening here and now is of paramount importance. • Let me make the change happen—let's just do it!	• Ensure the change is not confining and they have flexibility to do their own thing. • Do not worry so much about the ending stage. Move on to the new beginning. • Make sure there is some short-term payoff with the change. • Make the change happen quickly. Don't talk about it ad infinitum—just do it! • Slow down in the beginning stage to ensure mistakes aren't made.
Guardian	• Change must appear necessary. • Change, if approached properly, is positive. • Chaotic change is very uncomfortable. • Don't impose the change on me.	• Supply a clear explanation of the reason for the change with supporting data. • Allow longer time in the ending stage. • Provide time to discuss input and concerns before the change is final. • Allow time to analyze and find out where they are before starting the change. • Ensure they are allowed to design a process to implement the change.
Rational	• There are always new operating systems and approaches. • Change provides an opportunity to control my own destiny. • Change is constant and there is no need for emotional baggage in making transitions. • Let me create the new vision.	• Ensure the change they propose is worthwhile and not just created as part of their continual theoretical redesign process. • Allow them to help articulate the vision for change. • Use them to devise strategies for making change a reality. • Provide evidence of what can realistically be achieved within a specific time frame. • Encourage them to move into the beginning stage and conceptualize future direction quickly.

Table 8.3 Temperaments and Change (cont'd)

Temperament	Beliefs	Managing Through Transition
Idealist	• All team members and individuals should be involved in the change. • The change should provide opportunities for personal and professional development. • Change is a part of development. • Let me be the catalyst for change.	• Focus on the element of change that provides individuals and teams with greater opportunity for personal growth. • Anticipate objections they will have based on lack of personal growth opportunities. • Recognize their empathetic ability to know which team members are in the end, neutral, and beginning stage. • Expect them to "grieve" in the ending stage. • Use their future focus to move on to a new beginning.

Exercise 8.3

CHANGES FACING YOUR TEAM: PART TWO

1. In the chart below, write in team members' names and temperaments.

2. Review the changes you identified in Exercise 8.2.

3. Identify for each team member his or her approach to and beliefs about change.

4. Suggest strategies to help team members become more flexible in managing change.

Team Member	Temperament	Approach to Change	Strategies

Table 8.4 Functions and Creating a Rapid Response Team

Function	Strengths	Weaknesses
Extraverted Sensing (S_E): Experiencing	• Able to seize all current data in the moment • Pick out concrete data that others miss • Move quickly though the change process • Optimistic attitude toward change—attracted to variety	• May change direction too frequently • May miss hidden implication and meanings in change • May reach conclusion too quickly • May want to move on before others are ready
Introverted Sensing (S_I): Recalling	• Refer to past data when problem solving or approaching change • Approach problem solving in a sequential manner • Collate tangible data • Compare and contrast different approaches—create a rating scale	• May need time in the beginning to create some "history" • May bring prior negative experiences with change to the current change experience • May be negative about solutions that have not been tried before • May take too long processing/explaining historical data
Extraverted Intuition (N_E): Brainstorming	• Naturally able to brainstorm possible solutions to problems and new approaches to change • Focus on patterns and meanings in the problem/change • Resourceful and upbeat—normally see the opportunities in problems • Enthusiastic and supportive of new ideas and possibilities	• May not consider practical implementation • May want to make all changes at once and be reluctant to defer any ideas • May fantasize negatively and blow the problem up (if an inferior function) • May not consider the feasibility of options
Introverted Intuition (N_I): Visioning	• Reflect and then develop an entire solution to a problem • Picture entirely new ways of doing a task • Naturally future focused and tuned into the implementation in the outer world (T_E or F_E) • Naturally look to future ideas and solutions	• May be reluctant to accept anyone else's solution • May see the cause of the problem as an entirety instead of as components • May want to make the change despite practical reasons not to • May not be able to clearly articulate the change or solution

Table 8.4   Functions and Creating a Rapid Response Team (cont'd)

Function	Strengths	Weaknesses
Extraverted Thinking (T$_E$): Systematizing	• Help the team categorize and organize the elements in a problem • Create pros and cons list to evaluate criteria including cause-and-effect assumptions • Able to design the implementation of the solution • Anticipate the consequences of change and act to handle them	• May push for closure in problem solving too quickly • May be frustrated when they cannot understand a problem in terms of cause and effect • May become frustrated by those who have difficulty with or an emotional response to the change • May analyze the change process without consideration for the people
Introverted Thinking (T$_I$): Analyzing	• Use their own internal logical criteria in selecting the right solutions • Enjoy the objective process of analyzing possible solutions and critically evaluating the model for its effectiveness • Explore innovative ideas without the push for practical implementation • Observe the process and reflect and analyze it throughout the change	• Own logic may not agree with the team's solution • May want to design their own model for change • May spend too much time in the analysis of a problem • May want to continuously change and analyze as issues arise
Extraverted Feeling (F$_E$): Harmonizing	• Evaluate all problem-solving approaches in terms of appropriateness to group norms • Ensure that all team members support the decision • Understand what is important to team members and are able to understand decision-making factors accordingly • Ensure the team stays unified in a change and create a forum for everyone to provide feedback	• May buy in too much to other team members' "pain" in transitioning • May find it difficult to distance themselves and analyze cause-and-effect data • May not add their own perspective in order to maintain harmony and consensus • May have difficulty making transitions if there is discord
Introverted Feeling (F$_I$): Valuing	• Value individuals' different perspectives and allow them to express their opinions • Consider whether this is the right direction to be going in • Consider the ethics of the solution in relation to their own values • Understand what's important to each individual during a change	• May get caught up in how the change is unfair or wrong • May not work toward a consensus decision if it goes against their beliefs • Tend to idealize change as a solution to larger issues • May withdraw emotionally when their belief system is offended but may not talk about why

Table 8.5 Type and Creating a Rapid Response Team

Type	Strengths	Potential Challenges
ESTP, ISTP (**Thinking Artisan**)	• Figure out how to make the impossible happen and then become known as crisis managers • Take things to the limit • Love the neutral stage	• May jump in before understanding the ramifications • May focus on short-term glory and neglect the longer-term proactive solution • Can hit any target when in fire-fighting mode
ESFP, ISFP (**Feeling Artisan**)	• Nothing that they can't handle in the moment • Push the envelope to obtain desired results • Consider people when adapting to change	• If change goes against their values system, may be inflexible and leave • May act before thinking • Refuse to sacrifice people to achieve the end result
ESTJ, ISTJ (**Thinking Guardian**)	• If involved in the change, able to quickly create a logical implementation plan • Logically analyze root cause of problems and create contingency plans • Create an objective framework to understand change	• May resist change if there does not appear to be a logical reason for it • May need more time to complete the ending stage • May not deal well with arbitrary change.
ESFJ, ISFJ (**Feeling Guardian**)	• "Plug away" and stick to the process • Plan for contingencies and see the proactive resolution to the problem • Look for the root cause so as to save effort in the future	• May grieve during and need to celebrate the end of the transition • May be reluctant to let go of the team • May be reluctant to make a change if it is something they have never done before
ENTP, INTP (**Adaptable Rational**)	• Creative at identifying root cause and then brainstorming solutions to problems • Appear flexible if change is in alignment with their own mental model • Enjoy the process of change and are good at helping others to change	• May be stubborn in changing mental model if the change is in a different direction • May not do what they say they will do • May not be able to focus on one end result

Table 8.5   Type and Creating a Rapid Response Team (cont'd)

Type	Strengths	Potential Challenges
ENTJ, INTJ (Structured Rational)	• Deliver and get the job done • Do not allow double effort • Produce logistical regulation with expediency	• May vigorously defend the process already in place • May act as though a change has to be their idea • Can be ruthless at instigating their own structure
ENFP, INFP (Adaptable Idealist)	• Respond in the manner the situation calls for • Able to perceive abstract stimuli in the environment and brainstorm patterns and options • Work in bursts of energy	• May not follow through to deliverables • May implement more than one solution at a time and miss current practical details • May appear ineffective when quiet
ENFJ, INFJ (Structured Idealist)	• Willing to break with the status quo • Able to assist people through the transition process • Focus on what needs to be done and get it delivered	• May experience discomfort with unpredictable eventualities • May get overloaded to please everyone • May find it difficult to change plans

Contribution of Type

Consider the following perspectives around those team members with an Extraverting preference when introducing change and problem solving:

- Use their verbal fluency when problem solving.
- Expect them to externally process how they are responding to change.
- Make sure they stop and think before taking action.

Consider the following perspectives around those team members with an Introverting preference when introducing change and problem solving:

- Make sure, when you are solving problems, you allow them time to process and do not push for closure too quickly in making a decision.
- Remember they may not always share with you, at the time, their perspective on a transition. So it is important to create time for discussion.

- They may prefer to discuss issues with transition one on one with you rather than in front of the rest of the team.

- Make sure they do not take too long reflecting before taking action.

SAMPLE TEAM PROFILE: HUMAN RESOURCES TEAM

Background Information

This human resources team, profiled on the next page and in Figure 8.2 on page 222, is part of a fast-growing company in the network security and management field. The organization acquired seven companies in eighteen months, resulting in revenue growth from $150 million to $900 million in a period of five years. Some team members came from one of the companies that was bought, some from other organizations, and some from the original company. The team was responsible for managing compensation and benefits and recruiting, and providing HR generalist support and training to the employee workforce of approximately 6,000 people.

Due to the multiple acquisitions and the dynamic workforce, HR was facing problems in addressing the breadth of customer needs within a specific time frame. In addition, there was a conflict within the team between Linda and Sylvia, and the team leader wished to profile the team to identify possible causes and implement solutions to some communication issues. In addition, Claire often did not comprehend some of Linda's concerns.

Connects and Conflicts

- As illustrated in Figure 8.2, the team was very unevenly distributed with an obvious division between the SFJs and Claire, Rex, Tara, Sheridan, and Sylvia.

- Chigusa could have helped Linda in scripting her new ideas so that they appeared less "fluffy." They both shared dominant S_I: Recalling, but Chigusa then used T_E : Systematizing, as did Sylvia. She could have used her functions to bridge the gap.

- Tara seemed to play a role in bridging the differences between Claire and Linda.

SAMPLE TEAM PROFILE

Individual Analysis

Name	Temperament	1st/2nd Function		Type
Claire	Artisan	S_E	F_I	ESFP
Linda	Guardian	S_I	F_E	ISFJ
Sylvia	Rational	T_E	N_I	ENTJ
Rex	Artisan	S_E	F_I	ESFP
Tara	Idealist	F_I	N_E	INFP
Janet	Guardian	S_I	F_E	ISFJ
Charmaine	Guardian	F_E	S_I	ESFJ
Chigusa	Guardian	S_I	T_E	ISTJ
Marilu	Guardian	F_E	S_I	ESFJ
Mary	Guardian	S_I	F_E	ISFJ
Sheridan	Artisan	S_E	T_I	ESTP

Team Analysis

Temperaments: Guardians __6__   Artisans __3__

Idealists __1__   Rationals __1__

Team Temperament: __Guardian__

Team Leader Temperament: __Artisan__

Functions (First and Second Combined):

Perceiving S_E: __3__ S_I: __6__ N_E: __1__ N_I: __1__

Judging T_E: __2__ T_I: __1__ F_E: __5__ F_I: __3__

Preferences: E: __6__   I: __5__

S: __9__   N: __2__

T: __3__   F: __8__

J: __7__   P: __4__

First Function for the Team: __S_I: Recalling__

First Function for the Team Leader: __S_E: Experiencing__

Team Type: __ESFJ__

Team Leader Type: __ESFP__

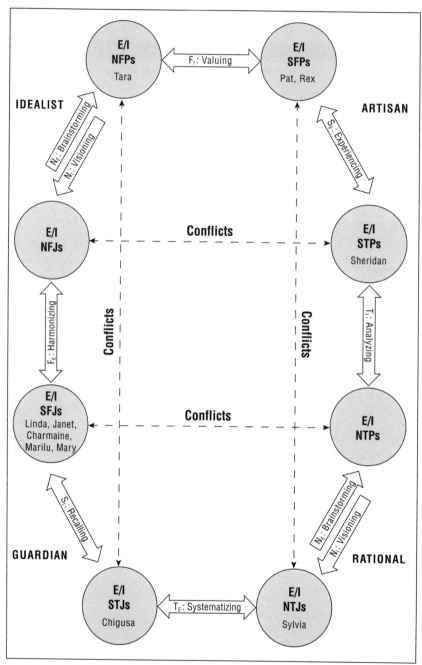

Figure 8.2 Sample Team Connects and Conflicts

Responding to the Environment

Based on the approach advocated in this chapter, the team leader and the team worked through the steps as follows:

- They first attempted to solve the problems caused by the volume of the workload.
- They made a decision to reorganize.
- They tried to implement the change (reorganization) to achieve results.

Team Problem Solving

A couple of problems arose regarding the team's performance. The director of the entire HR group (Claire) and the HR manager, Linda (the one reporting problems), undertook to create some solutions for these issues.

They each approached the problem-solving process fundamentally differently. Linda, as a Guardian using S_I: Recalling first and F_E: Harmonizing second, relied on historical data and considered what would be most appropriate for the other people on the team to solve the problem. Claire, an Artisan using S_E: Experiencing first and F_I: Valuing second, was constantly gathering new data, comparing and contrasting it with her internal values system to make decisions.

1. *Perceive the Problem*

   The challenges originally facing the team were highlighted when customers began complaining that the telephone response time was too slow and that individuals were not getting answers quickly enough about HR issues. Claire listened to comments from the workforce (Experiencing) and raised the issue with Linda. Linda initially believed that such issues had arisen before and that there was no need to take immediate action (Recalling). As the situation continued, she realized that this time the problem was longer running than in the past and action should be taken.

2. *Define the Problem*

   In the short term, two problems were defined: (1) "On average the phone is being answered only ____ percent of the time, with ____ staff and ____ resources" and (2) "Average time from the requests being called in, to the information being provided has risen from one day to three days. ____ internal customers are complaining about poor service."

3. *Analyze the Problem*

Categories to help adequately define the problem were as follows:

- Time of day
- Type of call
- Time to answer the call
- Type of information required
- People at each location
- Other tasks individuals were performing

Claire's role was critical at this stage. She would evaluate the data from multiple perspectives and decide whether the service they were providing was in alignment with her internal values system.

4. *Generate Alternatives*

Options generated initially included

- Change the phone answering process.
- Use voice mail more frequently.
- Reprogram Automatic Call Distributor to allocate call flow more effectively.
- Create a new group to answer the phone—an HR hotline.
- Reorganize the group.

In this part of the problem-solving process, the possible challenges in addressing the issues arose. Linda was reluctant to consider approaches that would result in a major reorganization of her team. She believed she had built a cohesive unit (Guardian values), and did not want to change the structure "just for the sake of change." In involving Claire's management team in generating ideas, Sylvia, a manager from another group, had a completely new vision for how the team could operate and prove successful (N_I: Visioning). She was to the point in articulating her new model (which Linda found annoying), and Claire was impressed.

5. *Evaluate Alternatives*

The team created a list of criteria with which to make a decision. Sylvia presented a logical cause-and-effect analysis (T_E: Systematizing) for the new reorganization, which Claire agreed with. Linda felt (using F_E: Harmonizing) that the team would not be comfortable with the change, but she was unable to clearly justify her perspective in a logical way.

6. *Make a Decision and Implement It*

As a result, the decision was made to reorganize the group.

Team Reorganization

The previous HR team was divided into two: one to deal with compensation and benefits and the other to deal with HR intervention, performance counseling, and coaching, and Sylvia was to establish the new team. Claire set the overall direction and then allowed Linda and Sylvia to create a new way of operating the now-divided team.

When this team reorganization was implemented, it created major challenges. Claire, the team leader (ESFP), approached the change in a straightforward way. The HR team had to be divided; the data were obvious (S_E: Experiencing). Alternative solutions had not worked. She analyzed whether this decision was in alignment with her internal values system (F_I: Valuing), made the decision quickly (Artisan), and defined the end result she was looking for. She told Sylvia to "make it happen." In the transitions model she had quickly moved through the ending and neutral stages, and was well immersed in the new beginning. Probably those with preferences for ESFP move through transitions more quickly than any other type, as long as the change does not conflict with their internal belief system. The other factor that made the transition easier was that she was not directly losing anything: Her job was the same, her workload was the same, and her status had actually risen slightly because she had "gained" another group.

Linda (ISFJ) had been the manager of the original HR team for a while and had not completed the ending stage of the transition process. She was protective of her team (Guardian) and had set up many systems and procedures to facilitate a smooth team operation. She still believed that there was no need to reorganize the group. To her this was the equivalent of a demotion (in the hierarchy). She had been Sylvia's manager originally and she did not think that Sylvia had the experience (using S_I: Recalling) to be promoted.

Sylvia (ENTJ) accepted the position that Claire offered because she had ideas for reconfiguring the team (N_I: Visioning) and providing better customer service. She found it easy to articulate this insight to others on the team, but Linda did not understand the approach because she had no historic data. In addition, Sylvia's direct, logical, precise language (Rational) alienated Linda, who wanted to consider the people on her team and make the best decision for them

(F_E: Harmonizing). Sylvia was in the neutral stage of transition—recognizing the benefit of the change but unable to move into the beginning stage, with lack of direct support from Claire and with resistance from Linda.

As Linda became more resistant to Sylvia's ideas, Sylvia became even more direct and confrontational with her, causing Linda to react negatively to the conflict (her second function was F_E: Harmonizing), and communication deteriorated from there. With Sylvia being the only Rational on the team, no one else understood that her approach was not insensitive or uncaring, merely direct.

Alternative Approach

- Claire, the manager, could have taken a more hands-on role in setting up this new team. She needed to facilitate some of the interaction between Sylvia and Linda, being careful to respect Linda's previous contribution and team membership, and also to respect the unique model Sylvia was suggesting.

- To help Linda move through the ending stage of the transition process, Claire needed to ensure that Linda was completely involved in all aspects of the change and find ways to replace some of the things Linda believed she was losing. For instance, Linda could have been made senior manager to compensate for the perceived drop in status.

- To support Sylvia and Linda as they entered the new beginning, Claire would need to take a more directive role and ensure that all concerns were raised and addressed. It was particularly important for Linda to have a clear understanding of her roles and responsibilities to show how she was still part of the overall team.

- Claire needed to realize that her laissez-faire management style was not adequate when the team was undergoing a major change. In addition she realized her style was viewed as "couldn't care less" by Linda, and for Sylvia it indicated a clear preference (which it wasn't). She needed to be clearer in her communication.

- The team needed to see beyond the "extreme" language Sylvia appeared to use in order to understand the core concepts.

- After the team profiling, the team was able to objectively analyze some of the issues it faced and decide ways out of the conflicts.

CREATING AND INTERPRETING
YOUR TEAM PROFILE

Use the information in Table 4.3 on page 112 and the Team Profile form in the appendix to create your team profile. Use the information in this chapter and in the case study provided to evaluate your team and identify the strengths and challenges it might face in the process of creating rapid response. Then use the questions in Table 8.6 on page 228 as the basis for diagnosing your team's performance. Use the Connects and Conflicts diagram in the appendix to remind you of the interrelationships of temperament, functions, and type.

Once you have assessed your team strengths and diagnosed any potential challenges to your team, it is time to decide what you can do, as a team, to raise your team SCORE in rapid response and become a more flexible team. Table 8.7 on page 229 provides a list of questions you can discuss with your team to act as a stimulus in formulating your own plan of attack.

	General Data	
Temperament	Table 1.1	Pages 24–25
Functions	Tables 2.2–2.5	Pages 41–44
	Tables 2.7–2.10	Pages 51–54
Type	Table 3.4	Pages 76–83
	Specific Data on Rapid Response	
Temperament	Table 8.2	Pages 211–212
	Table 8.3	Pages 214–215
Functions	Table 8.4	Pages 216–217
Type	Table 8.5	Pages 218–219

Table 8.6 Implications for Your Team: Rapid Response

Temperament/Connects & Conflicts	Function/Preferences
What temperaments are present on the team?	What is the first function on the team, and what implications does this have for solving problems? (For instance, if T_E: Systematizing is first, this would mean the ability to create a pros and cons list to evaluate criteria. This would also mean there might be pressure to solve a problem too quickly.) Remember to use Table 8.4 and the general tables in Chapter 2.
What temperaments are not present on the team?	
What might this say about the team's ability to solve problems? Remember to use Table 8.2 and the general tables in Chapter 1.	
What implications does this have for making any major changes? Remember to use Table 8.3 and the general tables in Chapter 1.	What is the first function for the team leader, and what does this mean in terms of strengths and weaknesses in creating a flexible team?
What is the team temperament?	
Using the temperament tables, what are the strengths of this team, considering its temperament, in solving problems? What are the potential challenges? (For instance, if the team temperament is Guardian, this might indicate that the team will look for the root cause of a problem but may be too cautious in its approach.)	What functions are not represented on the team as first or second used, and what impact could this have on the team solving problems? (For instance, if S_E: Experiencing is not represented, the team might miss picking up immediate signals of a problem.)
Using the temperament tables, what are the strengths of this team, considering its temperament, in managing transitions? (For instance, if the team temperament is Artisan, this might indicate that the team will enjoy the transition.)	What is the balance between Extraverting and Introverting and how might this affect the team in responding rapidly to the environment? (If the majority of team members have an Introverting preference, there may be a tendency to wait for others to take the initiative in resolving problems.)
What is the team leader's temperament? What implications does this have for ensuring the team responds rapidly to problems?	What is the team type and what does this indicate about the team's approach to responding rapidly to the environment? Use the descriptions of type in Chapter 3 and the information in the relevant tables for ideas.
Based on the team leader's temperament, how would he or she approach a transition?	What is the team leader's type? What are the team leader's strengths in responding rapidly to the environment? What are the potential challenges in this arena?

Table 8.7 Plan of Attack: Rapid Response

Temperament/Connects & Conflicts	Function/Preferences
How can we compensate for lacking a particular temperament as we solve problems?	How can we ensure that those with a preference for Extraverting pause and reflect before taking action? How do we make sure that those with a preference for Introverting have their needs for internal reflection met before we make a change?
How can we ensure that all temperaments on the team are aligned with changes we make?	
How can we capitalize on the strengths of all temperaments on our team in solving problems?	If the team has a predominantly Sensing preference, how can we ensure that future implications are considered when solving problems and making changes?
How can we avoid overusing any one temperament in making a transition?	If the team has a predominantly Intuition preference, how can we ensure that solutions are practical and the change necessary?
How can we reap the benefits our team temperament brings to responding rapidly to the environment?	If the team has a predominantly Thinking preference, how can we ensure that people are considered as a criteria in making decisions?
How can we compensate for potential challenges our team faces in responding rapidly to the environment?	If the team has a predominantly Feeling preference, how can we ensure that we are giving equal weight to logical options?
Looking at the Connects and Conflicts diagram for our team and the table on types, what can we do to ensure the team is cohesive as it approaches change?	If the team has a predominantly Judging preference, how can we ensure that the team remains flexible in making changes?
	If the team has a Perceiving preference, how can we ensure that a decision is made and adhered to in a timely manner?
	Based on the functions that we use in the team, how can we make sure we gather all possible information by using the four information-gathering functions when problem solving (Experiencing, Recalling, Brainstorming, and Visioning; see Figure 8.1)?
	Based on the functions that we use in the team, how can we make sure we consider all relevant criteria when deciding a plan of action (Systematizing, Analyzing, Harmonizing, and Valuing; see Figure 8.1)?

SUMMARY CHECKLIST

Before leaving this chapter, answer the following questions:

1. Have you identified any problems your team is currently facing?

2. Have you followed the entire problem-solving process with your team?

3. Have you identified changes in your team and evaluated any changes that could be postponed?

4. Have you identified for each team member which stage of the transition process he or she is in?

5. Have you identified specific strategies to help each team member through change?

9

Effective Leadership

WHO'S IN CHARGE?

*"Leadership. . . creates a set of conditions where people want
to do what needs to be done."*
—Unknown

This chapter focuses on the skills of effective team leaders and out-
lines the critical roles they play in enabling optimum team performance. The main role of leaders is to influence and inspire their
group, team, or organization to produce results. Effective team leadership falls into three major categories: achieving the objective, developing the individuals, and building the team. We will examine each
area in detail, providing exercises and coaching tips in order to hone
your skills. Also included in this chapter is an in-depth look at the
strengths and potential challenges that different temperaments, functions, and types manifest when heading a team, as leadership is influenced from the inside out. In addition, another team profile provides
a look at leaders with different leadership styles as they motivate their
team to raise its SCORE.

DEFINING TEAM LEADERSHIP

Leadership is one of the most discussed and most written about subjects
in current business literature. Team leaders are viewed as guides who
can make or break team performance. They lead so that the individuals
and the team as a whole move through the stages of team development
and perform effectively. However, once the team is performing effectively, almost any team member can take a leadership role. In fact,

leadership rotates depending on the task at hand, and the team will ultimately practice equal or shared leadership.

Before we delve into the characteristics of an effective team leader, it would be a good idea to determine your current leadership success. If you are leading a team or participating in a team, take a moment and answer the questions in Exercise 9.1.

Exercise 9.1

HOW EFFECTIVE ARE YOUR TEAM LEADERSHIP SKILLS?

	Yes	No
1. Does your team have a clear team purpose and defined team values?	____	____
2. Did you participate in defining the purpose and values?	____	____
3. Does the team have clear goals?	____	____
4. Did you participate in setting the team goals?	____	____
5. Do you have written objectives?	____	____
6. Do you give regular feedback to team members on their skills and accomplishments?	____	____
7. Do you participate in the decision-making process?	____	____
8. Do you communicate the team purpose and objectives to the rest of the organization?	____	____
9. Do you use the word *we* when describing team performance?	____	____

If you answered yes to more than seven questions, you are performing some of the functions of a team leader, even if you are not directly in that role. This chapter will be a useful tool in improving your leadership abilities.

EFFECTIVE TEAM LEADERSHIP

Team leaders must have the ability to take a task group and turn it into a high-performing team. However, selecting the team leader is not as imperative as providing the person selected with guidance and training in order to develop as the team develops.

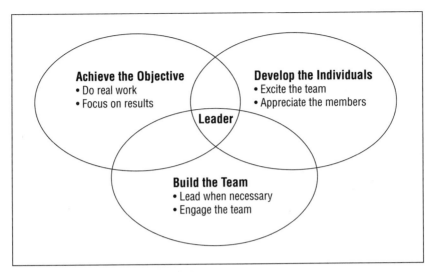

Figure 9.1   Team Leadership Defined

As illustrated in Figure 9.1, team leaders help the team achieve the objective through a focus on team results and by adding value through their own work. Leaders develop the individuals by exciting the team with their charisma and appreciating team members in order to bring out their best performance. They build the team by leading only when necessary and by stimulating high member involvement. An examination of each of these areas will help build a valuable understanding of team leadership.

Achieving the Objective

The team leader plays an important role in facilitating the achievement of team performance goals in two main arenas. First, the leader helps the team perform by constantly assessing the team SCORE in relation to the characteristics of high-performing teams. In this way, the team leader charts and checks the course to reaching the expected results.

Second, the team leader is responsible for many "behind the scenes" actions required to remove the barriers to team performance. Creating the right environment is a crucial part of the "real work" the leader must do, so that results can be produced by the team. This role spans several areas that include helping to reduce or eliminate barriers to team performance, ensuring that the team has the resources it needs to perform effectively, and acting as the main communication channel between the team and the rest of the organization and its customers. This second element of the team leader's position may not be as obvious, but it is of considerable importance to the team.

Developing the Individuals

Once the team is formed, the constant monitoring of talent and developing of individuals becomes paramount to creating a high-performing team. The team leader must give constant feedback and ensure that individuals feel motivated. By exciting team members about what they are there to do and coaching their performance with appropriate feedback, the leader unleashes people's hidden abilities.

Feedback

Feedback is any kind of attention you can get from or give to another person. It is a fundamental human need and is essential for a relaxed and happy life. Within a team, feedback is an imperative part of improving results, building self-esteem, and enhancing trust. As a team leader it is critical that you provide feedback to team members on a regular basis. There are numerous types of feedback.

- *Positive feedback* makes team members feel happy and useful by boosting spirits and generating enthusiasm. Examples of positive feedback include praise, thanks, attention, and interest.

- *Developmental feedback* is used when team members need to improve in a specific area. It is given so that the team member can take a negative behavior and turn it into a positive one.

- *Negative feedback* tends to hurt or denigrate and can make team members feel as though they have failed, rather than learning from an experience.

- *Zero feedback* is worse than negative feedback: It is simply the lack of any kind of feedback, positive or negative. With zero feedback, individuals are uncertain of where they stand. They feel insecure, unappreciated, and unclear about what is expected of them.

- *Physical feedback* involves some sort of physical contact, such as a pat on the back or a handshake.

- *Mental feedback* can be either verbal (that is, praise or thanks), or nonverbal (for example, nodding or smiling).

- *Conditional feedback* is input that is expected and planned. It comes in response to special events such as performance reviews, salary increases, and bonuses.

- *Unconditional feedback* is usually more fun than other kinds of feedback and greatly appreciated, as it comes as a surprise. As a result, unconditional feedback is an effective way of raising individual self-esteem. Examples include positive feedback from someone outside the team, customer letters of appreciation, and so on.

Many researchers have compared the effect of feedback to a bank's debit and credit balance. If team members have a credit balance of feedback, they probably feel positive and energized. If they have a debit balance, they are likely to feel depressed and less motivated. Use Exercise 9.2 to assess your style of giving feedback.

Coaching Principles

When meeting with your team members to provide feedback, it is critical to prepare the coaching session in advance to ensure you achieve the perfect balance between positive and developmental feedback. Following are some guidelines to optimize a coaching session:

- Think about the person you are meeting.
- Think about the area you wish to address. Be specific about the details in terms of either the positive behavior you want to

---

Exercise 9.2

FEEDBACK SELF-ASSESSMENT

Think about the last two times you gave positive feedback to your team members. *How* it was given (physical/mental) and *in what way* was it given (conditional/unconditional)?

Cite specific examples, such as, "I gave positive, mental, unconditional feedback today when I told Joe that he had done a great job on producing a failure analysis report. I told him that it was an important first step to defining the quality issues the team is trying to address."

Example One:

_____

_____

Example Two:

_____

_____

acknowledge and/or the behavior you wish to improve. Be sure you have adequate support data.

- Think about balancing the good news and the bad news to ensure the team member's self-esteem is protected.

- Consider the benefits of continuing or using the behavior discussed.

- Anticipate how the person might react and what type of questions he or she might ask.

Motivation

Herzberg's (1959) motivation theory distinquishes between *motivators* and *satisfiers*. Motivators are factors that inspire and motivate team members. They include the following:

- Accomplishment and achievement
- Feedback
- Job enrichment and growth
- Teamwork

Satisfiers are factors that, if absent, lead to unhappiness. However, the presence of satisfiers does not motivate individuals. Satisfiers include the following:

- Proper working conditions
- Company policy
- Personal stability
- Compensation and fringe benefits

In order to effectively motivate team members, team leaders must offer motivators and ensure satisfiers. Most team members are motivated by the opportunity to continue to grow and develop. Providing team members with new skills and knowledge, new challenges, and diversity in job assignments will contribute to keeping motivation levels high. In addition, different temperaments are encouraged in different ways. We will review this information later in this chapter.

Building the Team

Building the team as it moves through the various stages of team development constitutes the most critical responsibility of the team leader. The team leader's role and leadership need to change throughout the different developmental stages. Team leaders must be able to appropriately flex their technique to guide the team through the different stages, leading only when necessary and engaging the team through involvement. In this way the team develops a sense of ownership and belonging. However, most of us tend to fall into our natural style, rather than adjusting to the needs of the situation.

Styles of Leadership

According to Paul Hersey and Kenneth Blanchard's (1988) *Management of Organizational Behavior,* there are four distinct styles of leading: *directing, clarifying, collaborating,* and *delegating.* The styles are distinguished by the amount of task focus (direction) and relationship focus (support) exhibited by the leader. The style should be influenced by the stage of team development and the readiness of the team members.

- *Directing:* If one is highly task focused with little relationship emphasis, he or she is using the *directing* style of leadership.
- *Clarifying:* If one is highly task and relationship focused, he or she is using the *clarifying* style of leadership.
- *Collaborating:* If one is highly relationship focused but not very task focused, his or her style is *collaborative.*
- *Delegating:* If one is not very task or relationship focused, he or she is using a *delegating* style of leadership.

See Table 9.1 on page 238 for details on the four styles.

In high-performing teams, leadership is shared and team members participate in all areas. Forging this type of an environment is a substantial aspect of effective leadership. As a team leader, it is important to adapt your leadership style based on the needs of the team, not on your preferences.

TEAMS IN ACTION

Obviously temperament, functions, and type influence leadership from the inside out in two ways: first as they influence each individual's habitual leadership style, and second as the leader has to flex and adjust to individual team members.

The current consensus holds that anyone can learn to be an effective leader, given the right attitude, skills, and knowledge. There is no particular leadership type. The key to leading is knowing how to capitalize on your own strengths and those of your team, while effectively managing your own and team challenges. As temperament and type provide a better understanding of self and others, they truly provide an objective framework on which to develop your leadership skills.

Table 9.1   The Four Leadership Styles

Team Stage	Forming	Storming	Norming	Performing
Characteristics	• Member unclear about roles and goals • Superficial communication	• Conflict across team • Disagree about task, process, and goals	• Procedures in place • Team needs direction	• Team operating well collectively • Synergy among team members
Leadership Style	Directing	Clarifying	Collaborating	Delegating
Approach	Team leader tells the employee what, where, when, who, and how.	Team leader engages in two-way communication. In addition to giving direction as to what, where, when, who, and how, the leader now gives an explanation as to why. The team members can then ask questions for further clarifications.	Team leader engages in sharing ideas and facilitates joint decision making.	Team leader turns over responsibility for process, decision, and implementation to employee and monitors progress.
Interactions	• Gives structure • Time and task focus: little relationship focus • Comfortable in telling team members what to do • Closely supervises performance	• Provides opportunity for clarification: resolving conflicts • Focuses on task and relationship • Listens • Assigns workload	• Process orientation • Evokes, inspires • Gives information • Helps team design own system • Encourages and listens	• Allows autonomy • Trusts • Focuses on motivation • Lets team make decisions

Contributions of Temperament

Throughout history we have examples of different temperaments and their leadership approaches in such fields as government, military, arts, and business:

- *Artisans:* With their pragmatism and willingness to take action, famous Artisan leaders include John F. Kennedy, George Patton, Winston Churchill, and Elizabeth Taylor.
- *Guardians:* With their focus on concrete results and team cooperation, famous Guardian leaders include George Bush, George Washington, Queen Elizabeth II, and Colin Powell.
- *Rationals:* With their strategic vision and objective approach, famous Rational leaders include Thomas Jefferson, Albert Einstein, Napoleon Bonaparte, and Margaret Thatcher.
- *Idealists:* With their collaborative approach and future vision, famous Idealist leaders include Mohandas Gandhi, Princess Diana, Vladimir Lenin, and Albert Schweitzer.

Table 9.2 on pages 240 and 241 describes some general information about each temperament in the role of team leader, together with some coaching suggestions for each temperament to enhance leadership effectiveness.

Contributions of Functions

While every temperament has its own leadership style, the first and second functions the team leader uses will also bring different strengths and potential challenges to the team. Table 9.3 on pages 242 and 243 and Figure 9.2 on page 244 illustrate these concepts. Each of the characteristics, except where noted, illustrates how the function would appear as a first or second function.

Contributions of Type

We have also included, in Table 9.4 on page 245 and 246, the strengths and challenges each type brings to the leadership role. Remember that this table is a further extension of temperaments and functions but is used to highlight the unique components of each type.

Leaders with a preference for Extraverting may be

- Quicker to take action and initiate projects
- Less effective at listening to their team, particularly if the team members have an Introverting preference

Table 9.2 Temperament and Effective Leadership

Temperament	Strengths	Potential Challenges
Artisan *Coaching Suggestions:* • Be patient when the team appears to be stuck; recognize that smoothing the group process will enable the team to do better in the longer term. • If new data become available, investigate whether direction needs to be changed every time and immediately. • Respect some of the rules that guide team performance—if you break too many, you will lose the respect of the team.. • Try to focus on long-term direction.	• May be able to guide the team quickly through early stages of development • Understand what team members want (motive) and help them achieve it • Bring expedient solutions to problems facing the team—great tactical problem solvers • Focused on the now moment to enable the team to perform in the current situation • Build trust by knowing what to do before others recognize the situation • Persuasive abilities • Sharpen the professional skills of their team members • Quick thinking and resourceful	• When the team is in early stages of development, may not feel they are seeing direct, tangible outcome from their efforts • May not follow though on detailed implementation • May get impatient with group process issues with no immediate solution • May not think in terms of long-term strategy • May not heed past experience • May neglect the "rules" in order to get the job done • May manipulate others
Guardian *Coaching Suggestions:* • Understand that others are not as responsible in terms of detailed follow-through and commitment to the team, so do not judge team members too harshly. • Focus on giving positive feedback. • If team members are not living up to their commitments, discuss the shortfalls objectively; blaming and complaining alienates team members. • Make sure you stay alert to the team developmental stage and withdraw hands-on implementation when necessary.	• Build a strong team culture and uphold "traditions" • Responsible and reliable • Nurture their team—support members and facilitate results • Look out for the team within the organization • Establish policies, rules, and procedures to help smooth team interaction • Constantly monitor team performance and compare it to a standard • Build trust by assuming responsibility and fulfilling commitments • Pick up the slack within the team • Loyal to the team • Develop responsibility	• May be too hands-on during later stages of team development • May only give feedback on inadequate performance issues or to the person who does "best" • May get upset if team members do not stick to the rules • May get stressed if they feel they are not needed or allowed to fulfill their role • Feel unappreciated by others and complain when their overly dutiful nature pushes them to take on the responsibilities of others • May be impatient when a project gets delayed, even for good reasons • May be too authoritative

Table 9.2   Temperament and Effective Leadership (cont'd)

Temperament	Strengths	Potential Challenges
Rational *Coaching Suggestions:* • Make sure you focus on the group process and do not devalue people issues. • Be sensitive to how individuals receive your critical questioning skills. • Remember to give specific, positive feedback. • Be aware of your competitive nature and ensure you are not competing with team members.	• Help the team develop and understand its overall strategic direction • Act as an intermediary between the organization and the team, due to verbal fluency • Excellent analytical problem solvers • Able to help team members define goals • Understand the conceptual key elements of team effectiveness • Build trust through their expertise • Challenge team members to achieve • Cultivate knowledge	• May only point out errors and forget to give positive feedback • Focus on achieving the task and may undervalue the group process element • May be oblivious to some of the human interactions • May be tactless in giving negative performance feedback • May judge harshly and finally • Nothing is ever good enough • May drive to be ahead
Idealist *Coaching Suggestions:* • Make sure you give developmental feedback where necessary. • Recognize your tendency to avoid conflict, and learn conflict resolution skills. • Be more realistic in individual team member performance and team performance potential so that you reduce disappointment. • Make sure you recognize and make the tougher decisions.	• Recognize each team member's unique contribution • Provide individualized positive feedback • Use verbal fluency to act as a conduit of information and ideas to and from the organization • Help build bridges between different perspectives • Effective facilitators in most of the stages of team development • Want to inspire their employees and unleash their potential • Build trust through authenticity and solid relationships • Mentors; guide employees in personal and professional growth • Create a strong future focus for the team	• May have difficulty framing negative feedback • Managing conflict and team disputes may be stressful for them • May find it difficult to make some of the tough decisions that affect team members negatively • May not delegate effectively • May take on too much at once • May not focus enough on achieving the task • May need to be liked • May become overdependent on team relationships and not define an authoritative line • May expect too much from team members and be disappointed when they do not develop their potential

Table 9.3 Functions and Effective Leadership

Function	Strengths	Potential Challenges
Extraverted Sensing (S$_E$): Experiencing	• Use all current data in assessing team effectiveness • Focus on what needs to be changed right now for the team to perform • Alert to changes in the organizational environment • Action oriented, quick thinking, rapid response • Aim to be "champions" in the organization	• May change direction too frequently • May miss hidden implication and meanings, while absorbed in sensory data • May get bored quickly • May not get enough sensory input as the team begins to perform on its own • May lead the team into "adventure" when stability is desired
Introverted Sensing (S$_I$): Recalling	• Refer to previous team experiences for new ideas • Bring an organized, sequential thought process to monitoring and managing team performance • Take step-by-step approach to tasks and coaching • Ensure team projects are practically focused • Great at comparing and contrasting current state with past state	• May frustrate team members with comparisons to previous team experiences • May place too much emphasis on experience, overlooking potential • May not be comfortable dealing with abstract or unverified data • May not respond positively to new ideas and change
Extraverted Intuition (N$_E$): Brainstorming	• Able to brainstorm options and see new possibilities at every stage of team development • Future focused • See hidden patterns and meanings in organizational, team, and individual behavior • Resourceful and upbeat; normally see the positive in the environment • Great at helping the team solve problems	• May have trouble managing the practical details of leadership • May be too attracted to new ideas and changes • May not consider implementation issues around ideas and may overload team members with new projects • May not focus enough on the current team situation
Introverted Intuition (N$_I$): Visioning	• Provide an entire picture of future direction • Able to simplify the complex, discern the meaning • Broad long-range vision • Excellent at scenario planning • Provide an independent, fresh perspective	• May be stubborn in their ideas • May create a vision that seems unrealistic or unrelated to others • May not focus on the events at hand • May have trouble articulating their vision

Table 9.3 Functions and Effective Leadership (cont'd)

Function	Strengths	Potential Challenges
Extraverted Thinking (T_E): Systematizing	• Help the team categorize and organize workload • Able to put a specific action plan into place • Able to evaluate team effectiveness and make quick, objective decisions • Convince team and organization with solid, fact-based logic • Focus on implementation and logistics	• May overlook the human element when making quick decisions • May become impatient with delays in decision making • May be unrealistic in their implementation expectations • May not accept ideas or decisions without solid facts and proven data
Introverted Thinking (T_I): Analyzing	• Create logical models around team operation • Constantly analyze and seek to improve team performance • Evaluate team and test new theories of leadership • Focus on accuracy and precision of the task • Able to present an independent, alternative viewpoint for the team	• May be harsh with their logical analysis • May find facilitating team consensus a frustrating process • May not remember to consider the people issues • May use their own logic and deny that of others
Extraverted Feeling (F_E): Harmonizing	• Able to create a harmonious team environment by telling appropriate stories and connecting with individuals • Give ample positive feedback • Able to facilitate team discussions at the different stages of team development • Want to ensure the comfort and happiness of team members • Acutely aware of group process	• May be uncomfortable if conflicts arise in the team • May find it difficult to distance themselves and analyze cause-and-effect data • May neglect the task aspect of the team in order to facilitate a positive group process • May show emotions when frustrated
Introverted Feeling (F_I): Valuing	• Appreciate diverse identities on the team • Want to know what is important to team members and motivate them accordingly • Passionate leaders if they believe in the team purpose • Want genuine interaction among team members • Serve as the conscience to the team and set ideals for the team	• May find conflict difficult to manage • May not communicate their values until these values are contradicted • May be unwilling to compromise on things that are important to them • May focus on the good in others and downplay their faults; may allow for too many second chances

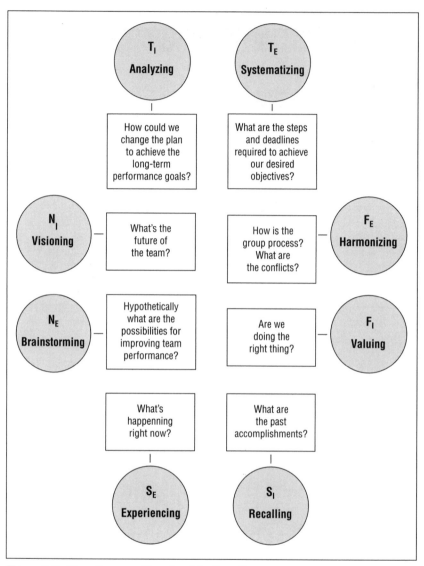

Figure 9.2 Functions and Leadership Questions

- More open—you will probably know where you stand with them
    Leaders with a preference for Introverting may
- Prefer to act one on one and through e-mail
- Not have as many meetings
- Appear to not take action or respond but will come through with action after they have had time to process

Table 9.4 Type and Effective Leadership

Type	Leadership Style Description
ESTP, ISTP (Thinking Artisan)	Leaders with preferences for STP are able to quickly recognize the realities of the moment and make quick, objective decisions in their functional areas. The ability to think on their feet and find tactical solutions to problems not experienced previously is critical to the success of their team. The focus is on action, getting the product or service out the door to meet the customer's needs. They are excellent troubleshooters and bring the resources necessary to get the job done. The focus on action may cause them to neglect activities that do not appear to produce results, such as meetings and strategic planning. In addition, calling a spade a spade could cause offense to some more conservative members of the team. Those with preferences for STP may need to step back from the sensory data and reflect more thoroughly before taking action. The push for results may cause them to push others for completion before they are ready.
ESFP, ISFP (Feeling Artisan)	Leaders with preferences for SFP combine an astute awareness of the physical world with tactical, functional knowledge to create a flexible strategy for their team. Their strong internal beliefs system guides them in deciding between different tactical approaches. They are strong, empathetic leaders with an innate ability to bridge differences within the group. With their instinctive understanding of motive, they are able to cue into what is important for team members and help them meet those needs. As leaders they have to ensure that they consider logical facts and data and do not rush too quickly into action without conducting an objective analysis. In addition, they may be perceived to be playing the fool too much as they rally those around them.
ESTJ, ISTJ (Thinking Guardian)	Leaders with preferences for STJ combine a rich historical data bank with logical, objective decision making and implementation planning in the external world. As a result, they are focused, organized, detailed logistical leaders. They bring a pragmatic and realistic approach to team workload and a respect for, and maintenance of, the traditions of the organization. They provide a fair and equitable working environment with a focus on decisive action. With their preference for historic data, they may face challenges when dealing with revolutionary versus incremental change, or when they have to implement new ideas where there is no precedent. They may need to be more flexible in their approach.
ESFJ, ISFJ (Feeling Guardian)	Leaders with preferences for SFJ approach leadership as caring yet directed managers. They create a relationship-oriented environment geared to supporting harmonious interaction and structured to enable team members to meet their needs. With their experience providing a rich source of data, they specialize in implementing process improvements by obtaining the buy-in of the team. Working in disorderly or chaotic organizations may be stressful to them because of their perceived inability to structure consistent results. In addition, they may find conflict painful and difficult, and a tough organizational culture may create stress for them.

Table 9.4   Type and Effective Leadership (cont'd)

Type	Leadership Style Descriptions
ENTP, INTP (Adaptable Rational)	Leaders with preferences for NTP bring to the table abstract information-gathering abilities balanced with internal, logical decision-making criteria. They are able to view multiple conceptual options and then evaluate each against an objective framework. They can be resourceful, visionary, and independent minded. They enjoy the freedom to work independently, solving abstract problems and designing the working systems. Areas they may wish to address are confusing others with complex explanations, arguing points too rigorously, and pointing out flaws in logic. Also, although data may not appear logical, there may be some valuable insights to be gained by considering subjective criteria.
ENTJ, INTJ (Structured Rational	Leaders with preferences for NTJ bring a clearly articulated logical vision of how the department needs to operate. They have a strong conceptual understanding of theoretical principles and a clear model of how these can operate in the organization. They are highly analytical and independent minded, with a strong push for action and closure in the external world. They are able to extract the essence in a given situation and able to articulate it clearly. Areas they may wish to address involve being sensitive to others' needs and remembering to deal with practical application as well as theoretical constructs. They may wish to remember to listen to others in their decision-making processes, as well as ensure that their models are integrated with team operations.
ENFP, INFP (Adaptable Idealist)	Leaders with preferences for NFP bring a strong internal belief system and the ability to investigate multiple possibilities in improving products and services. They will be excited about future options and curious about new technologies and systems. They bring a strong sense of commitment and build the strategy around the people they value. They appreciate uniqueness in others. An area they may wish to address is the tendency to start multiple projects. They may need to prioritize and eliminate some projects from the overall team workload. They may get overloaded by practical details and miss deadlines as a result. They may have difficulty in viewing the objective perspective in some decision making, and to overcome this they may need to reduce their level of perfectionism.
ENFJ, INFJ (Structured Idealist)	Leaders with preferences for NFJ bring a strong vision of how the company can operate and a core belief in the people in their team and company. They will drive to develop the potential in all their team members and will give excellent positive feedback when required. They have a clear understanding of how people and systems relate to each other and the ability to put things into writing. Areas they may wish to address: they may not be clear enough in the way they explain their vision to the world, and they may find conflict worrying. They may neglect to ask others for help as they protect their team from the rest of the organization. In addition, they will need to make sure they bring enough concrete practical applications to their vision of how the team should operate.

LEADERSHIP ACTIVITIES

As we discussed earlier in this chapter, the role of team leader involves achieving the objective, developing the individuals, and building the team. Each of these leadership activities varies depending on the temperaments, functions, and type of the other team members. Let's look now at how these factors overlay team leadership activities.

Achieving the Objective and Temperament

Table 9.5 on pages 248 and 249 lists the strengths and potential challenges each temperament brings to "getting the job done." Understanding this balance will allow you to adapt your leadership style accordingly.

Developing the Individual and Temperament

Each temperament varies in the type of feedback it likes to receive, the way it likes to be coached, and the factors that are motivating. What works for one temperament will not necessarily work for another. Team leaders need to remember the guidelines found in Table 9.6 on page 250 when working with different temperaments on their team.

Building the Team and Temperament

Forming

During this stage, you will probably notice some of the behaviors typical of each temperament. Usually people entering a group for the first time will be slightly cautious until they know what the team is supposed to do (Artisan), understand their roles and responsibilities (Guardian), know what expertise they can contribute (Rational), and determine if the relationship with others will be satisfying (Idealist). They will be listening for the topics and assignments that will help them meet their core needs. Each temperament, if not self-aware, will disregard or become impatient with some parts of the Forming process.

Artisans will be easily identified as they look for ways to influence the direction of the group. They will tend to make their presence known by wanting to immediately go into action, solve the problems facing the group, and get to the business at hand. They may not want to spend their time in long-range planning as they tend to be tactical planners. For example, they may say, "Let's do this, see what happens, then do the next step according to what's needed then." They may

Table 9.5 Temperament and Achieving the Objective

Temperament	Strengths	Potential Challenges
Artisan *Coaching Suggestions:* • Make sure plans are linked to long-term direction. • Build in short-term milestones to ensure progress is seen on large projects. • Be aware of the tendency to start new, exciting, and different projects.	• Often simplify planning by using short "to-do" lists with concrete action items • Desire to get it done and move on keeps them task focused • Put out "fires" quickly and effectively • Accurately recognize the steps necessary to implement an action plan • Will normally be to the point with e-mail and voicemail	• May view planning as a time-consuming, non-result-producing activity • May have a problem prioritizing because they want to do it all now • May plan only short-term tasks and struggle to link Key Result Areas to short-term plans • May want to react rather than plan
Guardian *Coaching Suggestions:* • Don't try to do it all. • Make sure you prioritize effectively between important and urgent. • Don't overplan—allow for contingencies, but not too many.	• Create clear step-by-step plans • Ensure that contingency plans are made to protect against unforeseen eventualities • Task focus leads to timely output • Know where to start a task and good at estimating time needed • Reliably come through with results • Good logistics planners	• May have problems prioritizing among multiple tasks • May lose the big picture when working on detailed implementation projects • May have difficulty adjusting to unexpected changes • May become resentful trying to do everything for everyone • May have difficulty eliminating the low-priority tasks—want to do it all

want to limit their role in the group and just do whatever is needed.

Guardians will come to this stage judging the quality of the leadership by observing how well the leader defines roles and responsibilities and assigns tasks in a fair and equitable manner. They expect the leader to manage the meeting in a traditional sense, and you may find them impatient with brainstorming and with sifting through complex data with which they have no experience. On the other hand, if they have already completed a similar project, they will bring to the table a wealth of experience that can cut short the learning curve and prevent repeating previous mistakes.

Rationals will communicate with the group about their specific field of knowledge or expertise. They will systematically design the methodology to create success for the project. Their focus will be on

Table 9.5 Temperament and Achieving the Objective (cont'd)

Temperament	Strengths	Potential Challenges
Rational *Coaching Suggestions:* • Consult with someone with a Sensing preference to ensure details are not underestimated. • Remember to consider the people in the plans. • Be aware of the tendency to want to create a new model.	• Approach planning using conceptual principles • Naturally able to link Key Result Areas with weekly and monthly planning • Prefer to use a system or model of planning • Like using a proactive approach to control results • Pragmatic approach; don't get distracted by relationships	• May be unrealistic when prioritizing due to an unclear understanding of how long each task takes to complete • May be more interested in ideas, theories, and strategic planning than in planning out all the details • May underestimate the detailed time requirements to complete the work
Idealist *Coaching Suggestions:* • Consider logical criteria when making a plan. • Consult with a Guardian or Artisan for practical implementation. • Focus on the short-term deliverables and be realistic.	• Want to create a plan that is integrated with the team purpose • Network—know where to go to get something done • Able to integrate Key Result Areas with weekly planning • Like having a direction and see the idea of planning positively	• May not comprehend the detailed, logistical steps required to make a project happen • May focus more on the people involved than on the task at hand • May lose focus if there are lots of tedious details • May continually project into the future rather than focus on the task at hand

completing the task in the most high-profile, competent way. They may get impatient with introductions as they will want to spend more time on deciding the strategic direction and operating principles for the group. They may be perceived by other team members as arrogant, but they will bring the ability to solve complex problems and view situations and challenges from an innovative conceptual perspective.

Idealists will come excited about the possibility that the group could make a difference to people as they work together to achieve a common goal. They will maintain a high degree of interest as long as the project has a focus on people and the relationships inside the team are attended to. You will observe them getting to know members of the team, not just on a superficial level but in a more meaningful way, and they will intuitively know what might motivate another team member. They will be particularly attentive to introductions and will find it irritating if others are not actively listening.

As a team leader you can recognize these different needs and guide the group process more effectively to help them meet these needs in a productive way.

Table 9.6 Temperament and Guidelines for Feedback, Coaching, and Motivation

Subject	Feedback	Coaching	Motivation
Artisan	• Give them frequent, specific, brief feedback. • Use colloquial language. • Notice their actions; unconditional feedback (as defined on page 235) is great. • Recognize tangible results.	• Have frequent interactions to discuss short-term tasks. • Don't try to micromanage—give them the direction and let them alone. • Make sure there is flexibility in their role and in the environment. • Make sure projects have short-term milestones.	• Seeing the direct tangible result from what they do • Freedom to do "their own thing" • Excitement and adventure
Guardian	• Give them specific feedback on concrete results. • They will normally want to hear areas for improvement. • Don't be effusive—they will be put off by extreme language. • Recognize their contribution to the team.	• Give clear, specific directions on projects and deliverables. • Leave them alone to follow through—they need minimal supervision. • Ensure responsibilities are clearly defined. • Make sure the workload produces concrete, tangible results.	• Membership on the team • Fulfilling responsibilities • Seeing achievements
Rational	• Give them logical, objective feedback. • They prefer to receive feedback from an "expert." • They prefer feedback on facts and data, rather than on personal issues. • Recognize their competence and intellect.	• Ensure their role has scope for critical thinking and analysis. • They like visionary leadership. • Coach on big picture and allow them to set strategic direction. • Coach to ensure they cover the details.	• Increasing their knowledge and competence • Control over their own direction • Intellectually interesting work
Idealist	• Be genuine. • They prefer warm, personal, positive feedback. • Recognize their uniqueness. • Give frequent feedback.	• They need personal leadership. • They prefer face-to-face interaction. • Give them big-picture direction. • Coach to ensure they cover the details.	• Meaningful work • Connections and personal relationships • Opportunity to help themselves and others develop their potential

Storming

In the Storming stage the team leader's role revolves mainly around managing team interaction and trying to create a cohesive direction for the team. Often the leader will be required to settle conflicts between team members at this point, as many differing perspectives will begin to clash. All temperaments will engage in differing behaviors in order to meet their core needs. Artisans may take whatever role allows them greatest freedom and will be fairly unpredictable from situation to situation. Guardians may act like victims so they can blame others for lack of performance. Rationals may use extensive critical questioning to ensure their ideas will be noticed as the best ones. Idealists may rescue someone by siding with a unique perspective but secretly undermine someone they view as a persecutor. As this stage continues, you will see the temperaments cycle through the stress response: Artisans will begin to retaliate, Guardians will complain and blame, Rationals will get tangled up in their thought processes, and Idealists will disconnect. You, as a leader, need to understand these stress responses and try to guide the team back to the overall purpose and direction.

The important thing to remember is that this is a critical stage in team development. If the team does not work out its differences and come to consensus, members will never reach the stage where the leader can delegate to them and they can become self-managing.

Norming

After dealing with the conflicts within the group and finally coming to some way of working together, the team will make a fundamental shift in the way it performs. Rather than the team leader making decisions, the team will make the decisions with the leader acting more as a participating member. If I were to walk into a meeting, I might not be able to immediately identify the leader of this team.

- Artisans are allowed to troubleshoot and specialize in tactical implementation, and are respected for their directness and pragmatic approach.
- Guardians are allowed to monitor process and progress and keep track of sequential progress toward the goal.
- Rationals are respected for their expertise and allowed to design the plan.
- Idealists are allowed to bring their coaching, mentoring, and visioning skills to the table and are listened to.

If the team leader remains too directing, the team will be unable to own its role definition and task assignment, and the team will not develop effectively.

Performing

In this stage the team is working harmoniously toward a common goal. Individual needs are being met; therefore the team can concentrate on the Key Result Areas and objectives for the team. Delivering the goods becomes a primary focus. All temperaments find successful team accomplishment a win, but their enjoyment comes from different "motivations."

- Artisans have found a way to make an impact and see direct, measurable output from their effort.
- Guardians have taken care of the group and kept order in such a way that results have been achieved.
- Rationals have evidence of their competence and mastery over what had once been a complex problem.
- Idealists feel that they have made a unique and special contribution.

In the Performing stage the team leader acts in an advisory role: Intervention could upset the group process. The team is now managing its own performance, and the team leader can act as a facilitator by coaching and guiding the team into new ways of operating and serving and, where required, as a content knowledge expert.

To summarize, we tend to be more comfortable using a specific style of management. Although most good team leaders have adapted their behaviors to suit the needs of the situation, in times of stress we revert back to what is easiest and most natural for us. As a team leader, it is important to adapt your leadership style based on the needs of the team.

Now that we have reviewed some general leadership principles, let's look at a team profile for an executive team.

SAMPLE TEAM PROFILE: EXECUTIVE TEAM

Background Information

This organization operated as a stand-alone division of a multinational company with its own marketing, engineering, product development, accounting, and manufacturing functions. However, it shared the sales function with the parent company.

The organization specialized in the manufacturing and production of connectors, which are used in a variety of applications and are a combination of plastic molding and electromechanical parts. Historically the connectors had been sold as discrete components.

The company had recently targeted a new market/approach for selling these connectors, combining them with other parts unique to a specific customer application. This required a new sales approach, and as a result the entire organization needed to change its structure and mode of operation.

The organization was divided into two offices. The East Coast division was responsible for maintaining and developing the existing "component" business. The West Coast office was responsible for developing the new combination approach. The management teams were also reorganized, and a relatively new team was established on the West Coast.

The West Coast team leader, Mike, wanted to use the analysis of temperament and type to help the executive team improve communication from the inside out, plus investigate strategies to enable the team to perform more effectively. The profile of the team is shown on page 255.

Connects and Conflicts

As you can see from the sample team profile and Figure 9.3 on page 256, the team had one person each from six different "bubbles." This meant that there was diversity in the team but that it might take longer to reach decisions as there was no strong faction. It also meant that Mike tended to influence the decision-making process more than he wished.

Mike and Pat often had strong discussions as Pat pushed Mike for concrete, logical decisions and Mike tended to have his own perspective with no tangible evidence.

Jay and John would conflict as John pushed for a logical, systematic model and Jay wanted the flexibility to work with the sales force.

Establishing Effective Leadership

Based on the approach advocated in this chapter, Mike worked through the steps as follows:

- He evaluated his leadership effectiveness.
- In *achieving the objective* he analyzed the critical components in SCORE to see how he could support team functioning, and decided how to intervene between the team and the company to smooth team operations.
- In *developing the individuals* he focused on providing positive feedback based on team member needs, coaching his direct reports and making sure they had key elements present in their positions that would motivate them.
- In *building the team* he identified the stage of team development and decided appropriate strategies that would help them move on to the next stage.

Assessing Leadership Effectiveness

Mike asked for feedback from his team. The feedback indicated that, while he felt the team had clear goals and direction, his team members did not feel the same way. With his INFJ type, his dominant function of N_I: Visioning, and his Idealist temperament, he had a clear picture of the direction of the company, but his team needed more specifics in terms of what that meant to them on a daily basis. Pat in particular, with his ESTP type, his first function of S_E: Experiencing, and his Artisan temperament, needed far more concrete data in terms of direction and objectives.

As a result of this informal leadership assessment, Mike decided to initiate an organizational assessment to identify organizational and team issues in greater detail.

Developing the Individuals

Providing Positive Feedback

Mike recognized that he tended to give positive feedback based on the characteristics that were important to him as an Idealist. Instead, he identified different strategies for providing positive feedback based more specifically on his team members' needs. To John, he said that he respected and admired the quality improvement model that John was introducing to the quality function. To Jay, he said that he welcomed the fresh insight into business development that Jay provided.

SAMPLE TEAM PROFILE

Individual Analysis

Name	Temperament	1st/2nd Function		Type
Mike	Idealist	N_I	F_E	INFJ
John	Rational	N_I	T_E	INTJ
Pat	Artisan	S_E	T_I	ESTP
Rob	Idealist	F_I	N_E	INFP
Sam	Rational	T_I	N_E	INTP
Jay	Artisan	F_I	S_E	ISFP

Team Analysis

Temperaments: Guardians __0__   Artisans __2__

Idealists __2__   Rationals __2__

Team Temperament: __Idealist/Artisan/Rational__

Team Leader Temperament: __Idealist__

Functions (First and Second Combined):

Perceiving S_E: __2__ S_I: __0__ N_E: __2__ N_I: __2__

Judging T_E: __1__ T_I: __2__ F_E: __1__ F_I: __2__

Preferences: E: __1__   I: __5__

S: __2__   N: __4__

T: __3__   F: __3__

J: __2__   P: __4__

First Function for the Team: __N_I: Visioning; F_I: Valuing__

First Function for the Team Leader: __N_I: Visioning__

Team Type: __INTP/INFP__

Team Leader Type: __INFJ__

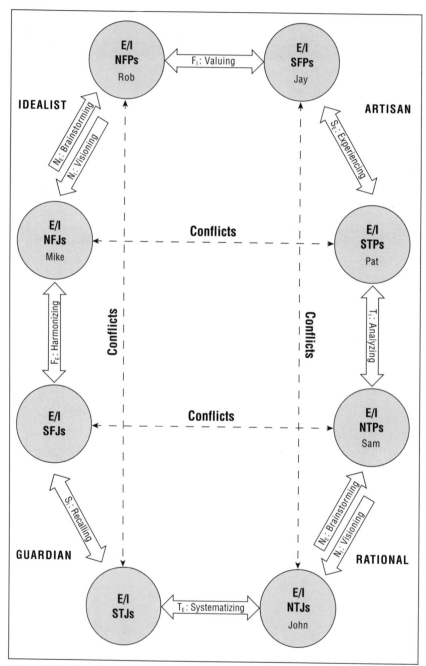

Figure 9.3 Sample Team Connects and Conflicts

Coaching

Pat, brought into the company to restructure operations, had been extremely successful but in the process had alienated some team members. Mike wished to use the framework of temperament and type to coach Pat. He began by recognizing the great job Pat had done. He then said that while Pat's communication style was direct and to the point, on occasion it had been viewed as offensive. They discussed how Pat could adapt his style without feeling confined. They decided that he could use any style he wished, but there were two team members with whom he would make a special effort to "soften" his style. The coaching session ended with further positive feedback.

Motivation

Based on each of his team members' temperaments, Mike believed that most were able to meet their core needs in their roles. Rob was able to create new possibilities for the company for the future (Idealist), Pat was able to change the "rules" and make production happen (Artisan), and Sam was able to create and implement a new operating model for the financial function (Rational).

Building the Team

Mike recognized that investing in time to define roles and responsibilities and setting specific plans in place would enable him to step back and use a more collaborating rather than directing style.

Other actions for the team:

- With no Guardians, the team found an internal manager who could bring in this perspective. This person attended team meetings and produced the added benefit of additional individuals in the company understanding more about the overall strategic direction.

- The team made a concerted effort to define action items and specify who was going to do what by when. John was helpful in undertaking this responsibility for the team with his secondary use of T_E: Systematizing.

- Mike learned to distance himself from his negative emotional response to what he perceived as conflict (F_E: Harmonizing), and the team became more aware that arguing for the sake of arguing was stressful to him.

- The team benefited from again picking up the strategic planning process and used the exercises in Chapter 5 to clarify their strategy and direction.

- The team had no direct sales force; sales reps were shared with the parent company, and this was creating a problem for ensuring an adequate flow of revenue. The team agreed to evaluate the current prospects and then prioritize them to provide Pat with a clearer, more specific plan to implement.

CREATING AND INTERPRETING YOUR TEAM PROFILE

Use the information in Table 4.3 on page 112 and the Team Profile form in the appendix to create your team profile. Use the information in this chapter and the case study provided to evaluate your team and identify the strengths and challenges it might face in the process of building effective leadership. Then use the questions in Table 9.7 on page 259 as the basis for diagnosing your team's performance. Use the Connects and Conflicts diagram in the appendix to remind you of the interrelationships of temperament, functions, and type.

Once you have assessed your team strengths and diagnosed any potential challenges within your team, it is time to decide what you can do, as a team, to raise your team SCORE in effective leadership. Table 9.8 on page 260 provides a list of questions you can discuss with your team to act as a stimulus in formulating your own plan of attack.

General Data		
Temperament	Table 1.1	Pages 24–25
Functions	Tables 2.2–2.5	Pages 41–44
	Tables 2.7–2.10	Pages 51–54
Type	Table 3.4	Pages 76–83
Specific Data on Leadership		
Temperament	Table 9.2	Pages 240–241
	Table 9.5	Pages 248–249
	Table 9.6	Page 250
Functions	Table 9.3	Pages 242–243
Type	Table 9.4	Pages 245–246

Table 9.7 Implications for Your Team: Effective Leadership

Temperament/Connects & Conflicts	Function/Preferences
What is your temperament?	What is the first function on the team, and what implications does this have for effective leadership? Remember to use Table 9.3 and the general tables in Chapter 2.
What strengths does this temperament bring to your leadership style? See Table 9.2 and the general information in Chapter 1.	
What potential challenges might you face with this leadership style?	What is the first function for the team leader, and what implications does this have in terms of strengths and challenges as a team leader?
What are the other temperaments on the team?	
How do they differ from you in the way they achieve the task? See Table 9.5.	What functions are not represented in the team as first or second used, and what impact could this have on the team?
How do they differ from you in the type of feedback they like? See Table 9.6.	What leadership styles are present on the team? What are the attributes they bring to the table and the possible handicaps? See Table 9.4 and the descriptions of type in Chapter 3.
How are they different from you in what they find motivating? See Table 9.6.	
What implications do these data have for the leadership of the team?	What is the team type and what does this indicate about the team's approach to leadership? Use the descriptions of type in Chapter 3 and the information in the relevant tables for ideas.
What is the team temperament?	
Using the temperament tables, what are the strengths of this team, considering its temperament, in effective leadership? What are the potential challenges? (For instance, if the team temperament is Idealist, this might indicate that the team is future focused but that it may not use enough objective data.)	What is the team leader's type? What are the team leader's strengths as a leader?
	What are the potential challenges in this arena?
What are the differences between the team temperament and the team leader's temperament? What might this mean to the team?	What impact will your team leader's preference for Extraverting or Introverting have on his or her leadership style?
What is the current stage of team development? What behaviors are you likely to see from each of the temperaments based on this data? See pages 247 through 252 on Building the Team and Temperament.	
Using the Connects and Conflicts diagram, what might be the challenges in leading effectively based on this profile?	

Table 9.8 Plan of Attack: Effective Leadership

Temperament/Connects & Conflicts	Function/Preferences
How can we work around any potential challenges in the team leader's temperament? See coaching suggestions in Table 9.2. (For instance, a team leader with a Guardian temperament may need to practice using the feedback sheet, Exercise 9.2).	If the team leader has a Sensing preference, how can the team ensure that the future possibilities are given enough weight by our team?
How can we capitalize on the strengths of each team member in achieving the objective? See Table 9.5.	If the team leader has an Intuition preference, how can the team ensure that the team direction is realistic?
How can we ensure all the team members are motivated? See Table 9.6.	If the team leader has a Thinking preference, how can the team ensure that motivating and coaching team members has enough emphasis?
How can we ensure we provide relevant feedback to all team members?	If the team leader has a Feeling preference, how can the team ensure that objective criteria are given the credence they deserve?
How can we manage the different temperaments more effectively through the stages of team development?	Based on the functions the team leader uses, how can we make sure we gather all possible information using the four information-gathering functions (Experiencing, Recalling, Brainstorming, and Visioning—see Figure 9.1)?
How can we avoid overusing one temperament as we lead our team?	
How can we reap the benefits our team temperament brings to effective leadership?	Based on the functions the team leader uses, how can we make sure we consider all relevant criteria when making a decision (Systematizing, Analyzing, Harmonizing, and Valuing—see Figure 9.1)?
How can we compensate for any potential challenges our team faces in effective leadership?	
Looking at the Connects and Conflicts diagram for our team and the table on type, what can we do to ensure that all team members are motivated and growing?	Based on the team leader's type, what can we do to use the leader's strengths and how do we manage the challenges?
	Which team members provide an alternative perspective in each of the areas above?

SUMMARY CHECKLIST

Before leaving this chapter, answer the following questions:

1. Have you assessed your leadership effectiveness?

2. Have you evaluated how else you could intervene with the organization to help your team work more effectively?

3. Have you assessed how you could give genuine feedback to your team members?

4. Have you identified someone you wish to coach and prepared for the coaching session?

5. Have you identified strategies for motivating team members more effectively?

6. Have you identified which stage of development your team is in?

7. Have you identified your responsibilities for the stage your team is in currently?

8. Have you analyzed your profile and defined its implications for effective leadership?

What's Next?

HOW TO MAINTAIN PEAK PERFORMANCE

"Everything changes but change itself."
—John F. Kennedy

You've read the book. Now what? You have any number of choices:

- You can leave well enough alone—after all, it's gotten you this far.

- You can use these new techniques until the next crisis and then return to all your old habits for the sake of expediency.

- Or, you can use your personal and team evaluations to create a plan of attack to raise your team's SCORE in each of the critical categories.

We all know that excellent team performance requires constant assessment and recognition of team accomplishments. This concluding chapter provides ideas that will appeal to all four temperaments in terms of recharging the team's batteries and maintaining the maximum team SCORE (See Table 10.1).

- **Artisans** will be excited to celebrate successes.

- **Guardians** will feel proud when recognizing achievements.

- **Rationals** will be stimulated by new intellectual learning.

- **Idealists** will feel enriched by team-building events and opportunities to reconnect.

Obviously, all temperaments will enjoy all four approaches, but make sure you use them at different times!

Table 10.1   Temperament and Maintaining Peak Performance

Temperament	Approach to Maintaining Peak Performance
Artisan	• Extremely sensitive to changes that might affect the team—for example, can detect changes in motive that may affect the team • Tuned into the here and now, may see changes in direction in the company/environment • Will think of innovative ways to celebrate team success • Will naturally see ways around rules to help the team perform • May be viewed as too fun-loving or flippant because of using creative ways of recognizing team performance; awards, off-sites, and so on may be perceived as extravagant • May not take a long-term view in evaluating results—what have we done well in the last month? • May not want to take time to evaluate team performance if no current problem exists
Guardian	• Constantly monitor achievements with goals and objectives and evaluate processes for efficiency • Always look for ways to build team cohesiveness • Have a clear memory of team's previous successes and challenges that can be brought to the evaluation process • Once a decision is made, will normally follow through • May forget to celebrate achievements, with their natural caution • May only recognize "the best" because everyone is supposed to act in a specific way • May view achieving concrete outcomes as more important than everyone interacting positively
Rational	• Will use logical criteria to accurately assess the team's current performance levels • Approach evaluating team performance from a long-term perspective, seeing future patterns and implications • Will use innovative approaches in repositioning the team, if necessary, to the organization • Naturally see the team's role from the strategic perspective • May be more concerned with creating new ways of operating than with reviewing current and past successes • May need help understanding the practical reality of what team members are facing • May forget to give positive feedback on achievements
Idealist	• Have excellent facilitation and verbal communication ability in discussing team evaluation • Have a clear understanding of individuals' contributions to team goals • Naturally give positive feedback and are aware of team achievements • Gravitate toward a consensus decision-making process and know the appropriate celebration for each person on the team • May miss consideration of practical options • May be unrealistic about where the team is succeeding • May be unrealistic about the challenges facing the team

CELEBRATING TEAM SUCCESSES: ARTISANS

Celebrating successes provides a sense of well-being and builds esprit de corps. These celebrations can be as simple as having a potluck or as sophisticated as organizing an off-site party for team members at an innovative location. Ideas for celebrations are listed below.

- Team dinner/picnic/barbecue
- Social event after work
- Outing to amusement park or show
- River rafting/ropes course
- Giveaway such as sweatshirt, T-shirt, or water bottle
- Awards and certificates
- Team Player of the Month
- Comp time
- Celebration of key milestones with cake or other refreshments
- Treasure hunt
- Contest

If you want to celebrate in style and innovatively, ask an Artisan for ideas!

RECOGNIZING ACHIEVEMENTS: GUARDIANS

Recognizing achievements is key especially for Guardians to maintain motivation and energy. Teams often view achievements as completion of major milestones, but they can also consist of multitudes of moments of truth—small successes that occur every day. Achievements can occur in both the task (getting the work done) and the group process (interacting together effectively) elements of teamwork.

Although we experience many small successes each day, instead of recognizing them either we are so consumed with current tasks that we miss them or we tend to focus on what has not worked, thereby reducing team confidence and lowering motivation levels. By recognizing major and minor accomplishments, teams not only build cohesiveness, moving up the communication pyramid (see Chapter 7), but also increase trust and morale.

In the future, remember to stop and recognize ongoing achievements and keep your eyes open for small successes you can use to build team spirit and productivity. To help you in recognizing team

Exercise 10.1

TEAM ACCOMPLISHMENTS

1. Ask each team member individually to list any major accomplishments he or she believes the team should recognize.

2. Ask team members to make a note of small successes.

3. Collate the data collected in answer to questions 1 and 2.

4. Discuss the results in a team meeting.

In reviewing the evaluations, the following questions can act as the stimuli for the team discussion:

- What accomplishments did the team identify?

- What results exceeded expectations and why?

- To what extent was there consistency in the accomplishments that were described?

- To what extent was there agreement on the results that arose?

- What were the reasons for the results?

successes, complete Exercise 10.1 above. Then, to help you to celebrate those successes, complete Exercise 10.2 on the next page.

PROVIDING NEW LEARNING OPPORTUNITIES: RATIONALS

For Rational team members, it is important to continue to learn and develop new mental models. Approaches that keep Rational team members immersed in team productivity include the following:

- Ensuring there are ongoing training programs.

- Making sure there are new intellectually challenging projects on a regular basis.

- Providing opportunities to attend conferences, exhibitions, lectures, and so on.

- Reassessing corporate strategy and direction.

- Analyzing complex problems to assess new approaches.

Exercise 10.2

CELEBRATING ACHIEVEMENTS

1. Identify two of your team's achievements. They can be small successes or larger project accomplishments.

2. Decide at least two ways that you will celebrate each achievement.

One achievement is:

_____

_____

The two innovative ways we will celebrate this achievement are:

_____

_____

One achievement is:

_____

_____

The two innovative ways we will celebrate this achievement are:

_____

_____

ENCOURAGING INTERACTION: IDEALISTS

Idealist team members will feel renewed if the team pursues multiple avenues of human interaction. Ideas for team-building events include the following:

- Conducting team strategy sessions to reaffirm purpose and direction.

- Using team-building exercises in regular team meetings. Books such as *Games Teams Play* (Berdaly, 1996) and *Games Trainers Play* (Newstrom and Scannell, 1980) can be used to stimulate unconventional interaction.

- Holding off-site meetings where team members get the chance to relate to one another on a personal level.

- Supporting an environment that provides opportunity for meaningful one-on-one interaction.

MY COMMITMENT TO ACTION

Complete Exercise 10.3 to help you in maintaining your team at peak performance level to maximize its SCORE.

SUMMARY

Everything you have learned in this book is negated without one thing: respect. If team members don't have respect for each other and for the leader, and if the team leader doesn't have it for each and every team member, the team will not succeed.

Teams need constant work in order to be successful. Don't forget to revisit the exercises and ideas in this book on a regular basis so that you can continue to drive your team's performance from the inside out.

Exercise 10.3

COMMITMENT TO ACTION

My temperament is _____

The strengths I bring in maintaining my team's peak performance are:

_____

_____

_____

The potential challenges I bring in maintaining my team's peak performance are:

_____

_____

_____

Things I plan to do to maintain my team's peak performance are:

What	**By when**

SUMMARY CHECKLIST

Before leaving this book, answer the following questions:

1. Are you regularly celebrating successes?

2. How often have you recognized major achievements and small successes?

3. How frequently have you provided opportunities for continuous learning and development?

4. Have you ensured there are regular times when the team can engage in meaningful interaction?

5. Have you decided what tools and techniques you are going to use and when to maintain your team's peak performance?

Appendix

Use the Team Profile form and the Connects and Conflicts diagram in this appendix in creating your team profile.

TEAM PROFILE

Individual Analysis

Name	Temperament	1st/2nd Function	Type

Team Analysis

Temperaments: Guardians _____   Artisans _____

Idealists _____   Rationals _____

Team Temperament: _____

Team Leader Temperament: _____

Functions (First and Second Combined):

Perceiving S_E: _____ S_I: _____ N_E: _____ N_I: _____

Judging T_E: _____ T_I: _____ F_E: _____ F_I: _____

Preferences: E: _____   I: _____

S: _____   N: _____

T: _____   F: _____

J: _____   P: _____

First Function for the Team: _____

First Function for the Team Leader: _____

Team Type: _____

Team Leader Type: _____

Team Profile Form

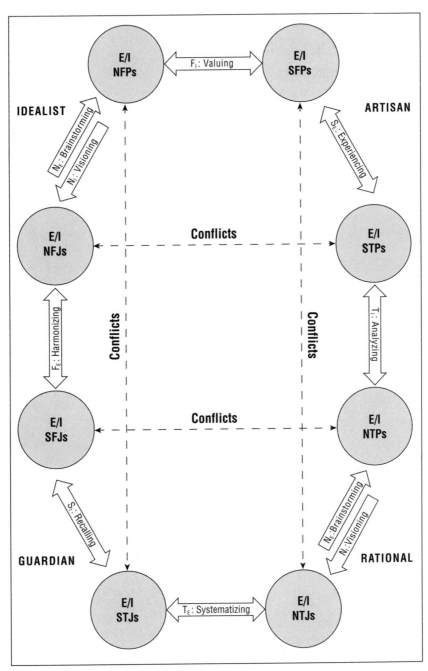

Connects and Conflicts Diagram

Bibliography

Berdaly, L. *Games Teams Play.* New York: McGraw-Hill, 1996.

Berens, L. V. *Understanding Yourself and Others.* New York: Telos, 1998.

Bridges, W. *The Character of Organizations.* Palo Alto, CA: Davies-Black, 1992.

Brownsword, A. W. *Type Descriptions.* Herndon, VA: Baytree, 1990.

Brownsword, A. W. *It Takes All Types.* Herndon, VA: Baytree, 1994.

Delunas, E. *Survival Games Personalities Play.* SunInk Publications, 1992.

Fitzgerald, C., and Kirby, L. K. *Developing Leaders.* Palo Alto, CA: Davies-Black, 1997.

Goldman, D. *Emotional Intelligence.* New York: Bantam Books, 1995.

Handy, C. *The Age of Unreason.* Boston: Harvard Business School Press, 1990.

Handy, C. *The Age of Paradox.* Boston: Harvard Business School Press, 1994.

Handy, C. *Beyond Certainty.* Boston: Harvard Business School Press, 1996.

Hersey, P., and Blanchard, K. H. *Management of Organizational Behavior: Utilizing Human Resources.* Upper Saddle River, NJ: Prentice-Hall, 1988.

Herzberg, F., Mausner, B., and Snyderman, B. B. *The Motivation to Work.* Piscataway, NJ: Transaction Publishers, 1993.

Hirsh, S. *MBTI Team Building Program.* Palo Alto, CA: Consulting Psychologists Press, 1992.

Hirsh, S. *Work It Out: Clues for Solving People Problems at Work.* Palo Alto, CA: Davies-Black Publishing, 1996.

Hirsh, S., and Kummerow, J. *Life Types*. New York: Warner Books, 1989.

Hirsh, S., and Kummerow, J. *Introduction to Type in Organizations*. (3rd ed.) Palo Alto, CA: Consulting Psychologists Press, 1998.

Huszczo, G. *Tools for Team Excellence*. Palo Alto, CA: Davies-Black, 1996.

Isachsen, O. *Joining the Entrepreneurial Elite*. Palo Alto, CA: Davies-Black, 1997.

Isachsen, O., and Berens, L. *Working Together*. San Juan Capistrano, CA: Institute for Management Development, 1988.

Katzenbach, J., and Smith, D. K. *The Wisdom of Teams*. New York: HarperCollins, 1993.

Keirsey, D. *Portraits of Temperament*. Del Mar, CA: Prometheus Nemesis Books, 1987.

Keirsey, D. *Presidential Temperament*. Del Mar, CA: Prometheus Nemesis Books, 1992.

Keirsey, D. *Please Understand Me II*. Del Mar, CA: Prometheus Nemesis Books, 1998.

Keirsey, D, and Bates, M. *Please Understand Me*. Del Mar, CA: Prometheus Nemesis Books, 1978.

Kriegel, R. J., and Patler, L. *If It Ain't Broke, Break It*. New York: Warner Books, 1992.

Kroeger, O., and Thuesen, J. M. *Type Talk*. New York: Delacorte Press, 1988.

Kroeger, O., and Thuesen, J. M. *Type Talk at Work*. New York: Delacorte Press, Bantam Doubleday, Dell, 1992.

Kroeger, O., and Thuesen, J. M. *16 Ways to Love Your Lover*. New York: Delacorte Press, Bantam Doubleday, Dell, 1994.

Kummerow, J. M., Barger, N. J., and Kirby, L. K. *Work Types*. New York: Warner Books, 1997.

Lawrence, G. *People Types and Tiger Stripes*. Gainsville, FL: Center for Applications of Psychological Type, 1995.

Myers, I. B., with Kirby, L. K., and Myers, K. D. *Introduction to Type*. (6th ed.) Palo Alto, CA: Consulting Psychologists Press, 1998.

Myers, I. B., and Myers, P. B. *Gifts Differing*. Palo Alto, CA: Davies-Black, 1995.

Myers, K. D., and Kirby, L. K. *Introduction to Type Dynamics and Development*. Palo Alto, CA: Consulting Psychologists Press, 1994.

Newstrom, J. W., and Scanell, E. *Games Trainers Play*. New York: McGraw-Hill, 1980.

Pearman, R. R. *Hardwired Leadership*. Palo Alto, CA: Davies-Black, 1998.

Pearman, R. R., and Albritton, S. C. *I'm Not Crazy, I'm Just Not You*. Palo Alto, CA: Davies Black, 1997.

Peters, T. J., and Waterman, R. H., Jr. *In Search of Excellence*. New York: Warner Books, 1988.

Quenk, N. *Beside Ourselves: Our Hidden Personality in Everyday Life*. Palo Alto, CA: Davies-Black, 1993.

Quenk, N. *In the Grip: Our Hidden Personality*. Palo Alto, CA: Consulting Psychologists Press, 1996.

Russell, P. *The Brain Book*. New York: Routledge, 1979.

Sharp, D. *Personality Types: Jung's Model of Typology*. Inner City Books, 1987.

Thompson, H. L. *Jung's Function-Attitudes Explained*. Wormhole Publishing, 1996.

Tieger, P. D., and Barron-Tieger, B. *Do What You Are*. Boston: Little, Brown, 1995.

Tuckman, B. W. "Development Sequences in Small Groups." *Psychological Bulletin, 63*, 1965.

Waterman, R. H. *The Renewal Factor*. New York: Bantam Books, 1988.

Waterman, R. H. *Adhocracy*. New York: Norton, 1993.

Waterman, R. H. *What America Does Right: Learning from Companies That Put People First*. New York: Norton, 1994.

Index

Analyzing. *See* Introverted Thinking

Artisan temperament: aesthetics, 12–13; approach to change, 13, 214; case study example of, 26–27, 60–61; characteristics of, 6, 12–14; coaching guidelines, 211, 240, 248, 250; communication style associated with, 178–179, 187–188, 191; conflicts, 86, 89; contextual thinker qualities, 12; decision-making functions associated with, 72, 75; disconnections, 88–89; feedback guidelines for, 250; importance of celebration of success for, 264, 266; leadership abilities, 239–240; as learners, 13; motivation guidelines, 250; objective fulfillment abilities, 248; overview of, 4; problem-solving abilities, 211; sensory stimulation, 12; stress effects, 13; team building approach, 247–248, 251–252; team performance effects, 24; team responsibilities and, 149, 151, 153; in team strategy setting, 124; type preferences, 68, 75–77, 85–86

BLM spectacles, 3–4

body language: of Artisan temperament, 179; definition of, 173; of Guardian temperament, 180–181; of Idealist temperament,184–185; of Rational temperament, 182–183

Brainstorming. *See* Extraverted Intuition

change: description of, 206–207; temperaments and, 210–211, 214–215; transition and, 207–208

clarifying style, of leadership, 237

coaching: for Artisan temperament, 211, 240, 248, 250; case study example of, 257; for Guardian temperament, 211, 240, 248, 250; for Idealist temperament, 212, 241, 249, 250; principles of, 235–236; for Rational temperament, 212, 241, 249, 250

collaborating style, of leadership, 237

communication: with Artisans, 178–179, 187–188, 191; barriers to, 173; building of, 176–177;